Absolute Be [barcode] s Guide to Algorithms

A Practical Introduction to Data Structures and Algorithms in JavaScript

ABSOLUTE
BEGINNER'S
GUIDE

Kirupa Chinnathambi

Pearson

Absolute Beginner's Guide to Algorithms

For information about buying this title in bulk quantities, or for special sales opportunities (which may include electronic versions; custom cover designs; and content particular to your business, training goals, marketing focus, or branding interests), please contact our corporate sales department at corpsales@pearsoned.com or (800) 382-3419.

For government sales inquiries, please contact governmentsales@pearsoned.com.

For questions about sales outside the U.S., please contact intlcs@pearson.com.

Visit us on the Web: informit.com

Library of Congress Control Number: 2023947403

Copyright © 2024 Pearson Education, Inc.

Hoboken, NJ

Cover image: Rozdesign/Shutterstock

ISBN-13: 978-0-13-822229-1
ISBN-10: 0-13-822229-0

1 2023

Pearson's Commitment to Diversity, Equity, and Inclusion

Pearson is dedicated to creating bias-free content that reflects the diversity of all learners. We embrace the many dimensions of diversity, including but not limited to race, ethnicity, gender, socioeconomic status, ability, age, sexual orientation, and religious or political beliefs.

Education is a powerful force for equity and change in our world. It has the potential to deliver opportunities that improve lives and enable economic mobility. As we work with authors to create content for every product and service, we acknowledge our responsibility to demonstrate inclusivity and incorporate diverse scholarship so that everyone can achieve their potential through learning. As the world's leading learning company, we have a duty to help drive change and live up to our purpose to help more people create a better life for themselves and to create a better world.

Our ambition is to purposefully contribute to a world where:

- Everyone has an equitable and lifelong opportunity to succeed through learning.

- Our educational products and services are inclusive and represent the rich diversity of learners.

- Our educational content accurately reflects the histories and experiences of the learners we serve.

- Our educational content prompts deeper discussions with learners and motivates them to expand their own learning (and worldview).

While we work hard to present unbiased content, we want to hear from you about any concerns or needs with this Pearson product so that we can investigate and address them.

- Please contact us with concerns about any potential bias at https://www. pearson.com/report-bias.html.

Figure Credits

Contents at a Glance

Table of Contents

Acknowledgments

As I found out, getting a book like this out the door is no small feat. It involves a bunch of people in front of (and behind) the camera who work tirelessly to turn my ramblings into the beautiful pages that you are about to see. To everyone at Pearson who made this possible, thank you!

With that said, there are a few people I'd like to explicitly call out. First, I'd like to thank Kim Spenceley for making this book possible, Chris Zahn for meticulously ensuring everything is human-readable, Carol Lallier for her excellent copyediting, and Loretta Yates for helping make the connections that made all of this happen years ago. The technical content of this book has been reviewed in great detail by my long-time collaborators Cheng Lou and Ashwin Raghav.

Lastly, I'd like to thank my parents for having always encouraged me to pursue creative hobbies like painting, writing, playing video games, and writing code. I wouldn't be half the rugged indoorsman I am today without their support ☺

Dedication

To my wife, Meena!

(For her support and timely insights throughout this book!)

About the Author

Kirupa Chinnathambi has spent most of his life teaching others to love web development as much as he does. He founded KIRUPA, one of the Web's most popular free web development education resources, serving 210,000+ registered members. Now a product manager at Google, he has authored several books, including *Learning React*. He holds a B.S. in computer science from MIT.

Tech Editors

Cheng Lou is a software engineer who has worked on various projects, such as ReactJS, Meta Messenger and ReScript. He's been passionate about graphics and general programming since the early Flash days, and is eager to keep its spirit alive.

Personal site: chenglou.me

Twitter / X: twitter.com/_chenglou

Aswhin Raghav serves as the Engineering lead for Project IDX at Google. He's also to blame for those pesky Firebase APIs. He's been building software and software teams for two decades at Twitter, Zynga, Thoughtworks, and Intel. He considers himself a specialist at building developer tools and facing the wrath of unhappy developers around the world. He lives with his wife and two kids.

Personal site: ashwinraghav.me

Twitter / X: twitter.com/ashwinraghav

1

INTRODUCTION TO DATA STRUCTURES

Programming is all about taking data and manipulating it in all sorts of interesting ways. Now, depending on what we are doing, our data needs to be represented in a form that makes it easy for us to actually use. This form is better known as a **data structure**. As we will see shortly, data structures give the data we are dealing with a heavy dose of organization and scaffolding. This makes manipulating our data easier and (often) more efficient. In the following sections, we find out how that is possible!

Onward!

Right Tool for the Right Job

To better understand the importance of data structures, let's look at an example. Here is the setup. We have a bunch of tools and related gadgets (Figure 1-1).

FIGURE 1-1

Tools, tools, tools

What we want to do is store these tools for easy access later. One solution is to simply throw all of the tools in a giant cardboard box and call it a day (Figure 1-2).

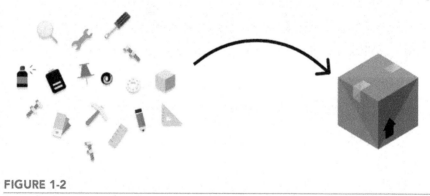

FIGURE 1-2

Tools, meet box!

If we want to find a particular tool, we can rummage through our box to find what we are looking for. If what we are looking for happens to be buried deep in the bottom of our box, that's cool. With enough rummaging (Figure 1-3)—and possibly shaking the box a few times—we will eventually succeed.

FIGURE 1-3

A rummager!

Now, there is a different approach we can take. Instead of throwing things into a box, we could store them in something that allows for better organization. We could store all of these tools in a toolbox (Figure 1-4).

FIGURE 1-4

Our metaphorical toolbox

A toolbox is like the Marie Kondo of the DIY world, with its neat compartments and organized bliss. Sure, it might take a smidge more effort to stow things away initially, but that's the price we pay for future tool-hunting convenience. No more digging through the toolbox like a raccoon on a midnight snack raid.

We have just seen two ways to solve our problem of storing our tools. If we had to summarize both approaches, it would look as follows:

- **Storing Tools in a Cardboard Box**

  - Adding items is very fast. We just drop them in there. Life is good.

  - Finding items is slow. If what we are looking for happens to be at the top, we can easily access it. If what we are looking for happens to be at the bottom, we'll have to rummage through almost all of the items.

  - Removing items is slow as well. It has the same challenges as finding items. Things at the top can be removed easily. Things at the bottom may require some extra wiggling and untangling to safely get out.

- **Storing Tools in a Toolbox**

  - Adding items to our box is slow. There are different compartments for different tools, so we need to ensure the right tool goes into the right location.

  - Finding items is fast. We go to the appropriate compartment and pick the tool from there.

- Removing items is fast as well. Because the tools are organized in a good location, we can retrieve them without any fuss.

What we can see is that both our cardboard box and toolbox are good for some situations and bad for other situations. There is no universally right answer. If all we care about is storing our tools and never really looking at them again, stashing them in a cardboard box is the right choice. If we will be frequently accessing our tools, storing them in the toolbox is more appropriate.

Back to Data Structures

When it comes to programming and computers, deciding which data structure to use is similar to deciding whether to store our tools in a cardboard box or a toolbox. Every data structure we will encounter is good for some situations and bad for other situations (Figure 1-5).

Phew! Just what we needed right now!

FIGURE 1-5

A good fit in this case

Knowing which data structure to use and when is an important part of being an effective developer, and the data structures we need to deeply familiarize ourselves with are

- Arrays
- Linked lists
- Stacks
- Queues
- Introduction to trees
- Binary trees
- Binary search trees
- Heap data structure
- Hashtable (aka hashmap or dictionary)
- Trie (aka prefix tree)

Conclusion

Over the next many chapters, we'll learn more about what each data structure is good at and, more important, what types of operations each is not very good at. By the end of it, you and I will have created a mental map connecting the right data structure to the right programming situation we are trying to address.

SOME ADDITIONAL RESOURCES

? Ask a question: **https://forum.kirupa.com**

Errors/Known issues: **https://bit.ly/algorithms_errata**

Source repository: **https://bit.ly/algorithms_source**

2

BIG-O NOTATION AND COMPLEXITY ANALYSIS

When analyzing the things our code does, we are interested in two things: time complexity and space complexity. Time complexity refers to how much time our code takes to run, and space complexity refers to how much additional memory our code requires.

Any code you will ever write will have a specific set of inputs that yields particular outputs. In an ideal world, we'd want your code to run as fast as possible and take up as little memory as possible in doing so.

However, the real world has its quirks, and your code might decide to take a leisurely stroll instead, depending on the size and characteristics of its input. While you can always glance at your wall clock to clock its performance for a specific input set, what we truly need is way to speak about how it performs with any set of inputs. And that's where the Big-O notation strides onto the stage.

Onward!

It's Example Time

To help us better understand the Big-O notation, let us look at an example. We have some code, and our code takes a number as input and tells us how many digits are present. If our input number is 3415, the count of the number of digits is going to be 4 (Figure 2-1).

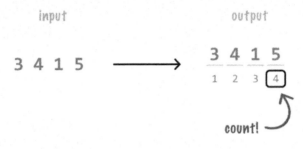

FIGURE 2-1

Count of digits in a number

If our input number is 241,539, the number of digits will be 6 (Figure 2-2).

FIGURE 2-2

For larger numbers, the number of digits will be larger as well

If we had to simplify the behavior, the amount of work we do to calculate the number of digits scales **linearly** (aka **proportionally**) with the size of our input number (Figure 2-3).

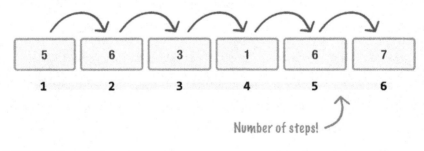

FIGURE 2-3

The number of steps scales linearly

The larger the number we provide as the input, the more digits we have to count through to get the final answer. The important detail is that the number of steps in our calculation won't grow abnormally large (or small) with each additional digit in our number. We can visualize this by plotting the *size of our input* versus the *number of steps* required to get the count (Figure 2-4).

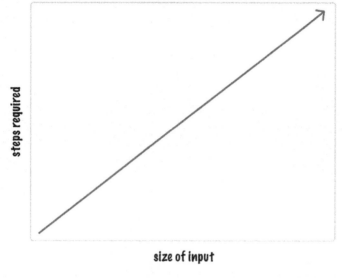

FIGURE 2-4

The amount of work scales linearly with the size of input

What we see here is a visualization of linear growth! Linear growth is just one of many other rates of growth we will encounter.

Let's say that we have some additional code that lets us know whether our input number is **odd** or **even**. The way we would calculate the oddness or evenness of a number is by just looking at the last digit and doing a quick calculation (Figure 2-5).

In this case, it doesn't really matter how large our input number is. The amount of work we do never changes. We always check the last digit and quickly determine whether the entire number is odd or even. We can simplify this by saying that our calculation here takes a **constant** amount of work (Figure 2-6).

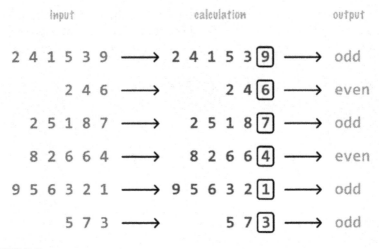

FIGURE 2-5

The last number is all we need to determine odd or even

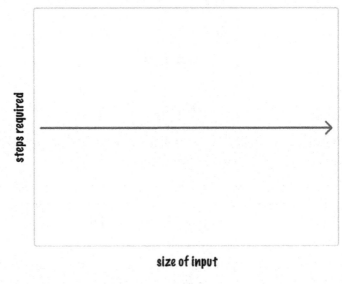

FIGURE 2-6

The amount of work is a constant

Notice that, in this graph of the steps required vs. the input size, the amount of work doesn't change based on the size of our input. It stays the same. It stays . . . constant!

It's Big-O Notation Time!

There is an old expression that you may have heard at some point in your life:

> Don't sweat the small stuff. Focus on the big things!

When it comes to analyzing the performance of our code, there is no shortage of little details that we can get hung up on. What is important is how much work our code does relative to the size of the input. This is where the Big-O notation comes in.

The Big-O notation is a mathematical way to express the **upper bound** or **worst-case scenario** of how our code runs for various sizes of inputs. It focuses on the most significant factor that affects an algorithm's performance as the input size gets larger. The way we encounter the Big-O notation in the wild takes a bit of getting used to. If we had to describe our linear situation from earlier, the Big-O notation would look like Figure 2-7.

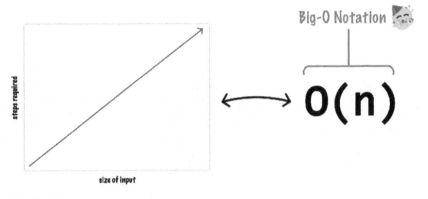

FIGURE 2-7

The Big-O notation for the linear relationship

The Big-O notation looks a bit like a function call, but we shouldn't think of it as such. If we had to decompose each part of this notation, it would be as follows:

- The *O* in Big-O, as well as O(. . .), stands for "order of." It represents the growth rate of the algorithm. To reiterate an earlier point, the growth rate can be measured in terms of time (how long it takes to run) or space (how much memory it uses).

- The *n*, or argument, for the O represents the number of operations our code will perform in the worst case.

For example, if we say our code has a Big-O notation of O(*n*), it means that our code's running time or space requirements grow linearly with the input size. If the input size doubles, the time or space required will also double. On the other hand, if our code has a Big-O notation of O(*n*²), it means that the algorithm's running time or space requirements grow quadratically with the input size. If the input size doubles, the time or space required will increase fourfold. The scary part is that quadratic growth isn't the worst offender, and we cover those in a few moments.

Now, what we don't do with Big-O notation is focus on extraneous modifiers. Using the linear case as an example, it doesn't matter if the *true* value for *n* is where we have O(2*n*) or O(*n* + 5) or O(4*n* − *n*/2), and so on. We only focus on the most significant factor. This means we ignore modifiers and simplify the time or space complexity of our code down to just O(*n*). Now, it may seem like going from O(*n*) to O(2*n*) will result in a lot more work (Figure 2-8).

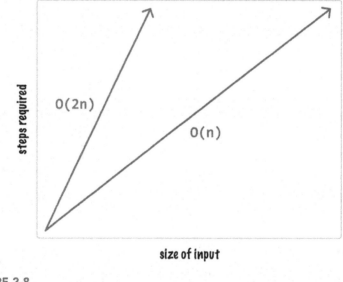

FIGURE 2-8

O(2n) versus O(n)

When we zoom all the way out and talk about really large input sizes, this differ-ence will be trivial. This is especially true when we look at what the other various classes of values for *n* can be! The best way to understand all of this is by looking at each major value for *n* and what its input versus complexity graph looks like (Figure 2-9).

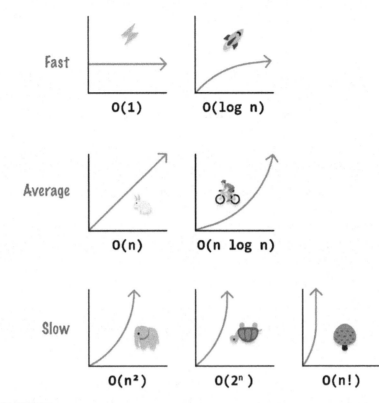

FIGURE 2-9

Input versus complexity graphs

Let's add some words and additional details to the preceding pictures to better explain the complexity:

- **O(1)—Constant Complexity:** This notation represents code that has a constant running time or space increase, regardless of the input size. It means that the execution complexity remains the same, regardless of how large the dataset becomes. Examples include accessing an element in an array by its index or performing a simple mathematical operation, such as calculating whether a value is even or odd.

- **O(log n)—Logarithmic Complexity:** Code with logarithmic time or space complexity has growth that scales slowly as the input size increases. These coding approaches typically divide the input into smaller parts repeatedly, such as in a binary search. As the input size doubles, the number of steps required increases by a small factor, not proportionally.

- **O(n)—Linear Complexity:** Linear time complexity means that the running time or space of our code grows linearly with the input size. As the input size increases, the time or space required also increases proportionally. Examples include iterating through an array or a linked list to perform an operation on each element.

- **O(n log n)—Linearithmic Complexity:** Algorithms with linearithmic complexity have running values that are a product of linear and logarithmic growth rates. These algorithms are commonly found in efficient sorting algorithms such as mergesort and quicksort.

- **O(n^2)—Quadratic Complexity:** Quadratic time complexity means that the running time or space growth of our code increases quadratically with the input size. These coding approaches often involve nested iterations, where the number of operations is proportional to the square of the input size. Examples include bubblesort and selection sort.

- **O(2^n)—Exponential Complexity:** Exponential time complexity represents code whose running time (or space taken up) grows exponentially with the input size. These coding approaches are highly inefficient and become impractical for larger input sizes. We get exponential time complexity when we solve problems with brute-force or exhaustive search strategies.

- **O(n!)—Factorial Complexity:** Factorial time complexity is the most severe and inefficient badge to tag a piece of code with. It represents coding approaches that have running times proportional to the factorial of the input size. As the input size increases, the number of required operations grows at an astronomical rate. We will run into factorial time and space complexity when we try to solve a problem using a brute-force approach that explores all possible permutations or combinations of a problem.

As we look at data structures and algorithms together, we will frequently use the Big-O notation to describe how efficient (or inefficient) certain operations are. That is why it is important for us to get a broad understanding of what the various values of Big-O represent and how to read this notation when we encounter it.

 NOTE   Big-O, Big-Theta, and Big-Omega

In some situations, we may run into other notations for describing the time or space complexity of how our code behaves. We saw here that Big-O represents the worst-case scenario. The Big-Theta (Θ) notation represents the average-case scenario, and the Big-Omega (Ω) notation represents the best-case scenario. When we see these non-Big-O notations make an appearance, we then know how to read them.

Conclusion

Okay! It is time to wrap things up. The Big-O notation is a mathematical notation used to describe the upper bound or worst-case scenario of a code's time or space complexity. To get all mathy on us, it provides an asymptotic upper limit on our code's growth rate. By using the Big-O notation, we can talk about code complexity in a universally understood and consistent way. It allows us to analyze and compare the efficiency of different coding approaches, helping us decide what tradeoffs are worth making given the context our code will be running in.

SOME ADDITIONAL RESOURCES

? Ask a question: **https://forum.kirupa.com**

Errors/Known issues: **https://bit.ly/algorithms_errata**

Source repository: **https://bit.ly/algorithms_source**

3

ARRAYS

We start our deep dive into data structures by looking at arrays. Arrays, as we will find out soon enough, are one of the most popular data structures that many other data structures use as part of their functioning. Remember the amazing toolbox we ran into in Chapter 1? Think of arrays as the sturdy outer shells that let you create compartments inside your toolbox – the nifty little organizers for your digital tools. They're like the toolbox's Tupperware containers, but for code!

In the following sections, we look at what arrays are, why they are so popular, situations they are good in (as well as ones they are bad in!), how to use them, and more.

Onward!

What Is an Array?

Let's imagine we are jotting down a list on a piece of paper. Let's call the piece of paper **groceries**. Now, in this paper, we write a numbered list starting with zero with all the items that we need to pick from the store (Figure 3-1).

FIGURE 3-1

The grocery list

This list of grocery items exists in the real world. If we had to represent it digitally, the data structure that we would use to store all of our grocery items would be an **array!** Here's why: **an array is a data structure that is designed for storing a collection of data in a sequential order.** If we turned our grocery list into an array, what we would have would look like Figure 3-2.

Each item in our grocery list is represented as an item in our array. These items are adjacent to each other, and they are **numbered sequentially, starting with zero**. Let's take our array and put it through some common data operations to help us better understand how it works.

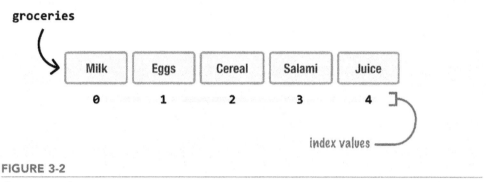

FIGURE 3-2

Our grocery list as an array

Adding an Item

With an array, one of the things we will frequently do is add items to it. Where exactly in the array we add our items is important. The location determines how much work is involved. Adding items to the end of our array is a walk in the park (Figure 3-3).

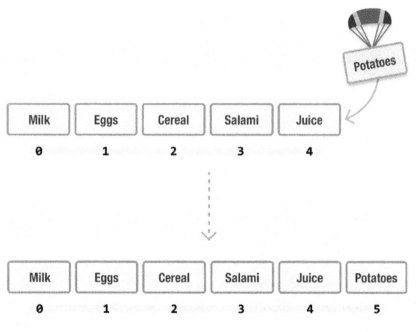

FIGURE 3-3

Adding items to the array

We append a new item to the end. This new item gets the next index value associated with it. Life is simple and good.

When we add an item at the middle or beginning of the array, we first have to make room for the new content (Figure 3-4).

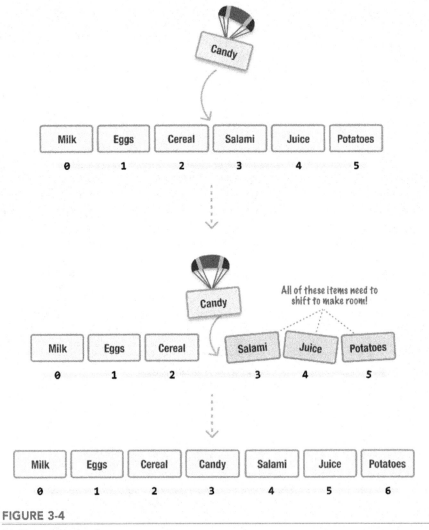

FIGURE 3-4

Making room for the new content

Because arrays are arranged sequentially, *making room* is a code word for shifting a bunch of array items over and recalculating their index positions. The more items we have to shift, the slower this operation becomes. The worst case is when we insert an item at the beginning, for this means that every item needs to be shifted with its index position updated. That's a whole lot of shifting!

Deleting an Item

When deleting an item from our array, the same challenges we saw earlier with adding items apply. If we are removing an item at the end, the disturbance is minimal (Figure 3-5).

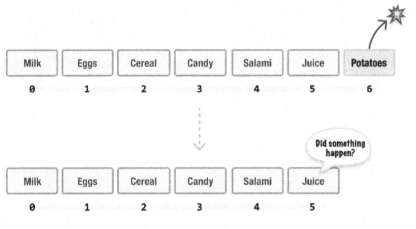

FIGURE 3-5

Deleting an item from the end

No other array item is affected. If we are removing an item from anywhere else, we need to ensure that all of our array items after the removed item are properly positioned and numbered (Figure 3-6).

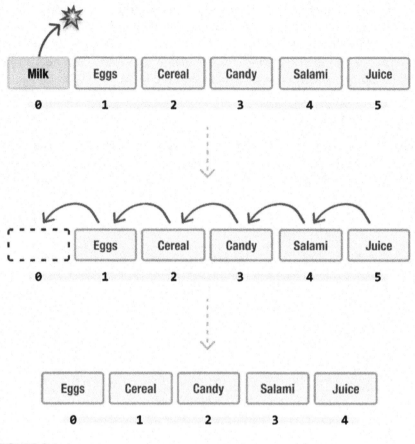

FIGURE 3-6

We need to ensure that all of our array items after the removed item are properly positioned and numbered

For example, we removed the first item from our array. Every other item in our array now has to shift and recount to account for this change. Phew!

Searching for an Item

Besides adding and deleting items, we will spend a lot of time searching for items. The most common approach is a linear search in which we start at the beginning of our array and go item by item until we find what we are looking for (Figure 3-7).

Depending on the exact shape of our data, there may be some optimizations we can make. For example, if we know our array's data is ordered in some way (alphabetically, numerically, etc.), we can employ a binary search to make our search go much faster (Figure 3-8).

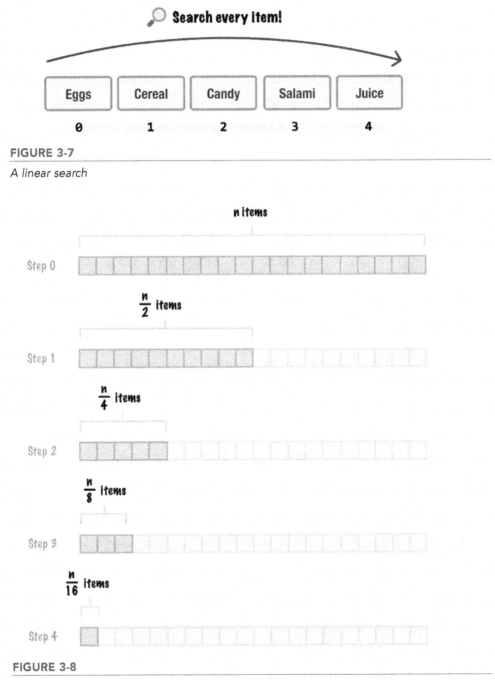

FIGURE 3-7

A linear search

FIGURE 3-8

A binary search goes faster

We cover binary searches, linear searches, and other search algorithms a bit later.

Accessing an Item

We have talked about the index position a few times so far, but it is time to go a bit deeper. The index position acts as an identifier. If we want to access a particular array item (via a search or otherwise!), we refer to it by its index position in the form of **array[index_position]**, as shown in Figure 3-9.

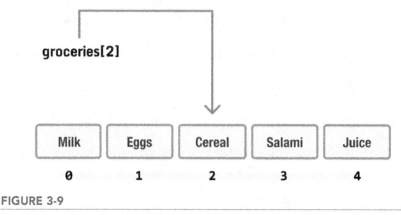

FIGURE 3-9

An array index position

A few tricks to keep in mind are that the first item will always have an index position of 0. The last item will always have an index position that is one less than the total number of items in our array. If we try to provide an invalid index position, we will get an error!

Array Implementation / Use Cases

An array is a fundamental data structure provided out-of-the-box in almost all programming languages, such as JavaScript! The following are some common examples of how we can use the array to perform some of the operations we called out in our grocery list example:

```
// Create our array!
let groceries = ["Milk", "Eggs", "Cereal", "Salami", "Juice"];
// Access the first item
let first = groceries[0];


// Access the last item
let last = groceries[groceries.length - 1];
```

```
// Access 3rd item
let cereal = groceries[2];
// Insert item at the end
groceries.push("Potatoes");

// Insert item at the beginning
groceries.unshift("Ice Cream");

// Insert item after the 3rd item
groceries.splice(3, 0, "Cheese");

// Remove last item
groceries.pop();

// Remove first item
groceries.shift();

// Delete the 3rd item
groceries.splice(2, 1);

// Find a particular item
let foundIndex = groceries.indexOf("Eggs"); // 1
let itemToFind = -1;
// Iterate through each item
for (let i = 0; i < groceries.length; i++) {
let currentItem = groceries[i];
// Return index of found item
if (currentItem == "Salami") {
itemToFind = i;
   }
}
```

For a thorough deep dive into learning the ins and outs of everything arrays do, check out my comprehensive arrays guide at www.kirupa.com/javascript/learn_ arrays.htm. If you aren't yet proficient with arrays, take a few moments and get really familiar with them. Many of the subsequent data structures and algorithms we'll be learning about use arrays extensively under the covers.

Arrays and Memory

When working in a modern, high-level programming language like JavaScript, we don't have to actively think about managing memory. All of the memory handling is taken care of for us. What we are about to look at goes a bit into the inner workings of our computers and the moments when knowing about what goes on will greatly improve our understanding of how things work—things, in our case, being arrays.

When we think of memory, let us simplify it as a series of regions into which we can store data (Figure 3-10).

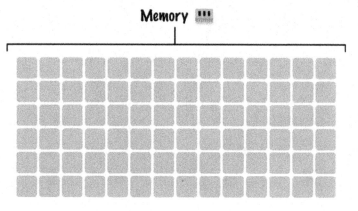

FIGURE 3-10

Memory as a series of regions

Now, our memory is never going to be as clean as what we see here. Our computer is juggling a bunch of other things that take up space (Figure 3-11).

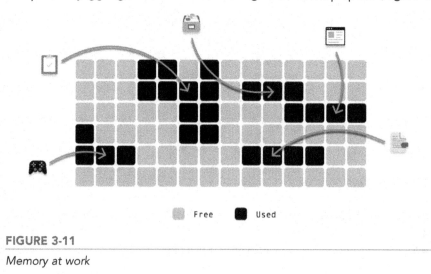

Free   Used

FIGURE 3-11

Memory at work

Any new items we add to our memory need to go into the available **free** regions. This gets us back to arrays. When we create an array, we first need to allocate some space in our memory where it can live. The thing about arrays is that they need to store their items in adjacent (aka contiguous) regions of memory. They can't be spread across *free* and *used* regions.

When we initialize an array, we allocate a fixed amount of space in memory and keep increasing this fixed amount as our array keeps growing. Let's say we create an empty array. Even though our array is empty right now, we allocate extra regions of memory (Figure 3-12).

Memory allocated for our array!

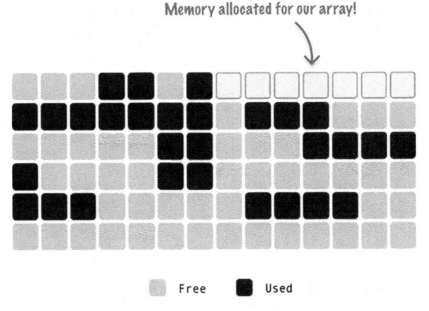

Free   Used

FIGURE 3-12

Memory allocation for the array

In our example, we have seven regions of memory allocated. As we add items to our array, they slowly start filling up our allocated memory (Figure 3-13).

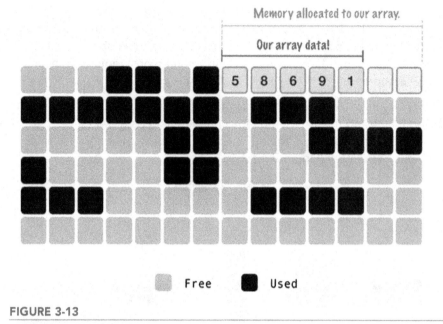

FIGURE 3-13

Filling up the array with data

We keep adding data into our array until we fill up all of our allocated space (Figure 3-14).

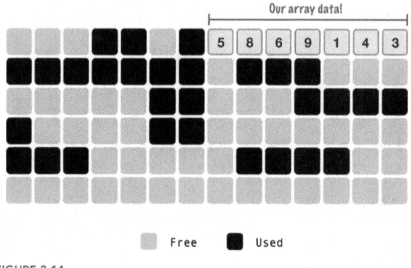

FIGURE 3-14

The array is filled with data

If we add an extra item, what happens next? There is no adjacent memory we can expand our array into. What happens next is that our operating system (or virtual machine) finds an uninterrupted section of memory into which our growing array can be moved (Figure 3-15).

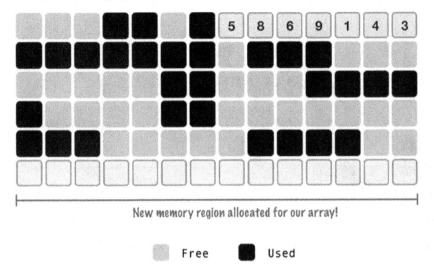

New memory region allocated for our array!

☐ Free   ■ Used

FIGURE 3-15

Finding an uninterrupted section of memory

Once it finds this region of memory, it is time to move our entire array to this new location (Figure 3-16).

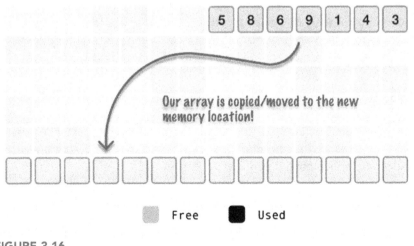

Our array is copied/moved to the new memory location!

☐ Free   ■ Used

FIGURE 3-16

The array data is moved to the new memory location

After our array is fully moved, which is definitely not a cheap operation because every item needs to go to a new position, we can add more array items, and the old memory location our array was in has free space into which other things can now go (Figure 3-17).

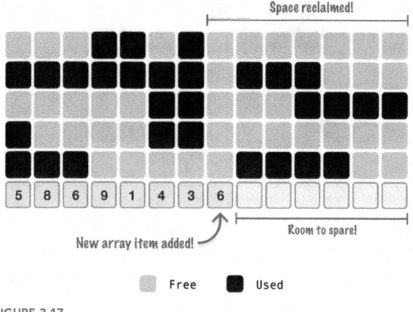

FIGURE 3-17

New data can now go into the memory locations freed up by the move

More traditional programming languages were strict about making sure you and I were thinking really hard about memory and how to ensure we don't go beyond it. Modern languages like JavaScript handle all of this for us, but the performance implications of going beyond our allocated memory size and needing to move our array to a larger region still do apply. We talk about that next.

Performance Considerations

In the previous sections, we got a glimpse of the sorts of activities that arrays are really fast at (and the activities they are slow at). Table 3-1 summarizes the performance and space considerations.

TABLE 3-1 Array Performance and Space Considerations

Action	Average	Worst
Space/memory	$\Theta(n)$	$O(n)$
Access by index	$\Theta(1)$	$O(1)$
Insert at end	$\Theta(1)$	$O(n)$
Insert elsewhere	$\Theta(n)$	$O(n)$
Delete	$\Theta(1)$	$O(n)$
Delete at end	$\Theta(1)$	$\Theta(1)$
Linear search	$O(n)$	$O(n)$
Binary search	$O(\log n)$	$O(n)$

Let's dive into a bit more detail on why our table has the values that it has by looking at each major class of operation!

Access

Array access is highly efficient and has constant time complexity ($O(1)$). This means that accessing an element at a specific index in an array takes the same amount of time, regardless of the size of the array. Arrays achieve this performance by storing elements in contiguous memory locations, allowing direct access to them by using the index.

Insertion

- Inserting an element at the beginning of an array is inefficient, for it requires shifting *all* the existing elements to make room for the new element. This operation has a time complexity of $O(n)$, where n is the number of elements in the array.

- Inserting an element at the end of an array is more efficient, particularly **when the array has sufficient adjacent memory capacity**. It can be done in constant time ($O(1)$).

- Inserting an element at a specific index within an array also requires shifting all the subsequent elements to make room. Thus, it has a time complexity of $O(n)$, where n is the number of elements in the array.

- As we saw earlier, there will be situations in which the array does not have sufficient adjacent memory capacity to add a new item. In such cases, the time will always go up to $O(n)$ because our array will need to move all of its contents to a newer, larger region of memory.

Deletion

- Deleting an element from the beginning of an array involves shifting all the subsequent elements to fill the gap, resulting in a time complexity of O(n), where n is the number of elements in the array.

- Deleting an element from the end of an array is efficient and can be done in constant time (O(1)).

- Deleting an element from a specific index within an array requires shifting all the subsequent elements to fill the gap, resulting in a time complexity of O(n), where n is the number of elements in the array.

Searching

There are two classes of search approaches we can take:

- **Linear search:** Searching for an element in an unsorted array requires iterating through each element until a match is found or the end of the array is reached. In the worst case, this operation has a time complexity of O(n), where n is the number of elements in the array.

- **Binary search:** Searching for an element in a **sorted array** can be done using binary search, which repeatedly divides the search space in half. This operation has a time complexity of O(log n), where n is the number of elements in the array. However, binary search requires a sorted array, so if the array is unsorted, an additional sorting operation may be needed, resulting in a higher time complexity.

We cover both linear and binary searches in greater detail later when covering algorithms, so keep this information under your hat until then.

Conclusion

Arrays are one of the more fundamental data structures we will use. Almost all programming languages, no matter how low-level, provide built-in support for arrays. There are several reasons for this. In programming, we deal with collections of data all the time. It would be odd to have to re-create the array for every project. The other reason has to do with how arrays work. They closely map continuous regions of memory, and it would be difficult for us (especially higher-level languages) to re-create an array data structure from scratch and maintain the performance that a more native implementation will provide. This is why, as we will see shortly, arrays are actually a part of other data structures that we will be looking at.

SOME ADDITIONAL RESOURCES

? Ask a question: **https://forum.kirupa.com**

Errors/Known issues: **https://bit.ly/algorithms_errata**

Source repository: **https://bit.ly/algorithms_source**

4

LINKED LISTS

Linked lists are pretty sweet. They provide an elegant solution for dealing with large amounts of data that are constantly changing, and they have some tricks up their sleeve for doing all of this dealing quickly and efficiently. In this chapter, we explore the ins and outs of linked lists, such as their basic structure, performance characteristics, code implementation, and more! It's going to be a hoot.

Onward!

Meet the Linked List

Linked lists, just like arrays, are all about helping us store a collection of data. In Figure 4-1, we have an example of a linked list we are using to store the letters A through E.

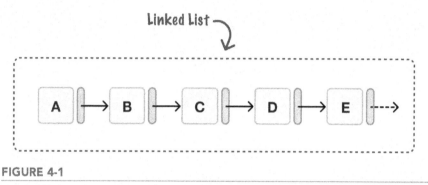

FIGURE 4-1

A linked list

Linked lists work by relying on individual nodes that are connected to each other. Each node is responsible for two things:

- Whatever data it is storing, such as a letter

- A next pointer (aka reference) that points to the next node in the list

It goes without saying that the node is a big deal. We can zoom in on a node and visualize it, as shown in Figure 4-2.

The abbreviated biography of a linked list is this: when we take a bunch of data, match them with nodes, and connect the nodes together via the next pointer, we have a linked list. How does a linked list become a linked list? How does it help us work with data? Let's walk through some more details and answer these questions!

Finding a Value

We have a linked list with a bunch of data, and we want to find something. This is one of the most common operations we'll perform. We find a value by starting with the *first* node (aka *head* node) and traversing through each node as referenced by the next pointer (Figure 4-3).

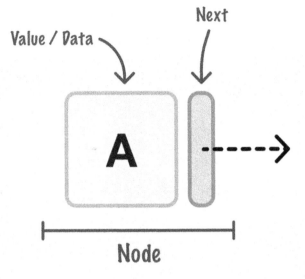

FIGURE 4-2

A node is made up of a value/datum and a pointer or reference

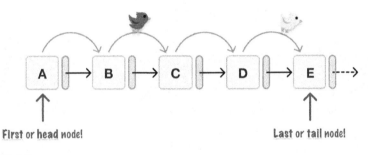

FIGURE 4-3

Traversing nodes

We keep jumping from node to node until we either

- Find the node whose value we are looking for, or
- Reach the last node (aka *tail* node) that marks the end of our list, and we have nowhere to go

If you think this sounds a whole lot like a linear search, you would be correct. It totally is . . . and all the good and bad performance characteristics that it implies. If you don't think so, that is okay. We look into linear search in greater detail in Chapter 17.

Adding Nodes

Now, let's look at how to add nodes to our linked list. The whole idea of adding nodes is less about *adding* and more about *creating* a new node and *updating* a few next pointers. We'll see this play out as we look at a handful of examples. Let's say that we want to add a node F at the end (Figure 4-4).

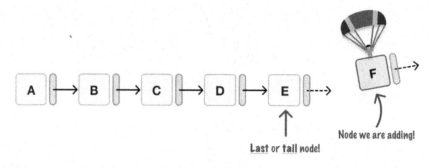

FIGURE 4-4

We want to add a new node F

What we need to do is update the next pointer for our *tail* or *last* E node to the new node F we are adding (Figure 4-5).

FIGURE 4-5

Updating the pointer for E

It doesn't matter where in our linked list we are adding our new node. The behavior is mostly the same. Let's say that we want to add a new node Q *between* our existing nodes of C and D (Figure 4-6).

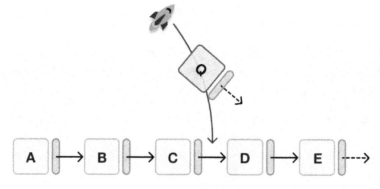

FIGURE 4-6

We want add a new node Q between C and D

To make this work, the steps we need to take are as follows:

1. Replace the next pointer on C to point to Q.

2. Replace the next pointer on Q to point to D.

This will result in the arrangement shown in Figure 4-7, which is exactly what we wanted.

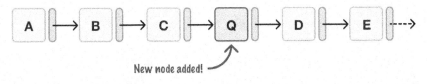

New node added!

FIGURE 4-7

Q has been added

An important detail to keep in mind is that it doesn't matter where in our linked list we are adding our node. Our linked list's primary job is to ensure the next pointers are updated to account for the newly added node. While this sounds complicated, it is a small amount of work. If we are adding a node to the beginning or end of our linked list, we make only one pointer-related update. If we are adding a node anywhere else but the beginning or end of our linked list, we make two pointer-related updates. That's pretty efficient!

Deleting a Node

When we want to delete a node, the steps we take are similar-ish to what we did when adding nodes. Let's say that we want to delete node D in our linked list (Figure 4-8).

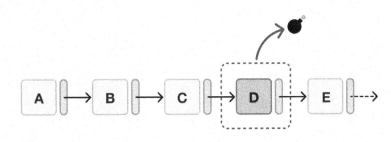

FIGURE 4-8

We want to delete node D

What we do is update the next pointer on node C to reference node E directly, bypassing node D (Figure 4-9).

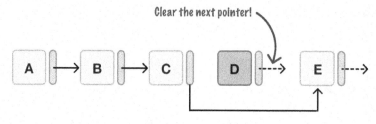

FIGURE 4-9

Updating the pointer on C to reference E, bypassing D

We also clear the next pointer on the D node. All of this makes node D unreachable via a traversal and removes any connection this node has with the rest of the nodes in our linked list. *Unreachable* does not mean *deleted*, though. When does node D actually get deleted? The exact moment varies, but it happens automatically as part of something known as **garbage collection**, when our computer reclaims memory by getting rid of unwanted things.

Linked List: Time and Space Complexity

It's time for some more fun! We started off our look at linked lists by talking about how fast and efficient they are. For the most common operations, Table 4-1 summarizes how our linked list performs.

TABLE 4-1   Linked List Performance

Action	Best	Average	Worst
Search	O(1)	O(n)	O(n)
Add/Insert	O(1)	O(n)	O(n)
Delete	O(1)	O(n)	O(n)

An important detail to keep in mind is that the exact implementation of a linked list plays an important role in how fast or slow certain operations are. One implementation choice we will make is that our linked list will have a direct reference to both the first (head) node and the last (tail) node.

Deeper Look at the Running Time

The Table 4-1 glosses over some subtle (but very important) details, so let's call out the relevant points:

- **Search**
  - Searching for an element in a singly linked list takes $O(n)$ time because we have to traverse the list from the beginning to find the element.
  - If what we are looking for happens to be the first item, then we return the found node in $O(1)$ time.

- **Add/Insert**
  - Inserting an element at the beginning or end of a singly linked list takes $O(1)$ time, as we only need to update the reference of the new node to point to the current head or tail of the list.
  - Inserting an element at a specific position in the list takes $O(n)$ time in the average and worst cases, for we have to traverse through the list to find the position.

- **Delete**
  - Similar to the adding case, deleting an element from the beginning or end of a singly linked list takes $O(1)$ time, as we only need to update the reference of the first or last node.
  - Deleting an element from a specific position in the list takes $O(n)$ time in the average and worst cases, for we have to traverse the list to find the element and then delete it.

Space Complexity

From a memory/space point of view, linked lists require $O(n)$ space. For each piece of data we want our linked list to store, we wrap that data into a node. The node itself is a very lightweight structure: all it contains is a thin wrapper to store our data and a reference to the next node.

Linked List Variations

As it turns out, linked lists aren't a one-size-fits-all phenomenon. We want to be aware of a few popular variations and talk through what makes them useful.

Singly Linked List

The singly linked list, spoiler alert, is the type of linked list we have been looking at in-depth so far (Figure 4-10).

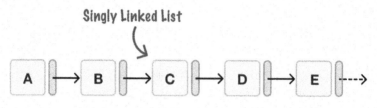

FIGURE 4-10

Our singly linked list

In a singly linked list, each node has exactly one pointer that references the next node. For many situations, this one-way behavior is perfectly adequate.

Doubly Linked List

In a doubly linked list, each node has two pointers, one to the previous node and one to the next node (Figure 4-11).

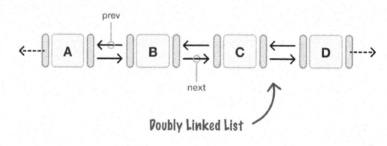

FIGURE 4-11

A doubly linked list

Using double links allows for easier traversal in both directions, similar to moving from a one-lane road to a two-lane one. We typically see a doubly linked list being used in implementations of associative arrays and other complex data structures.

Circular Linked List

In a circular linked list, the last node's next pointer points to the first node, creating a circular structure (Figure 4-12).

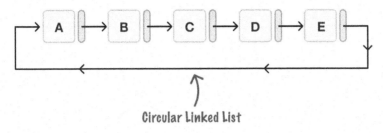

Circular Linked List

FIGURE 4-12

A circular linked list

This type of linked list can be used in situations where items need to be accessed in a circular fashion, such as a scheduling algorithm, picking the next player in a game of poker, and more. Speaking of poker, check out Figure 4-13.

Choosing the next dog to play (and cycle through) can be implemented with a circular linked list!

FIGURE 4-13

Poker is a circular activity

Sorry. I couldn't resist. If you mention poker, I am obligated to share this image.

Skip List

We saw that linked lists are fast. Skip lists make things even faster. A skip list is a linked list that includes additional "skip" links that act like shortcuts to make jumping to points in the list faster (Figure 4-14).

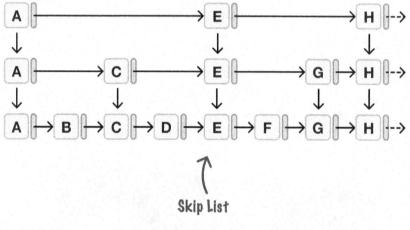

FIGURE 4-14

A skip list

Notice that each level of our skip list gives us faster access to certain elements. Depending on what data we are looking for, we will be traversing both horizontally as well as up and down each level to minimize the number of nodes we need to examine.

Skip lists are often used in situations where we need to perform frequent lookups or searches on a large dataset. By adding skip links to a linked list, we can reduce the amount of time it takes to find a specific element while still maintaining the benefits of a linked list (such as constant time insertion and deletion).

Implementation

With our linked list, a handful of operations are going to be critical for us to support:

- Creating a new linked list
- Adding an item at the beginning
- Adding an item at the end
- Adding an item before an existing item

- Adding an item after an existing item
- Checking if our linked list contains a specific item
- Removing the first item
- Removing the last item
- Removing a specific item
- Converting our items into an array
- Getting the length of our linked list

Here is our implementation that supports all of these operations:

```
class LinkedListNode {
  constructor(data, next = null) {
    this.data = data;
    this.next = next;
  }
}


class LinkedList {
  constructor() {
    this.head = null;
    this.tail = null;
    this.size = 0;
  }

  addFirst(data) {
    const newNode = new LinkedListNode(data, this.head);

    this.head = newNode;

    if (!this.tail) {
      this.tail = newNode;
    }

    this.size++;
  }
```

```
addLast(data) {
  const newNode = new LinkedListNode(data);

  if (!this.head) {
    this.head = newNode;
    this.tail = newNode;
  } else {
    this.tail.next = newNode;
    this.tail = newNode;
  }

  this.size++;
}

addBefore(beforeData, data) {
  const newNode = new LinkedListNode(data);

  if (this.size === 0) {
    this.head = newNode;
    this.size++;
    return;
  }

  if (this.head.data === beforeData) {
    newNode.next = this.head;
    this.head = newNode;
    this.size++;
    return;
  }

  let current = this.head.next;
  let prev = this.head;

  while (current) {
    if (current.data === beforeData) {
      newNode.next = current;
      prev.next = newNode;
```

```
        this.size++;
        return;
      }


    prev = current;
    current = current.next;
  }


  throw new Error(`Node with data '${beforeData}' not found in
list`);
  }


  addAfter(afterData, data) {
    const newNode = new LinkedListNode(data);

    if (this.size === 0) {
      this.head = newNode;
      this.size++;
      return;
    }


    let current = this.head;

    while (current) {
      if (current.data === afterData) {
        newNode.next = current.next;
        current.next = newNode;
        this.size++;
        return;
      }


      current = current.next;
    }


    throw new Error(`Node with data '${afterData}' not found in
list!`);
  }
```

```
contains(data) {
  let current = this.head;

  while (current) {
    if (current.data === data) {
      return true;
    }

    current = current.next;
  }

  return false;
}

removeFirst() {
  if (!this.head) {
    throw new Error('List is empty');
  }

  this.head = this.head.next;
  if (!this.head) {
    this.tail = null;
  }
  this.size--;
}

removeLast() {
  if (!this.tail) {
    throw new Error('List is empty');
  }

  if (this.head === this.tail) {
    this.head = null;
    this.tail = null;
    this.size--;
```

```
      return;
    }

    let current = this.head;
    let prev = null;

    while (current.next) {
      prev = current;
      current = current.next;
    }

    prev.next = null;
    this.tail = prev;
    this.size--;
  }

  remove(data) {
    if (this.size === 0) {
      throw new Error("List is empty");
    }

    if (this.head.data === data) {
      this.head = this.head.next;
      this.size--;
      return;
    }

    let current = this.head;

    while (current.next) {
      if (current.next.data === data) {
        current.next = current.next.next;
        this.size--;
        return;
      }
```

```
      current = current.next;
    }


    throw new Error(`Node with data '${data}' not found in list!`);
  }


  toArray() {
    const arr = [];


    let current = this.head;


    while (current) {
      arr.push(current.data);
      current = current.next;
    }


    return arr;
  }


  get length() {
    return this.size;
  }
}
```

To see this code in action, here are some example prompts:

```
let letters = new LinkedList();
letters.addLast("A");
letters.addLast("B");
letters.addLast("C");
letters.addLast("D");
letters.addLast("E");


console.log(letters.toArray()); // ['A', 'B', 'C', 'D', 'E']


letters.addFirst("AA");
letters.addLast("Z");
```

```
console.log(letters.toArray()); // ['AA', 'A', 'B', 'C', 'D', 'E',
'Z']

letters.remove("C");
letters.removeFirst();
letters.removeLast();

console.log(letters.toArray()); // ['A', 'B', 'D', 'E']

letters.addAfter("D", "Q");

console.log(letters.toArray()); // ['A', 'B', 'Q', 'D', 'E']

letters.addAfter("Q", "H");
letters.addBefore("A", "5");

console.log(letters.toArray()); // ['5', 'A', 'B', 'Q', 'H' 'D',
'E']

console.log(letters.length); // 7
```

To see a live example of all the preceding code, visit this Codepen demo: https://bit.ly/kirupa_linkedlist. In the future, if we need to use this `LinkedList` in our code, we can either copy/paste all of this code or reference it directly by adding the following script tag:

```
<script src="https://www.kirupa.com/js/linkedlist_v1.js"></script>
```

As we'll see shortly, the linked list plays a crucial role in how several other data structures and algorithms are implemented.

 NOTE   Linked Lists vs. Arrays

As mentioned in the previous chapter, arrays mirror how data is stored in our computer's memory. This implies that we need a contiguous block of memory precisely matching the size of the array to start using it. While arrays are optimized for direct access to elements, linked lists follow a different approach. They rely on the "next" pointer, which grants them flexibility and eliminates the need for contiguous memory. However, this design also makes linked lists less suitable for direct access operations. You win some, you lose some, right?

Conclusion

Phew! As we saw across the many words and diagrams, linked lists provide an efficient way to store and manipulate data. They allow for constant time insertion and deletion, and they can be easily traversed to perform operations such as searching. While they aren't the most efficient data structure out there, they can safely claim the top spot in their simplicity. As we will see in the next chapter, building a linked list in JavaScript is just as elegant as our explanation of how they work.

SOME ADDITIONAL RESOURCES

? Ask a question: **https://forum.kirupa.com**

☑ Errors/Known issues: **https://bit.ly/algorithms_errata**

☐ Source repository: **https://bit.ly/algorithms_source**

STACKS

Have you ever used Undo or Redo when working on something (Figure 5-1)?

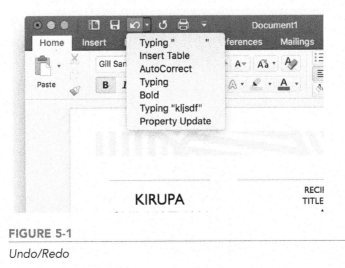

FIGURE 5-1

Undo/Redo

Have you ever wondered how your favorite programming languages tend to turn the things you write into sequential steps so that your computer knows what to do? Have you ever gone forward and backward in your browser? Do you like pancakes?

If you answered yes to any of the above questions, then you have probably run into the star of this tutorial, the **stack** data structure. In the following sections, we learn more about stacks and how you can use one in JavaScript.

Onward!

Meet the Stack

At some point in our lives, we have almost certainly seen a stack of things arranged on top of each other . . . such as pancakes, as shown in Figure 5-2.

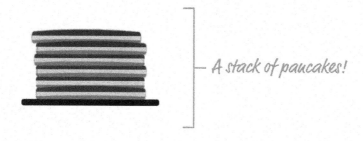

A stack of pancakes!

FIGURE 5-2

A stack

The thing about stacks of things is that we always add items to the top. We remove items from the top as well (Figure 5-3).

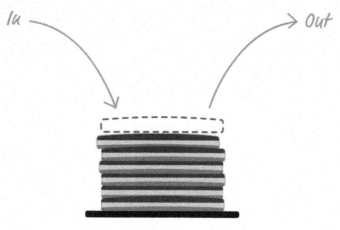

In ······ → *Out*

FIGURE 5-3

Add to and remove from the top of the stack

This concept also applies to things in the computer world. The stack is a well-known data structure we will frequently encounter where, just like our pancakes, we keep adding data sequentially (Figure 5-4).

We remove the data from the end of our stack in the same order we added them (Figure 5-5).

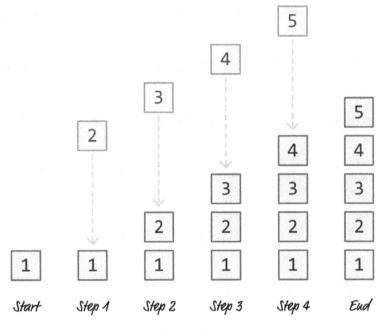

Start   Step 1   Step 2   Step 3   Step 4   End

FIGURE 5-4

Data is added sequentially to a stack

In computer speak, this is known as a **last in, first out** system—more commonly abbreviated **LIFO**. The data that you end up accessing (aka removing) is the last one we added. That's really all there is to know about stacks, at least conceptually.

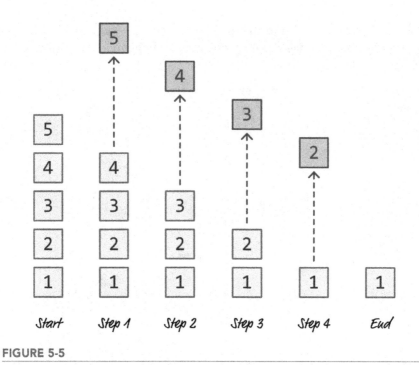

FIGURE 5-5

Data is removed from the end of the stack in the order it was added

A JavaScript Implementation

Now that we have an overview of what stacks are and how they work, let's go one level deeper. The following is an implementation of a `Stack` in JavaScript:

```
class Stack {
  constructor(...items) {
    this.items = items;
  }
  clear() {
    this.items.length = 0;
  }
  clone() {
    return new Stack(...this.items);
  }
  contains(item) {
    return this.items.includes(item);
  }
}
```

```
  peek() {
    let itemsLength = this.items.length;
    let item = this.items[itemsLength - 1];

    return item;
  }
  pop() {
    let removedItem = this.items.pop();
    return removedItem;
  }
  push(item) {
    this.items.push(item);
    return item;
  }
}
```

This code defines our `Stack` object and the various methods that we can use to add items, remove items, peek at the last item, and more. To use it, we can do something like the following:

```
let myStack = new Stack();

// Add items
myStack.push("One");
myStack.push("Two");
myStack.push("Three!");

// Preview the last item
myStack.peek(); // Three

// Remove item
let lastItem = myStack.pop();
console.log(lastItem) // Three

myStack.peek(); // Two
```

```
// Create a copy of the stack
let newStack = myStack.clone();

// Check if item is in Stack
newStack.contains("Three")  // false
```

The first thing we need to do is create a new `Stack` object. We can create an empty stack, as shown, or prefill it with some items, as follows:

```
let stuffStack = new Stack("One", "Two", "Three");
```

To add items to the stack, use the `push` method and pass in whatever you wish to add. To remove an item, use the `pop` method. If you want to preview what the last item is without removing it, the `peek` method will help you out. The `clone` method returns a copy of your stack, and the `contains` method allows you to see if an item exists in the stack or not.

The stack data structure is used quite a bit in other data structures and algorithms we'll be seeing throughout the book. We can copy/paste the code each time or reference this same implementation via **www.kirupa.com/js/stack_v1.js**.

Stacks: Time and Space Complexity

The runtime and memory performance of a stack is quite good. For the most common operations, such as the ones we support in our implementation, Table 5-1 summarizes how our linked list performs:

TABLE 5-1

Action	Best	Average	Worst
Push	O(1)	O(1)	O(1)
Pop	O(1)	O(1)	O(1)
Peek	O(1)	O(1)	O(1)
Search/Contains	O(1)	O(n)	O(n)
Memory	O(n)	O(n)	O(n)

A stack can be implemented as an array or as a linked list, but the differences in performance between those two implementation options is minimal. Let's dive a bit deeper into why our stack's performance numbers are what they are.

Runtime Performance

- **Push Operation:** Adding an element to the top of the stack (push operation) takes constant time complexity O(1). It doesn't matter how large the stack is; the push operation always requires the same amount of time.

- **Pop Operation:** Removing an element from the top of the stack (pop operation) also takes constant time complexity O(1). Similar to the push operation, it doesn't depend on the size of the stack.

- **Peek Operation:** Looking at the top element of the stack (peek operation) is also a constant time operation O(1).

- **Search/Contains Operation:** Searching for an element in the stack (e.g., checking if an element exists in the stack) takes linear time O(*n*). This operation involves traversing the entire stack and all of its items in the worst case.

Memory Performance

The memory performance of a stack in JavaScript is fairly efficient with O(*n*) growth, and this doesn't change based on whether the stack is implemented using arrays or linked lists. As we saw earlier, arrays in JavaScript are dynamically sized, so they can grow or shrink as elements are added or removed. However, this dynamic resizing might cause occasional memory reallocation, which can lead to some hiccups.

When using a linked list to implement the stack, memory allocation is done incrementally. There are no major reallocations similar to what we would have seen with arrays, so a linked list approach has its advantages when dealing with large stacks.

Conclusion

If you glance at the code, our stack implementation is just a wrapper over the `Array` object (for more about arrays in JavaScript, visit https://bit.ly/kirupaArrays). Because items are added to the end and removed from the end, using the array's push and pop methods works without any extra modification. The performance of adding and removing items from the end of an array is really good—constant time, or O(1), if you are keeping track.

SOME ADDITIONAL RESOURCES

? Ask a question: **https://forum.kirupa.com**

Errors/Known issues: **https://bit.ly/algorithms_errata**

Source repository: **https://bit.ly/algorithms_source**

6

QUEUES

In Chapter 5, we saw that stacks are a last in, first out (LIFO) data structure where items are added and removed from the end. Contrasting that, we have the other popular data structure, the **queue**. This is an interesting one that we'll learn more about in the following sections.

Onward!

Meet the Queue

Living up to its name, a queue is very similar to standing in line for something (Figure 6-1).

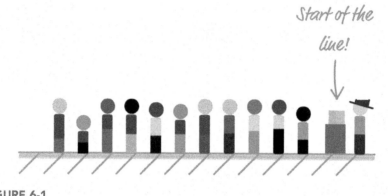

FIGURE 6-1

People lining up

The person standing at the front of the line is the first one to have shown up, and they are the first ones to leave as well. New people show up and stand at the end of the line, and they don't leave until the person in front of them has reached the beginning of the line and has left (Figure 6-2).

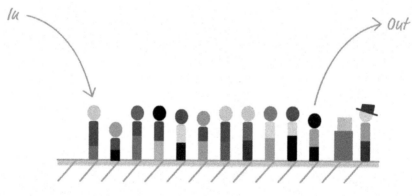

FIGURE 6-2

People leave the beginning of the queue, and they join at the end

Given that behavior, a queue follows a **first in, first out** policy, more commonly shortened to **FIFO**. Except for the little big detail about which items get removed first, queues and stacks are pretty similar otherwise.

When adding items, the behavior with stacks is identical (Figure 6-3).

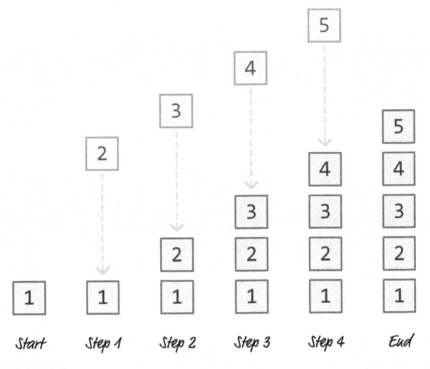

Start   Step 1   Step 2   Step 3   Step 4   End

FIGURE 6-3

Items get added to the top

Items are added to the end of the queue. When removing items, they are removed sequentially, starting with the first item that populated the data structure in a queue-based world (Figure 6-4).

Now, you may be wondering when you'll ever end up needing to use a queue. Besides helping you appreciate standing in line, queues have a lot of practical uses in the digital world. Pretty much any situation that requires you to maintain an order of something relies on a queue-like data structure. High-traffic situations like travel booking, waiting to purchase a ticket for a popular concert, prioritizing e-mails by an e-mail server, and more are all situations in which a queue is used. You'll see queues used a lot by various search algorithms as well, so queues are here to stay! Get friendly with them.

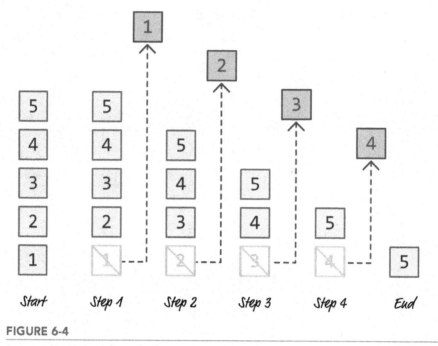

FIGURE 6-4

Items get removed from the bottom

A JavaScript Implementation

To turn all of those words and images into working code, take a look at the following Queue implementation:

```
class Queue {
  constructor() {
    this.items = new LinkedList();
  }
  clear() {
    this.items = new LinkedList();
  }
  contains(item) {
    return this.items.contains(item);
  }
```

```
  peek() {
    return this.items.head.data;
  }
  dequeue() {
    let removedItem = this.items.head.data;
    this.items.removeFirst();
    return removedItem;
  }
  enqueue(item) {
    this.items.addLast(item);
  }
  get length() {
    return this.items.length;
  }
}
```

Our implementation relies on a linked list to make some of the data operations much faster (as opposed to just using an array), so we need to either add our full `LinkedList` class via copy/paste or reference it from https://www.kirupa.com/js/linkedlist_v1.js.

The way we use a queue is by creating a `Queue` object, using the `enqueue` method to add items to the queue, and using the `dequeue` method to remove items from the queue:

```
// create new Queue object
let myQ = new Queue();

// add two items
myQ.enqueue("Item 1");
myQ.enqueue("Item 2");

// remove item
let removedItem = my.dequeue();   // returns Item 1
```

We can easily create a copy of our queue by using the `clone` method, check whether an item exists using `contains`, and peek at what the removed item might be (without actually removing it) by using . . . um . . . peek! The implementation very closely mimics that of our stack, but the important detail is that we are using a linked list and its implementation along as well.

Queues: Time and Space Complexity

For the most common queue operations, Table 6-1 summarizes how our queue performs across common operations:

TABLE 6-1

Action	Best	Average	Worst
Enqueue (Insert)	O(1)	O(1)	O(1)
Dequeue (Remove)	O(1)	O(1)	O(1)
Peek	O(1)	O(1)	O(1)
Search/Contains	O(1)	O(n)	O(n)
Memory	O(n)	O(n)	O(n)

A key detail for these performance numbers revolves around our using a linked list as the underlying data structure. If we used something like an array, operations that involve modifying the front of our list will take O(n) time as opposed to O(1) time with the linked list. We don't want that! Let's dive a bit deeper into why our queue's performance numbers are what they are.

Runtime Performance

- **Enqueue (Insertion):** The enqueue operation in a linked list-based queue has a constant time complexity of O(1) because elements are added to the rear of the linked list, and there is no need to shift or move existing elements.

- **Dequeue (Deletion):** The dequeue operation in a linked list-based queue also has a constant time complexity of O(1). Elements are removed from the front of the linked list, and like the enqueue operation, no shifting of elements is required.

- **Peek:** The peek operation, which allows us to access the front element without removing it, is also an O(1) operation. It directly retrieves the value from the head of the linked list.

- **Search:** Searching for an element in a linked list-based queue is less efficient than its insertion or deletion operations. The search operation requires traversing the linked list from the front to the rear, resulting in a linear time complexity of O(n), where n is the number of elements in the queue.

Memory Performance

The overall memory usage of a queue is O(n) where each element in the queue is represented by a node, which contains the data and a pointer/reference to the next node. Therefore, the space required grows linearly with the number of elements in the queue. With that said, there are a few additional details to keep in mind:

- **Dynamic Memory Allocation:** Linked lists are dynamically allocated, meaning that memory is allocated for each node as elements are added to the queue. This allows the queue to dynamically resize and efficiently handle varying numbers of elements.

- **Memory Overhead:** Linked lists require additional memory for maintaining the pointers between nodes. We know that already! This overhead, compared to an array-based implementation, can be a disadvantage when dealing with a large number of elements.

- **Cache Performance:** Linked lists can suffer from cache performance issues because the elements are not stored in contiguous memory locations. This might lead to more cache misses, affecting the overall performance for certain operations.

Not too shabby, right? A queue implemented using a linked list provides efficient insertion and deletion operations with a constant time complexity of O(1). Searching for an element in the queue is slower with a linear time complexity of O(n). When it comes to memory, things are pretty consistent with a linear O(n) growth based on the number of items our queue is storing.

Conclusion

Between what we saw earlier with stacks and what we saw just now with queues, we covered two of the most popular data structures that mimic how we model how data enters and leaves. A queue is known as a FIFO data structure where items get added to the end but removed from the beginning. This "removed from the beginning" part is where our reliance on a linked list data structure comes in. Arrays, as we have seen a few times, are not very efficient when it comes to removing or adding items at the front.

SOME ADDITIONAL RESOURCES

? Ask a question: **https://forum.kirupa.com**

Errors/Known issues: **https://bit.ly/algorithms_errata**

Source repository: **https://bit.ly/algorithms_source**

7

TREES

When we look around, a lot of the data we work with is hierarchical, with a clear relationship between a parent and child. Common examples include family trees, organizational charts, flow charts/diagrams, and more. Figure 7-1 is a famous example popularized by xkcd (https://xkcd.com/518/).

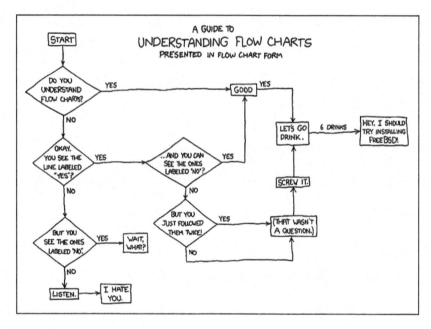

FIGURE 7-1

Visualizing the quirkiness of our programming lives nicely!

While we can *certainly* represent hierarchical data using linear data structures like arrays or linked lists, just as it is *certainly* possible to eat soup using a plate and fork, it isn't optimal. There are better ways. One of the better ways is the **tree** data structure.

In the following sections, we learn a whole lot about trees and set ourselves up nicely to go deeper into popular tree-related topics in the future.

Onward!

Trees 101

To retrace our steps a bit, a tree data structure is a way of organizing data in a hierarchical manner. Just as in nature, trees in our computer world come in many shapes and sizes. For our purposes, let's visualize one that looks like Figure 7-2.

We see a bunch of circles and lines connecting each circle. Each circle in the tree is known as a **node**. The node plays an important role in a tree. It is responsible for storing data, and it is also responsible for linking to other nodes. The link (visualized as a line) between each node is known as an **edge** (Figure 7-3).

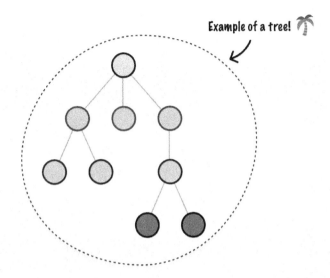

Example of a tree! 🌴

FIGURE 7-2

Example of a tree

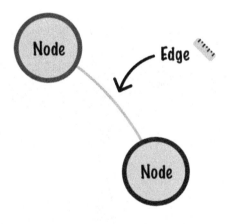

Node

Edge 📏

Node

FIGURE 7-3

Edges connect nodes

Now, just saying that our tree has a bunch of nodes connected by edges isn't very enlightening. To help give the tree more clarity, we give the nodes additional labels, such as **children**, **parents**, **siblings**, **root**, and **leaves**.

The easiest nodes to classify are the children. There are many of them, for a child node is any node that is a direct extension of another node. Except for the very first node at the very top, all of the nodes we see in Figure 7-4 fit that description and are considered to be children.

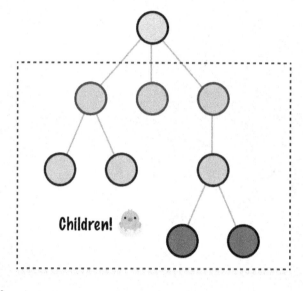

FIGURE 7-4

Child nodes

When we have child nodes, we also have parent nodes. A parent node is any node that has children (Figure 7-5).

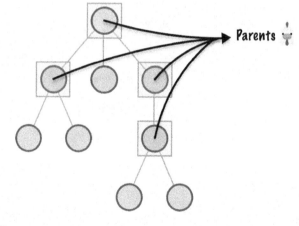

FIGURE 7-5

Parent nodes

One thing to call out is that the meaning of *parent* or *children* is relative depending on what part of the tree we are looking at. A node can be a child, a parent, a grandparent, a grandchild, and more, all at the same time (Figure 7-6).

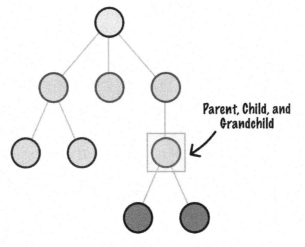

FIGURE 7-6

Nodes can be multiple family types

It is convention to never go beyond referring to a node as just a *child* or just a *parent*, though. Adding extra familial layers adds more complexity, especially because we have different ways of specifying the exact layer in the hierarchy a node is present in.

With that said, there is one more family relationship that we will encounter frequently. That one is *siblings*, which are all the children of the same parent (Figure 7-7).

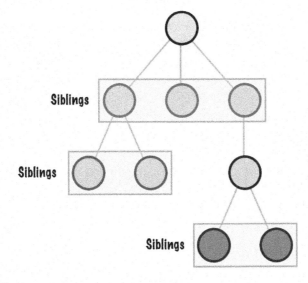

FIGURE 7-7

Sibling nodes

We are almost done here. Earlier, we said that all nodes are children except for the first node at the very top, which has no parent. This node is better known to friends, family, and computer scientists as the *root* (Figure 7-8).

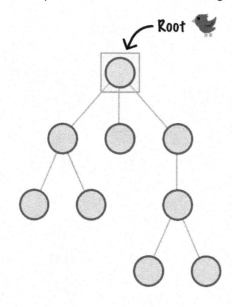

FIGURE 7-8

The all-powerful root node

While the root is a node that has no parent, on the other end are the nodes that don't have any children. These nodes are commonly known as *leaves* (Figure 7-9).

All righty. At this point, we covered the basic properties of trees and the many names we can give to each node depending on how zoomed in or zoomed out we are when looking at them. There are a few more tree properties and node groupings that have special names, but we'll cross those when we get to them later.

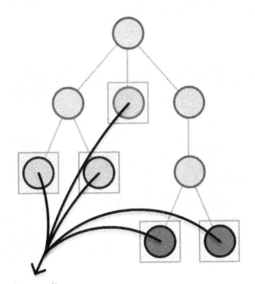

Leaves

FIGURE 7-9

Leaf nodes

Height and Depth

When we look at each node in our tree, the **height** and **depth** are little details used to describe the relative position of nodes within the tree. If we had to define both:

- The height of a node is the maximum number of edges that we must cross down to reach the furthest leaf node from the current node.

- The depth of a node is the number of edges we must cross up to reach the root node from the current node.

These definitions aren't the easiest ones to fully wrap our brains around. The easiest way to make sense of all this is by taking our example tree and seeing what the height and depth for each node will be. Take a close look at Figure 7-10.

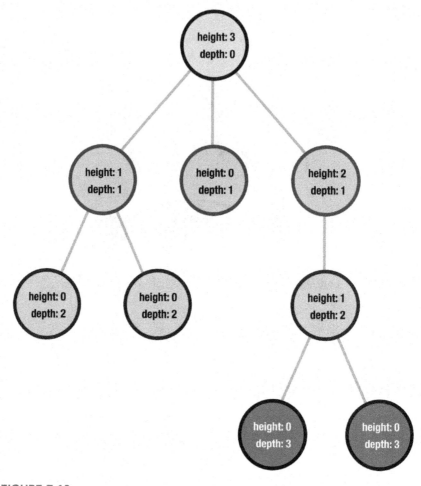

FIGURE 7-10

Tree height and depth explained

Some things to note: The value for height is *relative to each node*, depending entirely on how far away the furthest leaf node is. The value for depth is *global to the tree*, and it doesn't matter what the shape of our tree is. The root of the tree has a depth of 0, the next layer of children has a depth of 1, and so on.

Conclusion

All right, my leaf-loving friends, we've finally come to the end of our little deep dive through the zany world of the tree data structure. While thinking through how our data will fit into this tree-like format may seem a little daunting at first, we will go further in subsequent chapters to ensure we all become tree hugging experts! So, the next time you're feeling a little stumped, just remember to tree-t yourself to a nice cup of coffee, put on your thinking cap, and branch out . . . okay, I'll leaf now.

SOME ADDITIONAL RESOURCES

? Ask a question: **https://forum.kirupa.com**

Errors/Known issues: **https://bit.ly/algorithms_errata**

Source repository: **https://bit.ly/algorithms_source**

BINARY TREES

Earlier, we looked at the tree data structure and learned a whole lot about what all of the various nodes and edges mean. It's time to branch out (ha!) and go deeper. We are going to build upon that foundation by looking at a specific implementation of a tree data structure, the **binary tree**.

Onward!

Meet the Binary Tree

A binary tree, on the surface, looks just like a boring regular tree that allows us to store data in a hierarchical manner. Figure 8-1 is an example of what a binary tree looks like.

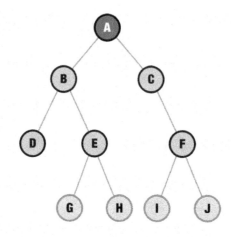

FIGURE 8-1

Example of a binary tree

What makes binary trees different is that, unlike regular trees where anything goes, we have three strict rules our tree must adhere to in order to be classified as a binary tree:

1. Each node can have only zero, one, or two children.

2. The tree can have only a single root node.

3. There can be only one path to a node from the root.

Let's dive a bit deeper into these rules, for they are important to understand. They help explain why the binary tree works the way it does, and they set us up for learning about other tree variants, such as the binary search tree.

Rules Explained

The first rule is that each node in a binary tree can have only zero, one, or two children. If a node happens to have more than two children, that's a problem (Figure 8-2).

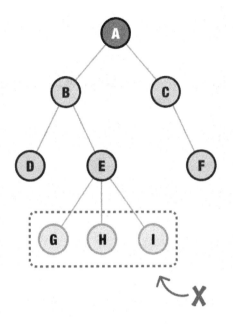

FIGURE 8-2

No more than two children allowed

The second rule is that a binary tree must have only a single root node (Figure 8-3).

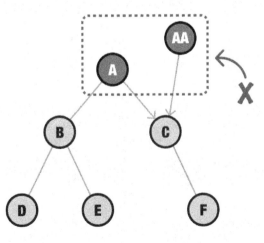

FIGURE 8-3

Can't have multiple root nodes

In this example, we have both the A node and the AA node competing for who gets to be the primary root. While multiple root nodes are acceptable in certain other tree-based data structures, they aren't allowed for binary trees.

Now, we get to the last rule. The last rule is that there can be only one path from the root to any node in the tree (Figure 8-4).

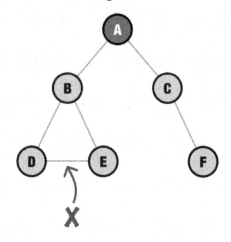

FIGURE 8-4

Can't have multiple paths between the root and a node

As we can see in this example, using node D as our destination, we can get there in two ways from our root. One way is by A - B - D. The other way is by A - B - E - D. We can't have loops / cycles like that and call the data structure a binary tree.

Binary Tree Variants

Binary trees, even with their stricter rules, appear in a handful of popular variants. These variants play a large role in how well our friendly binary tree performs at common data operations, how much space it takes up, and more. For now, we'll avoid the math and focus on the high-level details.

Full Binary Tree

The full binary tree, sometimes referred to as either a **strict binary tree** or **proper binary tree**, is a tree where all non-leaf nodes have their full two children (Figure 8-5).

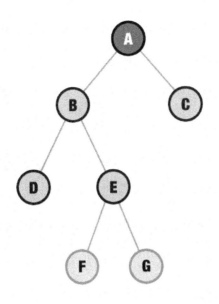

FIGURE 8-5

Example of a full binary tree

In this example, we can see that the non-leaf nodes A, B, and E have two children each.

Complete Binary Tree

A complete binary tree is one where all rows of the nodes are filled (where each parent has two children) except for the last row of nodes (Figure 8-6).

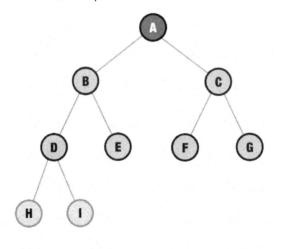

FIGURE 8-6

Every parent has two nodes

For this last row, there are some rules on how the nodes should appear. **If the last row has any nodes, those nodes need to be filled continuously, starting from the left with no gaps.** What you see in Figure 8-7 wouldn't be acceptable, for example.

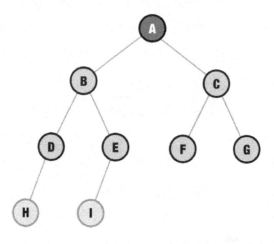

FIGURE 8-7

An incomplete binary tree

There is a gap where the D node is missing its right child, yet the I node is parented under the E node. This means we weren't continuously filling in the last row of nodes from the left. If the I node were instead inserted as the D node's right child, then things would be good.

Perfect Binary Tree

A perfect binary tree is one in which every level of the tree is fully filled with nodes (Figure 8-8).

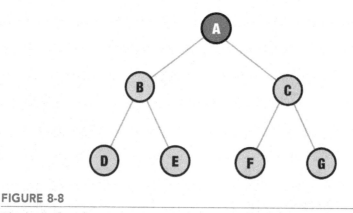

FIGURE 8-8

The look of perfection!

As a consequence of that requirement, all the leaf nodes are also at the same level.

Balanced Binary Tree

A balanced binary tree is a binary tree in which the height of the left and right subtrees of each node is not more than one apart. Figure 8-9 is an example of a balanced binary tree.

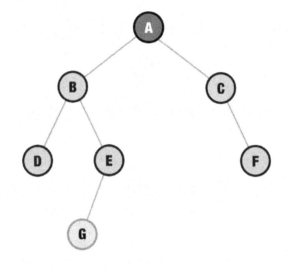

FIGURE 8-9

A balanced binary tree

In other words, this means that the tree is not lopsided. All nodes can be accessed efficiently.

Degenerate Binary Tree

In a degenerate binary tree, each parent node has only one child node (Figure 8-10).

The tree is essentially a linear data structure, like an array or linked list, with all nodes connected in a single path. Any advantages a tree-like structure provides are lost here; hence the *degenerate* classifier.

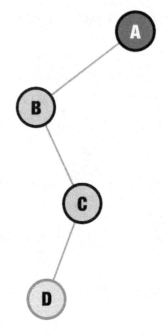

FIGURE 8-10

A degenerate binary tree

What about Adding, Removing, and Finding Nodes?

As with any data structure, common operations for us will be to add nodes, remove nodes, and find a particular node we are looking for. To echo a point I made earlier, binary trees in their generic state are not very efficient data structures. Learning how to perform common operations on them may be helpful as a general knowledge-gathering exercise, but the operations won't be too helpful in real-world situations. Instead of covering something that you will rarely benefit from, I'm going to put a pin on this topic and cover it in more detail as part of looking at a more efficient implementation of the binary tree, the **binary search tree**, later.

A Simple Binary Tree Implementation

Before we wrap things up, let's look at a simple binary tree implementation. The star of our implementation is the node, and here is how we represent this in JavaScript:

```
class Node {
  constructor(data) {
    this.data = data;
```

```
    this.left = null;
    this.right = null;
  }
}
```

We have a Node class, and it takes a data value as its argument, which it stores as a property called data on itself. Our node also stores two additional properties for left and right.

Let's re-create the following binary tree using what we have (Figure 8-11).

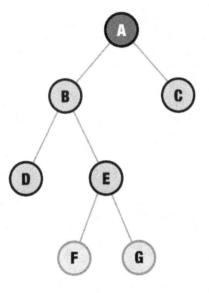

FIGURE 8-11

Example of the binary tree we are going to re-create

The full code for re-creating this binary tree using our Node class will look as follows:

```
class Node {
  constructor(data) {
    this.data = data;
    this.left = null;
    this.right = null;
  }
}
```

```
const rootNodeA = new Node("A");
const nodeB = new Node("B");
const nodeC = new Node("C");
const nodeD = new Node("D");
const nodeE = new Node("E");
const nodeF = new Node("F");
const nodeG = new Node("G");

rootNodeA.left = nodeB;
rootNodeA.right = nodeC;

nodeB.left = nodeD;
nodeB.right = nodeE;

nodeE.left = nodeF;
nodeE.right = nodeG;
```

Notice that we are creating a new Node object for each node in our tree, and the argument we pass in to the constructor is the letter value of each node:

```
const rootNodeA = new Node("A");
const nodeB = new Node("B");
const nodeC = new Node("C");
const nodeD = new Node("D");
const nodeE = new Node("E");
const nodeF = new Node("F");
const nodeG = new Node("G");
```

Our implementation of the Node object will support data ranging from simple (such as a letter) to overly complex. In some cases, our nodes will be made up of numbers. In other cases, our nodes will be made up of complex objects. We'll look at some more elaborate examples in later chapters.

Once we have our nodes created, we set each node's `left` and `right` properties to the corresponding child node:

```
rootNodeA.left = nodeB;
rootNodeA.right = nodeC;


nodeB.left = nodeD;
nodeB.right = nodeE;


nodeE.left = nodeF;
nodeE.right = nodeG;
```

If a node happens to be a leaf node, we don't do anything extra. It is safe to say that if a node doesn't have anything set for its `left` or `right` property, it is a leaf. It has no children.

Conclusion

In this chapter, through lots of words and countless diagrams, we learned about binary trees! The 411 is that a binary tree is a data structure that consists of nodes with an important constraint: **each node can have at most two child nodes**. The unique constraint of the binary tree allows us to use them to efficiently search, sort, and store data. Now, we didn't cover any of that here. The reason is that a binary tree by itself is too generic. The more useful variant of the binary tree is the **binary search tree**, and we look at it in Chapter 9.

SOME ADDITIONAL RESOURCES

   ? Ask a question: **https://forum.kirupa.com**

     Errors/Known issues: **https://bit.ly/algorithms_errata**

     Source repository: **https://bit.ly/algorithms_source**

9

BINARY SEARCH TREES

It's time for us to look at another awesome data structure, the **binary search tree.** If we squint at a binary search tree from a distance, it will look a whole lot like a binary tree (Figure 9-1).

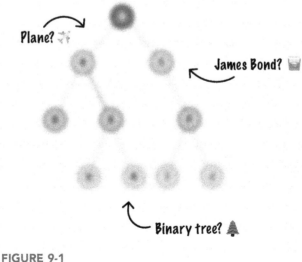

Plane? ✈

James Bond? 🥃

Binary tree? 🌲

FIGURE 9-1

This could be anything!

That's by design. Binary trees set a solid foundation with their node/edge rules and branching behavior that is desirable. Binary search trees improve upon plain binary trees by adding some extra logic on how they store data, and it is this extra logic that helps make them quite efficient when dealing with the sorts of data operations we may throw at it.

At a very high level, a binary search tree is designed in such a way that the location of each node is determined on the basis of the value it is storing. Nodes with smaller values go left, and nodes with larger values go right. Take a look at the binary search tree in Figure 9-2.

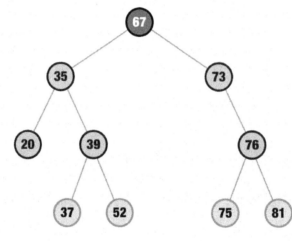

FIGURE 9-2

Example of a binary search tree

At each node, starting with the root, pay close attention to the node values and the values of their children, if applicable. At each layer:

- The child node to the left is less than the parent node's value.

- The child node to the right is greater than the parent node's value.

These two additional rules build on the three rules we saw for plain binary trees to give us our blueprint for how to think about binary search trees. What we are going to do next is dive deeper into how binary search trees work by looking at how to perform common add and remove operations.

Onward!

It's Just a Data Structure

When looking at the unique properties of trees, it is easy to get caught up in the weeds. If we take many steps back, a tree is just a data structure like our arrays, stacks, queues, linked lists, and more. It exists to help us manipulate or make sense of data. In the following sections, let's look at binary search trees and how we can add data to them, remove data from them, and more.

To help with this, let's start at the very top with a blank slate (Figure 9-3).

FIGURE 9-3

Future home of a binary search tree

Yes, that's right! We are going to start with an empty binary search tree and build our knowledge of how to work with them from there.

Adding Nodes

We are going to have our binary search tree store some numbers. The first number we want to store is 42, and Figure 9-4 is what our binary search tree will look like after we have added it.

FIGURE 9-4

The beginning of our binary search tree

It doesn't look like much of a tree, and that is because our binary search tree was empty. What we have is just a single node (which also happens to be the root!) with a value of 42.

Next, let's add the number 24 (Figure 9-5). Every new node we add from here on out has to be a child of another node. In our case, we have only our root node of 42, so our 24 node will be a child of it. The question is, will it go left, or will it go right?

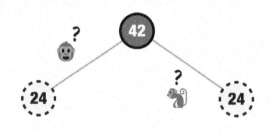

FIGURE 9-5

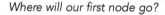

Where will our first node go?

The answer to this question is core to how binary search trees work. To restate what we mentioned earlier:

- If the value we are adding is less than the parent node, the value goes left.
- If the value we are adding is greater than the parent node, the value goes right.

We start at the root node and start looking around. In our tree, we have only one node, the root node of 42. The number we are trying to add is 24. Because 24 is less than 42, we add our node as a left child (Figure 9-6).

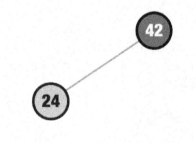

FIGURE 9-6

The smaller node relative to the parent goes left

Let's add another number. This time, the number we want to add is 99. We follow the same steps as earlier. We start at the root, 42. The value we are adding is 99, and it is greater than the root node. It goes right (Figure 9-7).

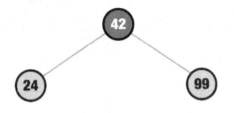

FIGURE 9-7

The 99 node goes to the right

We are not done with adding more numbers to our tree. Now that we have a few extra nodes beyond our root node, things get a bit more interesting. The next number we want to add is 15. We start at the root. The root value is 42, so we look left because 15 is less than 42. Left of 42 is the 24 node. We now check whether 15 is less than 24. It is, so we look left again. There are no more nodes to the left of 24, so we can safely park 15 there (Figure 9-8).

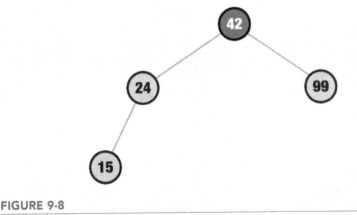

FIGURE 9-8

Our newly added node

You should see a pattern starting to emerge. When adding a new node, we ask, **Is the value greater than or less than the current node?** at each node we encounter, starting at the root. If we encounter a leaf node, this node now becomes our parent. Whether we are a child at the left position or right position is, again, based on whether the value of the node we are adding is less than or greater than our new parent.

We will go a bit faster now. The next value we want to add is 50. We start with our root node of 42. Our 50 value is greater than 42, so we look right. On the right, we have our 99 node. 99 is greater than 50, so we look left. There is no node to the left of our 99 node, so we plop our 50 value there (Figure 9-9).

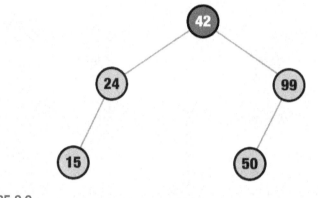

FIGURE 9-9

This node goes to the right branch from the root

The next value we want to add is 120. Using the same steps we've seen a bunch of times, this value will find itself to the right of the 99 node (Figure 9-10).

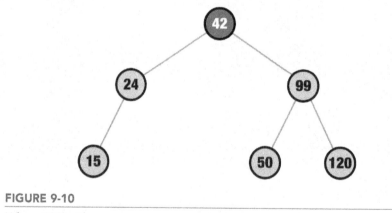

FIGURE 9-10

Where 120 ends up

The last number we are going to add is 64. Take a moment to see where it will land. If everything goes as planned, it will find itself as a right child of the 50 node (Figure 9-11).

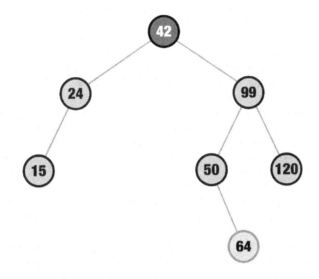

FIGURE 9-11

Our tree is getting popular!

Walking through our steps, we know that 64 is greater than our root node of 42. It is less than our 99 node, so we look left where we have the 50 node. The value 64 is greater than 50, so right of it . . . it goes!

By now, we have looked at a bunch of examples of how to add nodes to our binary search tree. The biggest thing to note is that every node we add ends up as a **leaf** somewhere in our tree. Where exactly it ends up is determined solely by its value and the value of the various nodes starting at the root that it needs to navigate through.

Removing Nodes

There will be times when we'll be adding nodes. Then there will be times when we will be removing nodes as well. Removing nodes from a binary search tree is slightly more involved than adding nodes, for the behavior varies depending on which node we are removing. We walk through those cases next.

Removing a Leaf Node

If the node we are trying to remove is a leaf node, this operation is straightforward. Continuing our binary search tree example from earlier, let's say we want to remove our leaf node with the value of 64 (Figure 9-12).

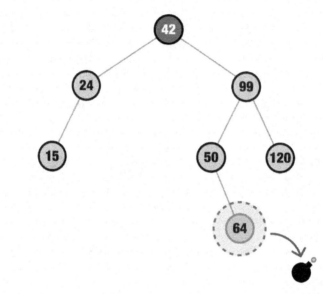

FIGURE 9-12

We want to remove the 64 node

When we remove it, well . . . it is removed (Figure 9-13). That's it.

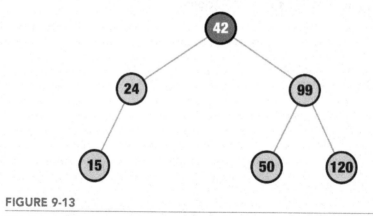

FIGURE 9-13

The 64 node is removed

There is nothing else for us to do. Because it is a leaf node, nothing else in our tree is impacted. That isn't the case with what we are going to see next.

Removing a Node with a Single Child

Removing a leaf node was straightforward. We just removed it. What if, instead of removing a leaf node, we are removing a node that has a single child. For example, let's say we want to remove the node with the value of 24 (Figure 9-14).

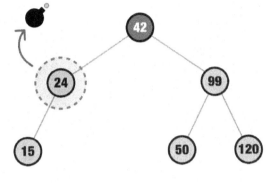

FIGURE 9-14

Removing the 24 node

When we remove a node with a single child, that child takes the place of the removed node. In our example, when we remove the 24 node, the 15 node takes its place (Figure 9-15).

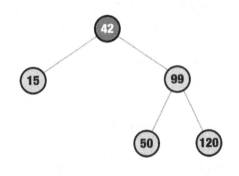

FIGURE 9-15

The child node takes the place of the parent node

Because of how we add nodes to our binary search tree in the first place, promoting a child node to its parent position will not break the overall integrity of our tree, where values to the left of each node are smaller than values to the right of each node.

There is another point to clarify. When we are talking about the behavior of deleting a node with a single child, we mean a single **immediate** child. Our immediate child can have more children of its own. Take a look at Figure 9-16.

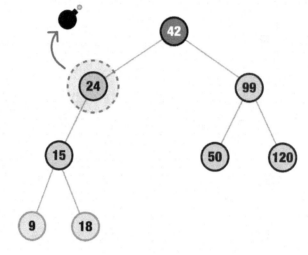

FIGURE 9-16

What will happen when we remove the 24 node?

We want to remove our 24 node, and it has the 15 node as its child. The 15 node has two children of its own, but this detail doesn't change the behavior we are describing. As long as the parent node we are removing has only a single immediate child, that single immediate child will take the parent's place and bring along any children it may have as well (Figure 9-17).

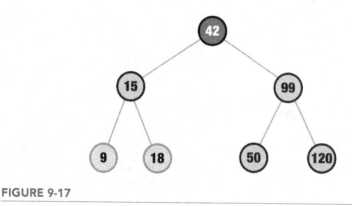

FIGURE 9-17

Phew! The 24 node has been removed

If we walk through all the nodes in the tree after this shift, we'll again see that the integrity of the tree is still maintained. No node is out of place.

Removing a Node with Two Children

We are now at the last case. What happens when we remove a node that happens to have two children. Take a look at the example in Figure 9-18 where we wish to remove the 99 node.

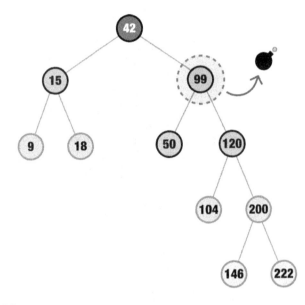

FIGURE 9-18

Removing a node that contains both children

When removing a node with two children, we can't just pick one of the children nodes and call it a successful operation. If we do that, we may find that our tree is no longer valid. Some of the nodes may find themselves in the wrong places.

What we do in this case is look in the right subtree for the node with the next highest value, also known as the **inorder successor**. For our situation where we are removing our node with a value of 99, the right subtree is as shown in Figure 9-19.

Which node in our subtree has the *next highest value* from 99? To describe the same thing differently, when we look at all the children to the *right* of our 99 node, which node has the smallest value? The answer to both of these questions is the node whose value is 104. What we do next is remove our 99 node and replace it with our 104 node (Figure 9-20).

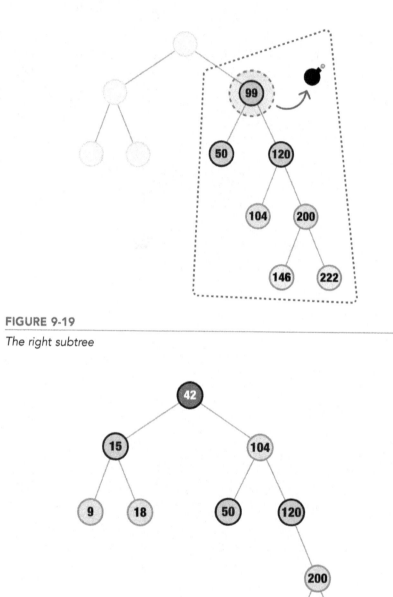

FIGURE 9-19

The right subtree

FIGURE 9-20

This removal required a swapping of node values

When we look at our binary search tree after this removal and swap, the integrity of all of the nodes is maintained. This isn't an accident, of course. The inorder successor node will always have a value that ensures it can be safely plopped into the place of the node we are removing. That was the case with our 104 node that took over for our 99 node. That will be the case for other nodes we wish to remove as well.

Implementing a Binary Search Tree

If we had to summarize all of the words and diagrams into a few simple rules for adding and removing nodes, it would be the following:

For adding nodes, do the following:

1. If the tree is empty, create a new node and make it the root.

2. Compare the value of the new node with the value of the root node.

3. If the value of the new node is less than the value of the root node, repeat steps 2 and 3 for the *left subtree of the root node*.

4. If the value of the new node is greater than the value of the root node, repeat steps 2 and 3 for the *right subtree of the root node*.

5. If the value of the new node is equal to the value of an existing node in the tree, return a message to indicate that the node was not added.

6. Create a new node and add it as either the left or right child of the parent node where the new node should be inserted.

7. Rebalance the tree if necessary to maintain the binary search tree property.

For removing nodes, do the following:

1. Find the node to be removed. If we can't find the node in the tree, return a message to indicate we couldn't remove the node.

2. If the node to be removed has no children, simply remove it from the tree.

3. If the node to be removed has one child, replace it with that child.

4. If the node to be removed has two children, find its inorder successor:

    a. To find the inorder successor, go right once, then left as far as possible.

    b. Replace the node to be removed with the inorder successor.

5. Rebalance the tree if necessary to maintain the binary search tree property.

Go through the above steps and make sure nothing sounds too surprising. They are almost the TL;DR version of what we saw in the previous sections. Our code is mostly going to mimic the preceding steps. In fact, let's look at our code now!

Our binary search tree implementation is made up of our familiar Node class and the BinarySearchTree class:

```
class Node {
  constructor(data) {
    this.data = data;
    this.left = null;
    this.right = null;
  }
}

class BinarySearchTree {
  constructor() {
    this.root = null;
  }

  insert(value) {
    // Create a new node with the given value
    const newNode = new Node(value);

    // If the tree is empty, the new node becomes the root
    if (this.root === null) {
      this.root = newNode;
      return this;
    }

    // Traverse the tree to find the correct position for the new
node
    let currentNode = this.root;

    while (true) {
      if (value === currentNode.data) {
        // If the value already exists in the tree, return
undefined
        return undefined;
      } else if (value < currentNode.data) {
        // If the value is less than the current node's value, go
left
```

```
        if (currentNode.left === null) {
          // If the left child is null, the new node becomes
          // the left child
          currentNode.left = newNode;
          return this;
        }
        currentNode = currentNode.left;
      } else {
        // If the value is greater than the current node's value,
        // go right
        if (currentNode.right === null) {
          // If the right child is null, the new node becomes
          // the right child
          currentNode.right = newNode;
          return this;
        }
        currentNode = currentNode.right;
      }
    }
  }
  remove(value) {
    // Start at the root of the tree
    let currentNode = this.root;
    let parentNode = null;

    // Traverse down the tree to find the node to remove
    while (currentNode !== null) {
      if (value === currentNode.data) {
        // If we found the node to remove, proceed with removal
process
        if (currentNode.left === null && currentNode.right ===
null) {
          // Case 1: Node has no children
          if (parentNode === null) {
            // If the node is the root of the tree
            this.root = null;
          } else {
            // If the node is not the root of the tree
```

```
          if (parentNode.left === currentNode) {
            parentNode.left = null;
          } else {
            parentNode.right = null;
          }
        }
        return true;
      } else if (currentNode.left !== null &&
                  currentNode.right === null) {
        // Case 2: Node has one child (left child only)
        if (parentNode === null) {
          // If the node is the root of the tree
          this.root = currentNode.left;
        } else {
          // If the node is not the root of the tree
          if (parentNode.left === currentNode) {
            parentNode.left = currentNode.left;
          } else {
            parentNode.right = currentNode.left;
          }
        }
        return true;
      } else if (currentNode.left === null &&
                  currentNode.right !== null) {
        // Case 2: Node has one child (right child only)
        if (parentNode === null) {
          // If the node is the root of the tree
          this.root = currentNode.right;
        } else {
          // If the node is not the root of the tree
          if (parentNode.left === currentNode) {
            parentNode.left = currentNode.right;
          } else {
            parentNode.right = currentNode.right;
          }
        }
        return true;
```

```
    } else {
      // Case 3: Node has two children
      // Find the inorder successor of the node to remove
      let successor = currentNode.right;
      let successorParent = currentNode;

      while (successor.left !== null) {
        successorParent = successor;
        successor = successor.left;
      }

      // Replace the node to remove with the inorder successor
      if (successorParent.left === successor) {
        successorParent.left = successor.right;
      } else {
        successorParent.right = successor.right;
      }

      currentNode.data = successor.data;
      return true;
    }
  } else if (value < currentNode.data) {
    // If the value we're looking for is less than
    // the current node's value, go left
    parentNode = currentNode;
    currentNode = currentNode.left;
  } else {
    // If the value we're looking for is greater than
    // the current node's value, go right
    parentNode = currentNode;
    currentNode = currentNode.right;
  }
}

// If we reach this point, the value was not found in the tree
return false;
  }
}
```

Take a brief glance through the preceding lines of code. The comments call out important landmarks, especially as they relate to the binary search tree behavior we have been looking at. To see this code in action, here is an example:

```
let myBST = new BinarySearchTree();

myBST.insert(10);
myBST.insert(5);
myBST.insert(15);
myBST.insert(3);
myBST.insert(7);
myBST.insert(13);
myBST.insert(18);
myBST.insert(20);
myBST.insert(12);
myBST.insert(14);
myBST.insert(19);
myBST.insert(30);
```

We are creating a new binary search tree and adding some nodes to it. This tree will look like Figure 9-21.

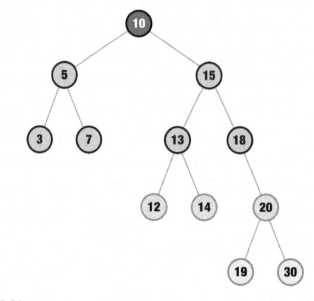

FIGURE 9-21

Our new binary tree

Let's say that we want to remove the 15 node:

```
myBST.remove(15);
```

Our tree will rearrange itself to look like Figure 9-22.

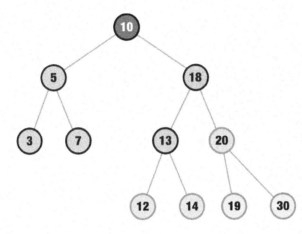

FIGURE 9-22

Our binary tree after removing the 15 node

The 15 node is gone, but the 18 node takes its place as the rightful inorder successor. Feel free to play with more node additions and removals to see how things will look. To easily see how all of the nodes are related to each other, the easiest way is to inspect your binary search tree in the Console and expand each left and right node until you have a good idea of how things shape up (Figure 9-23).

If you want to go above and beyond, you can create a method that will print an ASCII-art representation of a tree in our console, so do let me know if you have already done something like that.

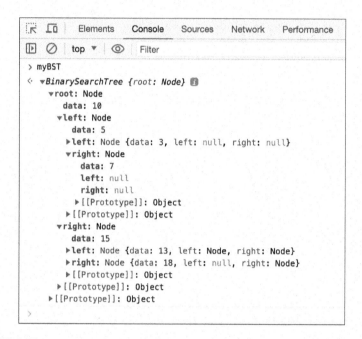

FIGURE 9-23

Output of running our code

Performance and Memory Characteristics

The performance of our binary search tree is related to how balanced or unbalanced the tree is. In a perfectly balanced tree, the common operations like searching, inserting, and deleting nodes will take **O(log *n*)** time (Figure 9-24).

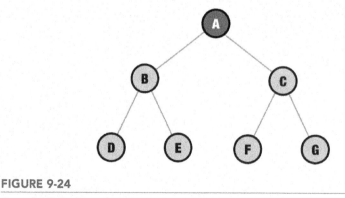

FIGURE 9-24

A perfectly balanced tree

This is because we can avoid taking very uniquely long paths to find any single node. The worst-case scenario is when our tree is heavily unbalanced (Figure 9-25).

In this tree, if our node happens to be deep in the right subtree, we'll be exploring a lot of nodes relative to the total number of nodes in a tree. This gets us closer to a running time of O(n), which is the worst-case scenario.

As for the amount of memory a binary search tree takes up, that doesn't depend on how balanced or unbalanced our tree is. It is always O(n) where each node takes up a fixed amount of memory.

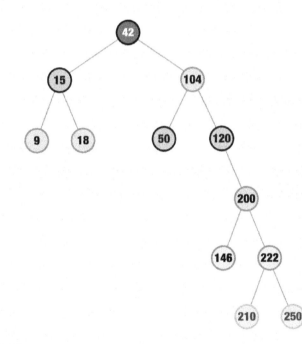

FIGURE 9-25

Our final binary search tree

Conclusion

Binary search trees are pretty sweet. They are a type of binary tree with some added constraints to make them more suited for heavy-duty data wrangling. The constraints are to ensure the left child is always smaller than the parent and the right child is always greater. There are a few more rules around how nodes should arrange and rearrange themselves when they get added or removed.

This type of structure allows us to efficiently perform search, insert, and delete operations in O(log n) time complexity, making binary search trees a popular data structure. However, as we saw a few moments ago, the performance of a binary search tree can be impacted by its balancedness. For heavily unbalanced trees, this can lead to worst-case scenarios with the time complexity of O(n).

SOME ADDITIONAL RESOURCES

? Ask a question: **https://forum.kirupa.com**

 Errors/Known issues: **https://bit.ly/algorithms_errata**

 Source repository: **https://bit.ly/algorithms_source**

10

HEAPS

If you are anything like me, you probably have a bunch of ideas and too little time to act on them. To help bring some order, we may rely on a tool that is designed to help us prioritize tasks (Figure 10-1).

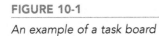

FIGURE 10-1

An example of a task board

There are a billion tools out there for managing our projects, and they all do a variation of the following things:

- Allow us to catalog all of the items that we want to work

- Give us the ability to prioritize things

- Provide a way to help us easily see what the highest priority items are

- Allow us to add and remove items while maintaining our prioritized order

Building our own tool that does all of this sounds like a fun activity, but we are going to stay focused on the data structures side of the house. There is a very efficient data structure that we can use to represent all of the things we want to do, and that data structure is the **heap**. We learn all about it in the following sections.

Onward!

Meet the Heap

The funny-sounding heap data structure allows us to retrieve the highest priority item in constant O(1) time and fast insertion and removal of items in logarithmic O(log n) time. This makes the heap pretty awesome, and Figure 10-2 shows what it looks like:

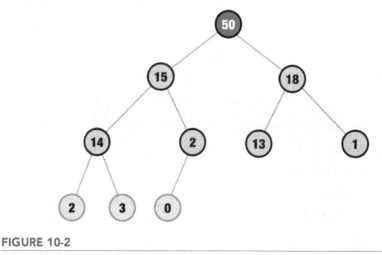

FIGURE 10-2

Example of a heap

This particular heap variation is known more formally as a **max-heap**, where priority is based on how large a number we are dealing with. The highest priority item will be the one with the largest number, and this item will always be at the root of our tree. The rest of the tree will be made up of other smaller numbers—all appropriately layered on the basis of their value.

The other variation of a heap is a **min-heap**, where lower numbers end up having a higher priority (Figure 10-3).

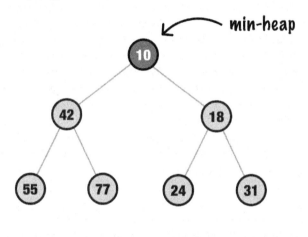

min-heap

* We don't talk about ~~Bruno~~ min-heaps.

FIGURE 10-3

Meet the min-heap

We won't be talking about min-heaps today. When we talk about heaps, we'll default to talking about the max-heap variant, for a min-heap is just the opposite of how max-heaps decide what items to prioritize. This bias toward heaps being assumed to be max-heaps is consistent with how heaps are talked about broadly, but to avoid this confusion, we may see heaps referred to explicitly as *max-heap* or *min-heap* in some books and online resources.

Getting back to looking at our heap, two details are quickly noticeable:

- Our heap is a binary tree where each node has at most two children.

- The value of each node is greater than or equal to the values of its children.

When we talk about the **heap property**, what we mean is that our heap epitomizes both of these two details. More on that in a bit.

Now, here is the kicker that makes heaps really sweet. What we are dealing with isn't just any binary tree. It is a **complete binary tree** where all rows of the nodes are filled left to right without any gaps. This leads to a very balanced-looking tree (Figure 10-4).

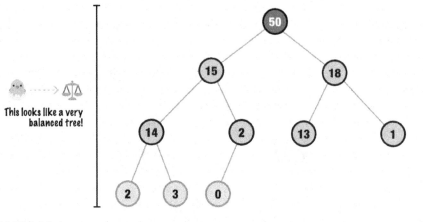

This looks like a very
balanced tree!

FIGURE 10-4

Example of a balanced tree

This is a detail that we'll highlight when talking about performance in a little bit, for a balanced binary tree avoids the problems where we end up with a long chain of nodes that cause poor performance. In a balanced binary tree, the height of the tree is O(log n), which is ideal for many types of data operations.

Common Heap Operations

The goal of our heap, besides looking really cool, is to allow us to quickly remove the highest priority item. As part of allowing us to do this, we also need the ability to add items to our heap. These are the two primary operations we need our heap to support, so we spend the next few sections detailing what both of these operations look like.

Inserting a Node

Let's start with inserting a node, which is also the place to start when we have a blank slate and want to build our heap from scratch. The first item we want to add is the item with the value 13 (Figure 10-5).

FIGURE 10-5

Our first node

This is our first item, and it becomes our root node by default. This is the easy case. For all subsequent items we wish to add, we need to follow these rules:

1. We add the new node to the bottom level of the heap, on the leftmost available spot, with no gaps. This ensures that the tree remains complete.

2. We compare the value of the new node with the value of its parent node. If the value of the new node is greater than the value of its parent node, we swap the new node with its parent node. We repeat this process until either the new node's value is not greater than its parent's value or we have reached the root node.

3. After swapping, we repeat step 2 with the new parent and its parent until the heap property is restored.

The important detail to note is that all we are checking between the parent and child is that the parent has a larger value than the child. This is a much less constrained approach than what we have with binary search trees where there are a few more constraints. All of this will make more sense as we walk through some more insertions.

We now want to insert node 10. We add it to the bottom level of our heap on the first leftmost available spot (Figure 10-6).

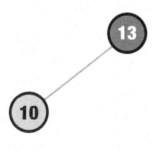

FIGURE 10-6

Adding the 10 node

Our 10 value is less than the parent value of 13, so this is a valid heap structure that maintains our heap property. The next number we want to add is 5. We add it to the leftmost available spot at the bottom of our heap (Figure 10-7).

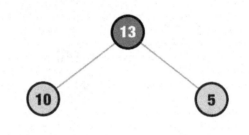

FIGURE 10-7

Adding the 5 node

Our newly inserted 5 value is less than the parent 13 value, so our heap property is still maintained. The next number we want to add is 24. We insert it at the left-most spot in our bottom row (Figure 10-8).

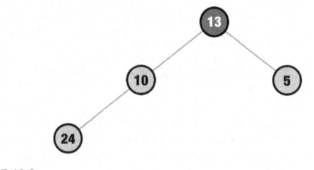

FIGURE 10-8

Our new node is added at the leftmost part of our tree

Now, is 24 less than the parent value of 10? No. So, we swap the parent and child to ensure the child is always less than the value of the parent (Figure 10-9).

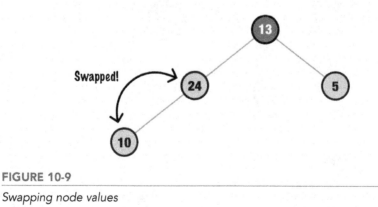

FIGURE 10-9

Swapping node values

We repeat our parent–child check with our newly swapped 24 node and its new parent. Is 24 less than 13? The answer again is no, so we swap the nodes one more time (Figure 10-10).

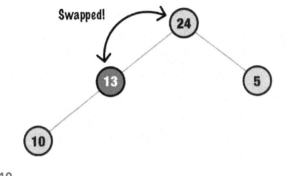

FIGURE 10-10

Swapping node values again

At this point, our 24 node reaches the root. It doesn't have a parent to compare itself against, so our heap is now in a good state again. There is a name for what we just did. It is called **bubbling up**, where we insert our node at the bottom and keep checking (and swapping, if needed!) against the parent to ensure the heap property is maintained.

We'll go a bit faster now. The next node we want to add is 1. We add it to the leftmost location on our lowest level (Figure 10-11).

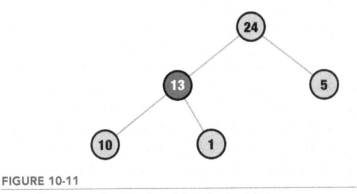

FIGURE 10-11

Repeating the earlier steps for adding the 1 node

This is valid, and no further adjustments need to be made. The next value we want to add is 15. We insert this as the left child of the 5 node (Figure 10-12).

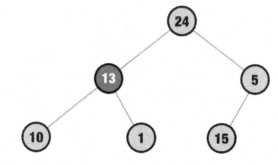

FIGURE 10-12

Let's see what happens when we add the 15 node

The parent (5) is lower than our newly added child (15), so we swap the 15 and 5 (Figure 10-13).

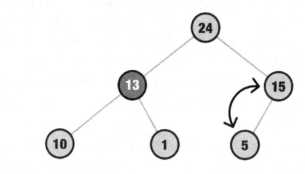

FIGURE 10-13

Swapping node values

Our newly swapped 15 node is correctly less than our parent node, whose value is 24, so we are back to maintaining our heap property.

The next number we add is 36. Our 36 starts off as the right child of our 15 node. That location is only temporary! To maintain the heap property, our 36 node will swap with the 15 node and then swap with the 24 node as well (Figure 10-14).

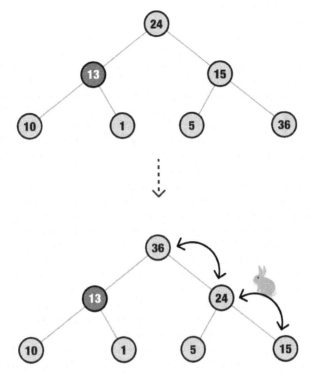

FIGURE 10-14

Maintaining the heap property through further swaps

Our node containing the newly added 36 is now the largest number in our heap and is located at the root. Good job, 36! Let us add one last item—the number 3 (Figure 10-15).

We add it at the leftmost level on the bottom level, and our node containing the 3 value is a child of the 10 node. This maintains the heap property, so we don't need to do anything additional. Our heap is in a good spot, and we have just seen what inserting nodes into a heap looks like and the role bubbling up plays in ensuring our nodes are properly positioned.

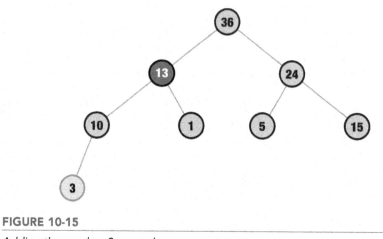

FIGURE 10-15

Adding the number 3 to our heap

Removing the Root

The next heap operation we look at is how to remove the root node, aka our heap's maximum and most important value. As we will see in a few moments, removing the root has some interesting behaviors that are very different than what we saw earlier when adding items to our heap. Let's get started, and we'll continue with the heap example we had earlier.

What we want to do is remove the root node whose value is 36 (Figure 10-16).

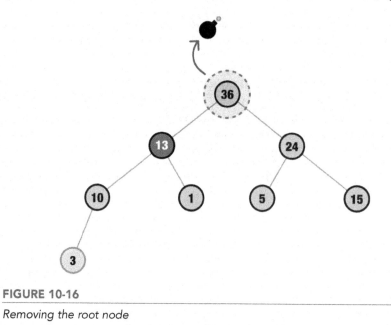

FIGURE 10-16

Removing the root node

When removing the root node from a heap, we still want to ensure that the heap property is maintained. This means that the new root node should be the largest value in the heap, and the binary tree should be restructured so that it remains complete.

Here are the steps to remove the root node from our heap:

1. We remove the root node from the heap and replace it with the last node in the heap.

2. We compare the value of the new root node with the values of its children. If the value of the new root node is less than the value of either of its children, we swap the new root node with the larger of its children. We repeat this process until either the new root node's value is greater than or equal to the values of its children or it has no children. This process is called **bubbling down**.

3. After swapping, we repeat step 2 with the new child node and its children until the heap property is restored.

Let's put these steps into action by walking through what happens when we remove our root node 36. The first thing we do is remove our 36 root node and swap it with the last node in our heap, which will always be the rightmost node at the lowest level of our heap (Figure 10-17).

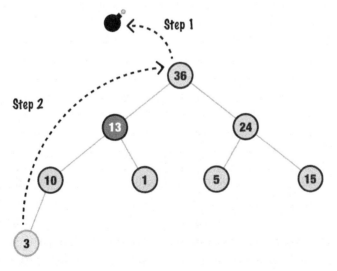

FIGURE 10-17

Rebalancing our tree after removing the root node

When we remove our 36 node and swap it with our 3 node, our heap will look as shown in Figure 10-18.

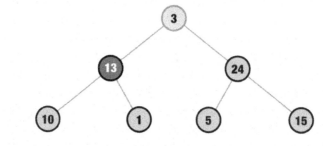

FIGURE 10-18

The root has been replaced with our last node

Next, we start our bubbling-down operation and compare our newly appointed root node with its children to see if it is less than either of its children. If it is less than either of the children, we swap it with the largest child. In our case, our root value of 3 is less than both its child values of 13 and 24. We swap it with the largest child, which would be 24 (Figure 10-19).

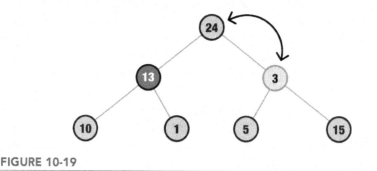

FIGURE 10-19

Time to rebalance

We aren't done yet. We now repeat our parent–child check at the new location our 3 node is in. In this case, our 3 node is less than both its child values of 5 and 15. So, we swap our 3 node with the larger of its children, the 15 node (Figure 10-20).

At this point, our 3 node is a leaf with no children to compare its value against. This means it is now at its intended location, and our heap property is now restored.

Let's go through the removal steps just one more time to make sure we have all of our i's dotted and t's crossed. Our new root node has a value of 24, and we want to remove it (Figure 10-21).

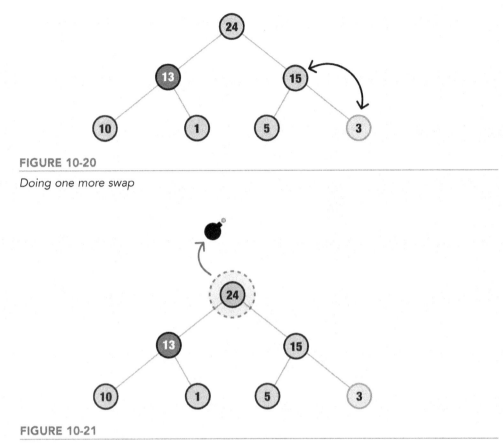

FIGURE 10-20

Doing one more swap

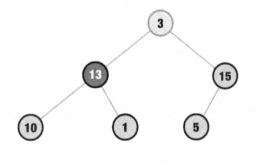

FIGURE 10-21

Let's remove node 24

The first thing we do is remove it and replace it with our last node, which is our 3 node again (Figure 10-22).

FIGURE 10-22

The last node takes the place of the removed root node

After we do this, we compare our 3 node with the values of its children. It is less than both of them, so we swap it with the largest of its children, the 15 node (Figure 10-23).

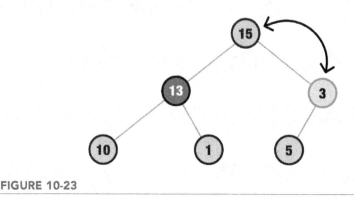

FIGURE 10-23

Time to maintain the heap property

After this swap, we are not done yet. We now check whether our 3 node happens to be less than any of its children. Its only child is the 5 node, and 3 is not less than 5. We do one more swap (Figure 10-24).

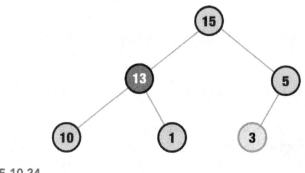

FIGURE 10-24

All is well with our heap

At this point, our 3 node is back where it belongs, our root contains our heap's largest value, and all child nodes are safely located in their own rooms. The world is right again.

Heap Implementation

Now that we have a good idea of how a heap works when we are adding items or removing the root node, it's time to look at how exactly we will build it.

Heaps as Arrays

One cool and interesting detail is how our heap is represented under the covers. Yes, we have been talking about it as if it is a binary tree. But we are not going to be representing it as a binary tree in our implementation. We are going to be representing it as an array in which each item represents a node in our heap.

Let's look at a visual first (Figure 10-25), then talk about how exactly this mapping works.

Tree representation:

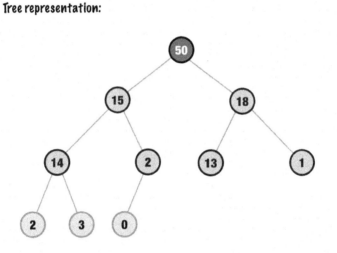

Array representation:

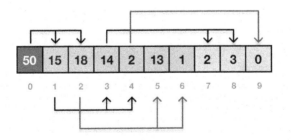

FIGURE 10-25

The relationship between a heap and an array

Pay attention to how each array item represents the parent–child relationship of each node in our tree. There are a series of calculations we can use to map between nodes in our tree and the flat list of items in our array:

- To find the parent of a node at index i, we can use the formula Math.floor(i-1)/2 to calculate its parent index. Note that this formula applies only to nodes other than the root node, since the root node has no parent.

- To find the left child of a node at index i, we can use the formula 2i+1 to calculate its left child index. Note that this formula applies only if the left child index is within the bounds of the array.

- To find the right child of a node at index i, we can use the formula 2i+2 to calculate its right child index. Note that this formula applies only if the right child index is within the bounds of the array.

When we look at the items in our array (and their children and parents), the calculations should track nicely.

The Code

The following JavaScript takes all of the words and diagrams we have seen so far and turns them into working code:

```
class Heap {
  constructor() {
    // The heap is stored as an array
    this.heap = [];
  }


  // Add a new element to the heap
  insert(value) {
    // Add the new element to the end of the array
    this.heap.push(value);
    // Restore the heap property by bubbling up the new element
    this.#bubbleUp(this.heap.length - 1);
  }


  // Remove the maximum element from the heap
  extractMax() {
    // If the heap is empty, return null
```

```
      if (this.heap.length === 0) {
        return null;
      }
      // If the heap has only one element, remove and return it
      if (this.heap.length === 1) {
        return this.heap.pop();
      }
      // Otherwise, remove the root element (maximum value) and
replace it
      // with the last element in the array
      const max = this.heap[0];
      const end = this.heap.pop();
      this.heap[0] = end;
      // Restore the heap property by bubbling down the new root
element
      this.#bubbleDown(0);
      return max;
    }


    // Restore the heap property by bubbling up the element
    // at the given index
    #bubbleUp(index) {
      // If the element is already at the root, return
      if (index === 0) {
        return;
      }
      // Find the index of the parent element
      const parentIndex = Math.floor((index - 1) / 2);
      // If the element is greater than its parent, swap them
      if (this.heap[index] > this.heap[parentIndex]) {
        [this.heap[index], this.heap[parentIndex]] = [this.
heap[parentIndex], this.heap[index]];
        // Continue bubbling up the element from its new index
        this.#bubbleUp(parentIndex);
      }
    }
```

```
  // Restore the heap property by bubbling down the element
  // at the given index
  #bubbleDown(index) {
    // Find the indices of the left and right child elements
    const leftChildIndex = 2 * index + 1;
    const rightChildIndex = 2 * index + 2;
    // Initialize the index of the largest element to be
    // the current index
    let largestIndex = index;
    // If the left child element is larger than the current
element,
    // update the largest index
    if (leftChildIndex < this.heap.length &&
        this.heap[leftChildIndex] > this.heap[largestIndex]) {
      largestIndex = leftChildIndex;
    }
    // If the right child element is larger than the current
element,
    // update the largest index
    if (rightChildIndex < this.heap.length &&
        this.heap[rightChildIndex] > this.heap[largestIndex]) {
      largestIndex = rightChildIndex;
    }
    // If the largest element is not the current element, swap them
and
    // continue bubbling down the element from its new index
    if (largestIndex !== index) {
      [this.heap[index], this.heap[largestIndex]] =
              [this.heap[largestIndex], this.heap[index]];
      this.#bubbleDown(largestIndex);
    }
  }


  // Return the maximum element in the heap without removing it
  getMax() {
    return this.heap[0];
  }
```

```
  // Return the size of the heap
  size() {
    return this.heap.length;
  }


  // Check whether the heap is empty
  isEmpty() {
    return this.heap.length === 0;
  }
}
```

Our heap implementation supports the following operations:

- **insert**: Adds new items to our heap
- **extractMax**: Removes the root node that contains the highest priority (aka largest) value from our heap and returns it
- **getMax**: Gives us the value of our root node with the highest priority (aka largest) value, but it doesn't remove it from the heap
- **size**: Gives us the count of how many nodes are in our heap
- **isEmpty**: Lets us know if our heap is empty or not

The way we would use this code and many of the preceding operations is as follows:

```
let myHeap = new Heap();
myHeap.insert(14);
myHeap.insert(18);
myHeap.insert(50);
myHeap.insert(1);
myHeap.insert(3);
myHeap.insert(15);
myHeap.insert(2);
myHeap.insert(2);
myHeap.insert(0);
myHeap.insert(13);
```

```
console.log("Size of heap: " + myHeap.size()); // 10

console.log(myHeap.getMax()); // 50

console.log("Size of heap: " + myHeap.size()); // 10

console.log(myHeap.extractMax()); // 50

console.log("Size of heap: " + myHeap.size()); // 9

console.log(myHeap.extractMax()); // 18
console.log(myHeap.extractMax()); // 15
console.log(myHeap.extractMax()); // 14

console.log("Size of heap: " + myHeap.size()); // 6
```

We are re-creating the example heap we saw earlier and putting many of the operations we called out into action.

Performance Characteristics

In a heap, we called out earlier that removing the root node and inserting items into our heap are the two fundamental operations we care about. Let's look into how these fare from a performance point of view.

Removing the Root Node

There are two concepts relevant to removing the root node:

- Time complexity: $O(\log n)$, where n is the number of elements in the heap

- Space complexity: $O(1)$

Removing the root node in a heap involves two main steps: swapping the root node with the last leaf node in the heap, and then re-heapifying (via the #bubbleDown method in our code) the heap by sifting the new root node down the heap until the heap property is restored.

The first step of swapping the root node with the last leaf node takes constant time because we are just updating two array elements. For example, Figure 10-26 represents what is happening.

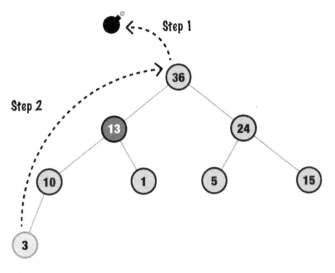

FIGURE 10-26

Our earlier example of what happens when we remove a root node

The second step of re-heapifying the heap takes logarithmic time because we must compare the new root node with its children and swap it with the larger of the two until the heap property is restored. Because the height of a complete binary tree is O(log *n*), where *n* is the number of nodes in the tree, the worst-case time complexity of removing the root node from a heap is O(log *n*).

Inserting an Item

There are two concepts relevant to inserting an item into a heap:

- Time complexity: O(log *n*), where *n* is the number of elements in the heap

- Space complexity: O(1)

Inserting an item into a heap involves two main steps: inserting the new item at the end of the heap and then re-heapifying (via the #bubbleUp method in our code) the heap by sifting the new item up the heap until the heap property is restored.

The first step of inserting the new item at the end of the heap takes constant time because we are simply appending a new element to the end of the array, like the 15 we are adding to the heap (Figure 10-27).

Because we are using an array to implement our heap, adding items to the end is pretty fast as well. That's something our arrays are really, REALLY efficient at.

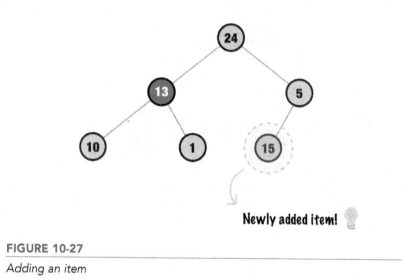

Newly added item!

FIGURE 10-27

Adding an item

The second step of re-heapifying the heap takes logarithmic time because we must compare the new item with its parent and swap it with the parent if it is larger. We keep repeating this until the heap property is restored. Just like with our root removal case earlier, because the height of a complete binary tree is O(log *n*), where *n* is the number of nodes in the tree, the worst-case time complexity of inserting an item into a heap is also O(log *n*).

Performance Summary

Putting all of this together, removing the root node and inserting items into a heap both have a worst-case time complexity of O(log *n*), where *n* is the number of elements in the heap. The space complexity of these operations is O(1) because we only need to store temporary variables during the re-heapification process.

Conclusion

To tie it all up, heaps are an incredibly useful data structure that greatly simplify a wide range of algorithms and problems. By organizing elements in a binary tree structure that satisfies the heap property, heaps enable two things:

- Efficient retrieval of the maximum element in constant time
- Fast insertion and removal of elements in logarithmic time

Because of their efficiency, heaps are used in a variety of applications, such as heapsort, priority queues, and Dijkstra's algorithm for finding the shortest path in a graph. Yes, they can also make our goal of building a task organizer really snappy (Figure 10-28).

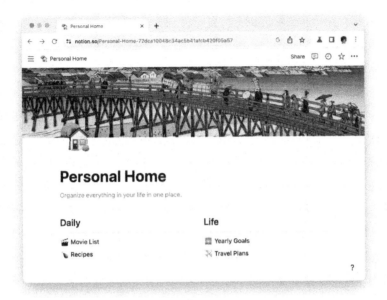

FIGURE 10-28

Another example of a task organizer

Furthermore, heaps can be easily implemented using an array, which makes them particularly efficient in terms of memory usage. What's not to love about heaps?

SOME ADDITIONAL RESOURCES

? Ask a question: **https://forum.kirupa.com**

Errors/Known issues: **https://bit.ly/algorithms_errata**

Source repository: **https://bit.ly/algorithms_source**

11

HASHTABLE (AKA HASHMAP OR DICTIONARY)

When it comes to data structures, the hashtable holds a special place in all of our hearts. It takes storing and retrieving values really quickly to a whole new level. For this reason, we'll find hashtables used in the many, MANY situations where we need to cache data for quick access later. We'll see hashtables used by other data structures and algorithms for their functioning. In this chapter, we go deep into what makes hashtables (often also referred to as *hashmaps* or *dictionaries*) really awesome.

Onward!

A Very Efficient Robot

Here is the setup that will help us explain how hashtables work. We have a bunch of food that we need to store (Figure 11-1).

Food! Food! Food! Food! Food!

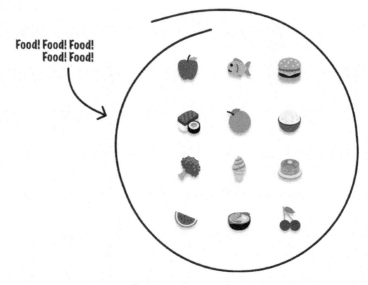

FIGURE 11-1

Let's talk about food!

We also have a bunch of boxes to store this food into (Figure 11-2).

Boxes to store our food into! →

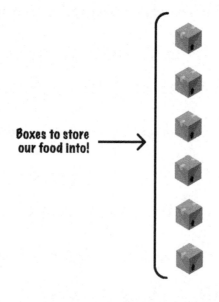

FIGURE 11-2

Boxes

Our goal is to take some of our food and store it in these boxes for safekeeping. To help us here, we are going to rely on a trusted robot helper (Figure 11-3).

FIGURE 11-3

A helpful (and trusted) robot

As our first action, we decide to store our watermelon. Our robot comes up to the watermelon and analyzes it (Figure 11-4).

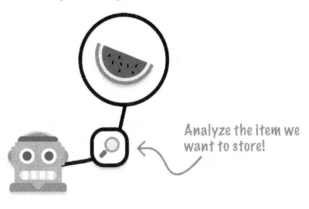

FIGURE 11-4

Our robot analyzing our watermelon

This analysis tells our robot which box to put our watermelon into. The exact logic our robot uses isn't important for us to focus on right now. The important part is that, at the end of this analysis, our robot has a clear idea of where to store our watermelon (Figure 11-5).

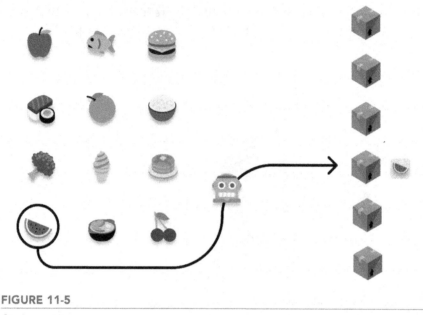

FIGURE 11-5

Storing an item

Next, we want to store the hamburger. The robot repeats the same steps. It analyzes it, determines which box to store it in, and then stores it in the appropriate box (Figure 11-6).

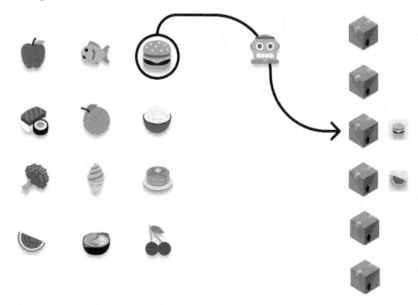

FIGURE 11-6

Storing another item

We repeat this process a few more times for different types of food that we want to store, and our robot analyzes and stores the food in the appropriate box (Figure 11-7).

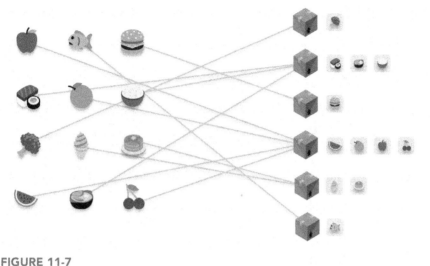

FIGURE 11-7

All of our items are now stored

Now, we are going to shift gears a bit. We want to retrieve a food item that we had stored earlier. We are in the mood for some fish, so we tell our robot to retrieve our fish. We have an exact replica of the fish (possibly a picture!), and the first thing our robot does is analyze the replica. This analysis helps our robot to determine which box our actual edible fish is stored in (Figure 11-8).

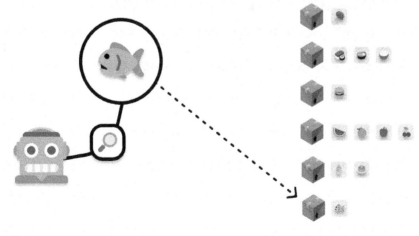

FIGURE 11-8

Time to retrieve an item

Once it has figured out where our fish is, it goes directly to the right box and brings it back to us (Figure 11-9).

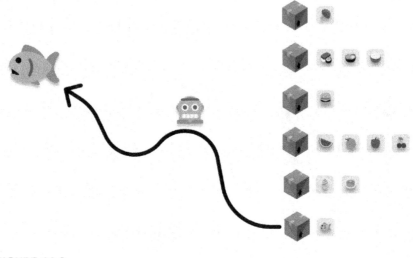

FIGURE 11-9

Our robot knows exactly where an item is

The important thing to note, just as we saw earlier when our robot was storing items, is that our robot goes directly to the correct box. It doesn't scan other boxes looking for our fish. It doesn't guess. Based on its analysis of the fish replica, it knows where to go and it goes there without any dilly-dallying.

From Robots to Hashing Functions

The example we saw earlier with our robot very efficiently storing and retrieving items sets us up nicely for looking at our next intermediate stop, the **hashing function**. Let's bring our robot back one last time (Figure 11-10).

FIGURE 11-10

Our robot is back!

What exactly does our robot do? It analyzes the item we want to store and maps it to a location to store it in. Let's adjust our visualization a little bit (Figure 11-11).

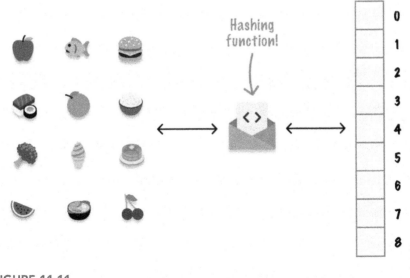

FIGURE 11-11

A hashing function

Our robot has been replaced by something we are calling a **hashing function**. The generic boxes we had for storage are now replaced with a more formal structure, with index positions, which looks a bit like an array.

So, what in the world is a hashing function? A hashing function is nothing more than a bunch of code. This code takes a value as an input and returns a unique value (known as a **hash code**) as the output. The detail to note is that the output *never changes* for the same input. For example, we throw our plate of pancakes at our hashing function, and the output could be storage position #5 (Figure 11-12).

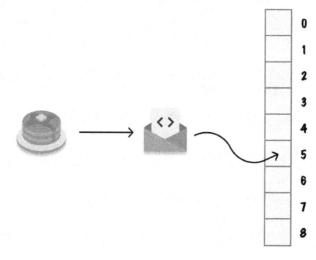

FIGURE 11-12

Where our pancakes will be stored

Every single time our hashing function encounters this exact pancake, it will always return position #5. It will do so very quickly. We can generalize this relationship between the input, the hashing function, and the output as shown in Figure 11-13.

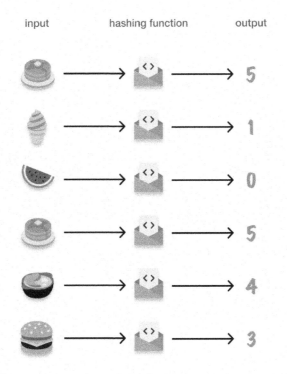

FIGURE 11-13

What our hashing function returns

Our output here represents numbers that go from 0 to 5, but it can be anything. It all depends on how our hashing function is implemented, and we'll look at an example of a hashing function a bit later on here.

From Hashing Functions to Hashtables

It is time! We are now at the point where we can talk about the star that builds on everything we've seen so far, the **hashtable** (aka **hash table**, **hashmap**, or **dictionary**). Starting at the very beginning, a hashtable is a data structure that provides lightning-fast storage and retrieval of key-value pairs. It uses a hashing function to map keys to values in specific locations in (typically) an underlying array data structure (Figure 11-14).

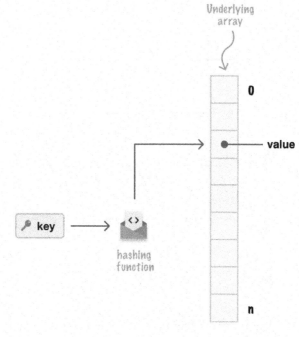

FIGURE 11-14

We somehow always end up with an array, don't we?

What this means is that our hashtables can pull off constant-time, aka O(1), lookup and insertion operations. This speedy ability makes them perfect for the many data-caching and indexing-related activities we perform frequently. We are going to see how they work by looking at some common operations.

Adding Items to Our Hashtable

To add items to our hashtable, we specify two things:

1. **Key:** Acts as an identifier we can use to reference our data later

2. **Value:** Specifies the data we wish to store

Let's say that we want to add the following data in the form of a **[key, value]** pair where the key is a person's name and the value is their phone number:

- Link, (555) 123-4567

- Zelda, (555) 987-6543

- Mario, (555) 555-1212

- Mega Man, (555) 867-5309

- Ryu, (555) 246-8135

- Corvo, (555) 369-1472

If we visualize this data as living in our hashtable, it looks like Figure 11-15.

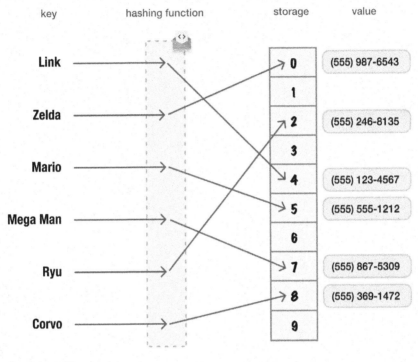

FIGURE 11-15

Another look at how hashing works

The input is both our keys and values. The key is sent to our hashing function to determine the storage location. Once the storage location is determined, the value is placed there.

Reading Items from Our Hashtable

Continuing our example from earlier, let's say we want to read a value from our hashtable. We want to get Mega Man's phone number. What we do is provide our hashtable with our key Mega Man. Our hashing function will quickly compute the storage location the phone number is living at and return the correct value to us (Figure 11-16).

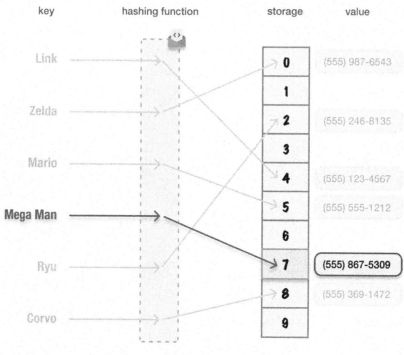

FIGURE 11-16

Retrieving a phone number efficiently

If we provide a key that doesn't exist (for example, Batman), our hashtable will return a message such as *undefined* because the hashing function will point to a storage location that doesn't exist.

JavaScript Implementation/Usage

Almost all modern programming languages provide a hashtable implementation, so we won't attempt to re-create one here. In JavaScript, we have our `Map` object that supports common operations like adding, retrieving, and removing items. We can use the `Map` as follows:

```
let characterInfo = new Map();

// set values
characterInfo.set("Link", "(555) 123-4567");
characterInfo.set("Zelda", "(555) 987-6543");
characterInfo.set("Mario", "(555) 555-1212");
```

```
characterInfo.set("Mega Man", "(555) 867-5309");
characterInfo.set("Ryu", "(555) 246-8135");
characterInfo.set("Corvo", "(555) 369-1472");

// get values
console.log(characterInfo.get("Ryu")); // (555) 246-8135
console.log(characterInfo.get("Batman")); // undefined

// get size
console.log(characterInfo.size()); // 6

// delete item
console.log(characterInfo.delete("Corvo")); // true
console.log(characterInfo.size()); // 5

// delete all items
characterInfo.clear();
console.log(characterInfo.size()); // 0
```

Behind the scenes, a hashing function is used to ensure our values can be quickly accessed when provided with their associated key. We can assume that this hashing function is a good-quality one. If you are curious to see what a basic hashing function might look like, take a look at the following:

```
function hash(key, arraySize) {
  let hashValue = 0;

  for (let i = 0; i < key.length; i++) {
    // Add the Unicode value of each character in the key
    hashValue += key.charCodeAt(i);
  }

  // Modulo operation to ensure the hash value fits within
  // the array size
  return hashValue % arraySize;
}
```

```
// Create a new array allocated for 100 items
let myArray = new Array(100);

let myHash = hash("Ryu", myArray.length);
console.log(myHash) // 20
```

For any character-based input we throw at it, this hashing function will return a number that fits safely within our 100-item `myArray` array. Here is an interesting problem. What if we want to store 101 items? Or what if we want to store 1000 items? Let's imagine that, for these cases, we are in a language other than JavaScript where going beyond the fixed size of the array will throw an error.

What if the following happens?

```
let newHash = hash("Yur", myArray.length);
console.log(myHash) // 20
```

Notice that the returned hash value for Yur is the same 20 as it is for Ryu. This doesn't seem desirable, so let's discuss it next!

Dealing with Collisions

In a perfect world, our hashing function will return a unique storage location for every unique key (and value) we ask it to store. This perfect world requires two things:

1. Our hashing function is designed in such a way that it is capable of generating a unique key for each unique input.

2. We have enough storage available that each value has its own location to place itself in.

In our actual world, neither of these things is true. While our hashing functions are good at generating unique keys, they aren't perfect. There will be moments when, for certain types of input, our hashing functions return the same hash code that points to the same storage location. When we are storing a lot of items, we may run out of actual storage locations to put our unique items into.

Both of these situations result in what is known as a **collision**, and it results in our storage locations holding multiple values, as highlighted in the example in Figure 11-17).

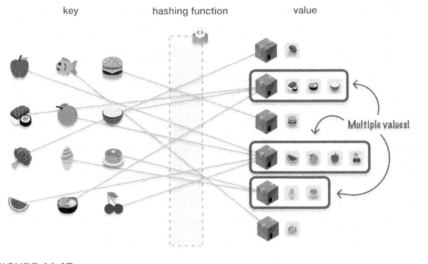

key   hashing function   value

Multiple values!

FIGURE 11-17

Example of collisions

What happens when a storage location is now storing multiple values? For the most part, nothing too eventful to our hashtable *functionality*. Our hashtable implementations will handle this situation gracefully.

Performance and Memory

While collisions don't impact functionality, they do have the potential to impact *performance*. When a storage location stores a single item, we have the best constant time O(1) performance. When a single storage location holds many items, or in the worst case, every single item we are throwing at our hashtable, then the performance drops to O(n), as shown in Figure 11-18.

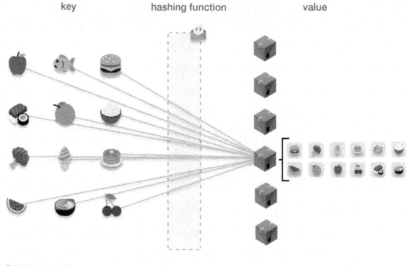

FIGURE 11-18

Worst-case scenario where all items are stored in a single box

This behavior makes this particular hashtable no better than an array or linked list where we employ a linear search. Cases in which every item we store (or close to every item we store) lives in a single storage location are rare. They typically point to a poorly defined hashing function, and there are many techniques modern hashtable implementations use to avoid getting into this pickle of a situation.

As for the amount of space a hashtable takes, it is linear. Every item we store needs to be represented in our hashtable. There is some extra overhead to deal with the hashing function and provide scanning capabilities if a single storage location has multiple values, but this doesn't change the linear growth characteristics.

If we had to summarize in a nice table, we would see what is shown in Table 11-1.

TABLE 11-1   Hashtable Performance and Memory

Action	Average	Worst
Space	$\Theta(n)$	$O(n)$
Retrieval	$\Theta(1)$	$O(n)$
Insertion	$\Theta(1)$	$O(n)$
Delete	$\Theta(1)$	$O(n)$

These are some good results! All of the warnings and worst-case scenarios aside, there isn't a more efficient data structure for allowing us to quickly store and retrieve values, and we'll see this play out when we see our hashtable used by other data structures and algorithms.

> ### NOTE   Is a Hashtable a Dictionary?
>
> We mentioned a few times that a hashtable is sometimes referred to as a *hashmap* or a *dictionary*. Different programming languages use these names or similar ones to provide hashtable capabilities. The controversial one here is the dictionary. If we are strict in our interpretation, a dictionary is not a hashtable. It is a data structure that allows us to store key and value pairs, but it often doesn't implement a hashing function.
>
> Complicating this story a bit, some dictionary implementations can use a hashtable under the covers. An example of this is the dict object we have in Python. It is a dictionary, but it uses a hashtable under the covers for all of the efficiency perks we learned about.
>
> **To answer our question directly, is a hashtable also a dictionary? It depends!**

Conclusion

The beauty of hashtables lies in their ability to provide constant-time performance for key-based operations like insertion, retrieval, and deletion. By using a hash function to compute the index of each element, hashtables eliminate the need for linear searches and enable direct access to data, making operations incredibly fast. All of this is still true even for large amounts of information.

This performance superpower makes hashtables particularly useful in scenarios where quick access to data is critical, such as implementing caches, symbol tables, or dictionaries. Moreover, hashtables have built-in mechanisms to handle collisions where two key inputs produce the same hash code. Hashtables are like the unicorns of the data structure world!

SOME ADDITIONAL RESOURCES

? Ask a question: **https://forum.kirupa.com**

Errors/Known issues: **https://bit.ly/algorithms_errata**

Source repository: **https://bit.ly/algorithms_source**

12

TRIE (AKA PREFIX TREE)

We are on some web page, we encounter an input field, and we start typing. As we type, we start seeing partial results based on the few characters we have already typed (Figure 12-1).

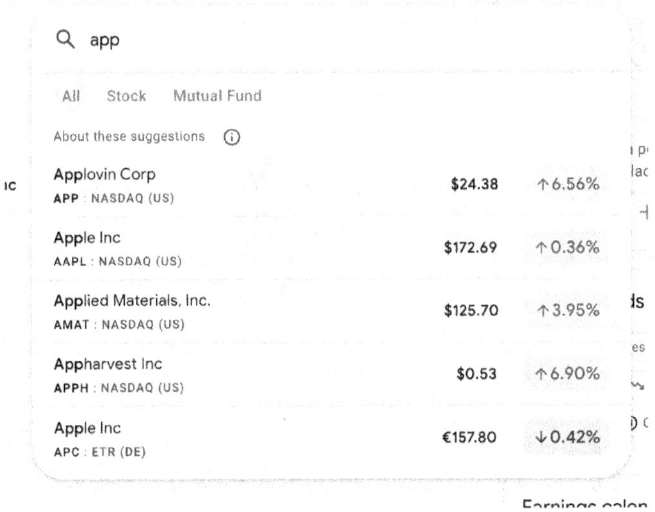

FIGURE 12-1

An example of autocomplete

As we keep typing, the partial results keep getting refined until it nearly predicts the word or phrase we were trying to type fully. This autocompletion-like interaction is one we take for granted these days. Almost all of our user interfaces (aka UIs) have some form of it. Why is this interesting for us at this very moment?

Behind the scenes, there is a very good chance that the data structure powering this autocomplete capability is the star of this chapter, the **trie** (sometimes also called a **prefix tree**). In the following sections, we learn more about it.

Onward!

What Is a Trie?

Let's get the boring textbook definition out of the way:

A trie (pronounced "try") is a data structure that breaks phrases or words down into their individual alphabets and stores them in a way where adding, deleting, finding, or even auto-completing phrases is efficient.

Yeah . . . that definition isn't particularly helpful in explaining what a trie is or does (Figure 12-2).

FIGURE 12-2

What is a trie?

This calls for an example and visual walkthrough to examine the most common operations we'll be performing on a trie.

Inserting Words

What we want to do is store the word *apple* inside a trie. The first thing we do is break our word into individual characters: *a, p, p, l,* and *e.* Next, it's time to start building our trie tree structure.

The start of our trie is an empty root node (Figure 12-3).

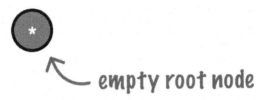

FIGURE 12-3

An empty root node

Our next step is to take the first letter (*a*) from the word (*apple*) we are trying to store and add it to our trie as a child of our root node (Figure 12-4).

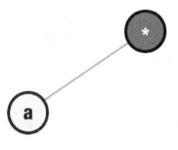

FIGURE 12-4

Our child

We repeat this step for the next letter (*p*) and add it as a child of our *a* node (Figure 12-5).

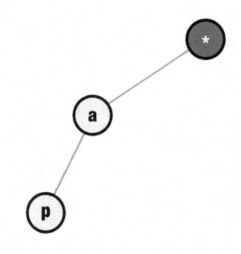

FIGURE 12-5

The letters of the word continue being added as children

We keep taking each letter of our word and adding it as a child of the previous letter. For *apple*, the final trie structure would look like Figure 12-6.

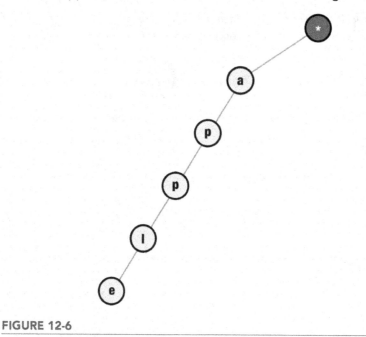

FIGURE 12-6

The word apple stored in a trie

There is one additional thing that we do once our entire word is represented in the tree. We tag the last letter of our input to indicate that it is complete (Figure 12-7).

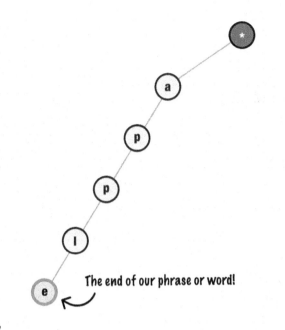

FIGURE 12-7

Designating the end of our word

We'll see later why marking the end is important. For now, let's go ahead and add a few more words to our trie. We are going to add *cat*, *dog*, *duck*, and *monkey*. When we add *cat* and *dog*, our trie will look like Figure 12-8.

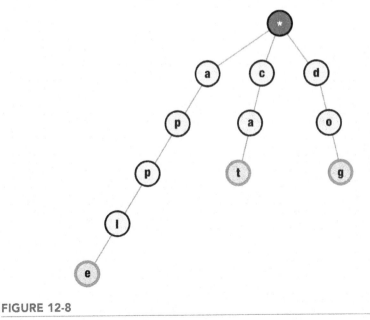

FIGURE 12-8

More words stored in our trie

The next word we are going to add is *duck*. Notice that the first letter of our word is *d*, and we already have a *d* node at the top as a child of our root. What we do is start from our existing *d* node instead of creating a new *d* node. The next letter is *u*, but we don't have an existing child of *d* with the value of *u*. So, we create a new child node whose value is *u* and continue on with the remaining letters in our word.

The part to emphasize here is that our letter *d* is now a common prefix for our *dog* and *duck* words (Figure 12-9).

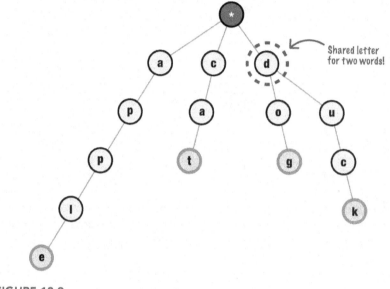

FIGURE 12-9

Our letter d has two words starting from it

The next word we want to add is *monkey,* and this will be represented as follows once we add it to our tree (Figure 12-10).

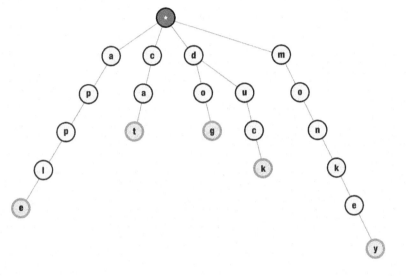

FIGURE 12-10

Our trie is getting pretty large!

Because the starting letter *m* is not already a child of our root, we create a new node for *m*. Every subsequent letter in *monkey* follows from it. We are almost done here, so let's go a little faster as well.

The next word we want to represent is *dune*. We know the letters *d* and *u* are already in our trie, so what we do is add the letters *n* and *e* that build off the common prefix, *du* (Figure 12-11).

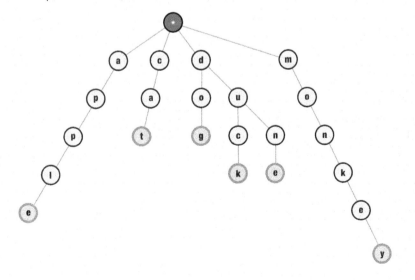

FIGURE 12-11

We build off of common prefixes

The next two words we want to add are *app* and *monk*. Both of these words are contained within the larger words of *apple* and *monkey* respectively, so what we need to do is just designate the last letters in *app* and *monk* as being the end of a word (Figure 12-12).

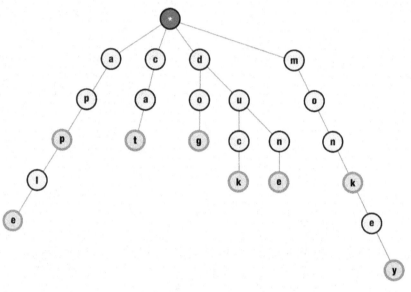

FIGURE 12-12

A word within a word

Ok. At this point, our trie contains *apple, app, cat, dog, duck, dune, monkey,* and *monk*. We have enough items in our trie now. Let's look at some additional operations.

Finding Items

Imagine we add all the words from Webster's dictionary to a trie. Now, picture yourself trying to manually determine whether a word is a valid entry in the dictionary. Let's explore how we can leverage our trie to efficiently search for a word. Continuing with our trie from earlier, let's say we want to see if the word *eagle* exists. What we do is break our input word into its individual characters: *e, a, g, l, e.*

We check whether the first letter exists as a child of our root node (Figure 12-13).

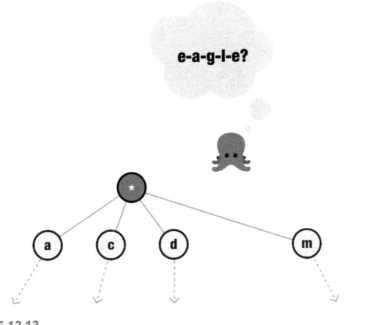

FIGURE 12-13

The start of a search

The starting letters we have are *a, c, d,* and *m.* The letter *e* isn't present, so we can stop the search right here. If the first letter isn't available, we can safely state that all subsequent letters won't be present either.

Our next task is to see if the word *monk* exists in our trie. The process is the same. We check whether the first letter of the word we are looking for (*m*) exists as the first letter in our trie. The answer is yes (Figure 12-14).

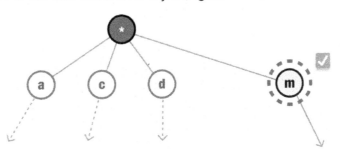

FIGURE 12-14

We find the m for monk in our trie

We then continue down the path of the *m* node and check whether the second letter (*o*) is an immediate child (Figure 12-15).

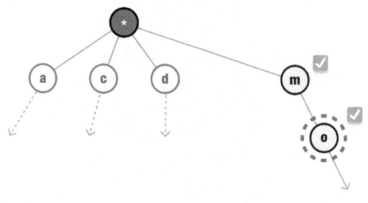

FIGURE 12-15

We check letter by letter

In our case, *o* is an immediate child of *m*. Notice that our search is very narrowly focused on the branches of the *m* node only. We don't care about what is happening in the other nodes. Continuing on, now that our first two letters match, we keep repeating the same steps and checking whether the third and fourth letters match as well (Figure 12-16).

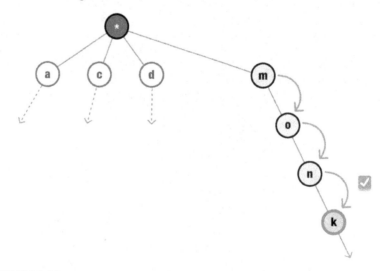

FIGURE 12-16

We stay on the same branch

The remaining letters in *monk* match what we have in our trie. Depending on the operation we are doing, there may be one more step:

1. If we are checking whether the **complete word** exists in our trie, then we check to make sure the last letter is designated as the end of a word. In our case, *monk* was added to our trie as a final word, and the letter *k* has been marked as the end of it. We are good on this front.

2. If we are checking whether the **prefix** exists in our trie, then we don't have to check whether the last character is also marked as the end of the word. Our word *monk* would still pass the test, but so would other prefixes leading up to here, such as *m, mo,* and *mon.*

This distinction between a complete word and prefix when we are searching our trie becomes important in various situations. The complete word search is important if we want to check whether *monk* was added to our trie at some point as a full word. If we wanted to find all words that start with *monk*, then the prefix search is the approach we use. We'll see some examples of both of these approaches when diving into our implementation later.

Deleting Items

The last step we look at is how to delete an item from our trie. Because we went into detail on how to add and find items in our trie, how we delete items is more straightforward. There are a few additional tricks we need to keep in mind. In our trie, let's say that we want to delete the word *duck* (Figure 12-17).

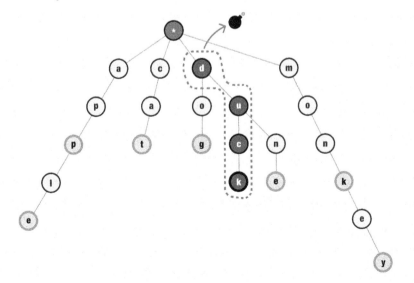

FIGURE 12-17

Deleting items is a bit more involved

What we can't do is just traverse this tree and delete all the characters because:

- We first need to make sure that the word we are deleting actually exists in our tree.

- We also need to ensure that if a particular letter is shared by other words, we don't remove it. In the case of *duck*, the letter *d* is shared with *dog* and *dune*, and the letter *u* is shared with *dune*.

- We also need to ensure that the letter we are removing isn't part of another word.

So, what do we do? Well, we have our three checks to perform. We first check to make sure the word we are deleting exists in our tree, and we check the last node by making sure it is flagged as being the end of our word. If all of that checks out, at this point, we are at the last character of the word we are interested in removing (Figure 12-18).

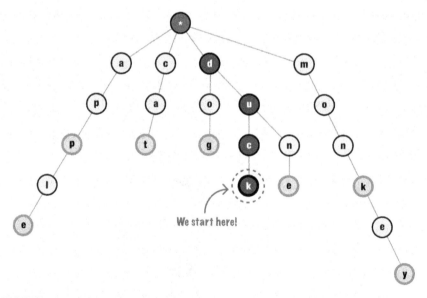

FIGURE 12-18

Deletions start with the last letter

What we do next is traverse up our tree in reverse order. For each letter we encounter, we check that the current node has no other children and is not the end of another word. If the node we encounter passes these checks, we remove the node and keep moving up the tree. This process continues until we encounter a node that has other children or is the end of another word. At that point, the deletion process stops.

For our example where we want to remove *duck* from our trie, we start at the end with the letter *k*. This node is safe to delete, so we delete it. We then move up to the letter *c*. This node is also safe to delete, so our trie now looks like Figure 12-19.

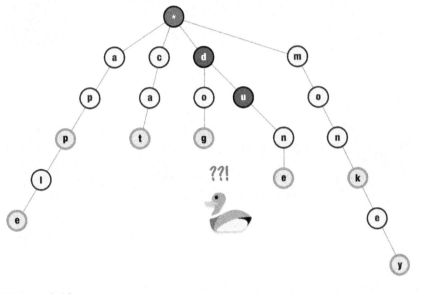

FIGURE 12-19

The duck value is no longer in the trie

The next letter we run into is *u*, and *u* has additional children. It is a shared prefix where it is on the path to the letter *n* that is part of the word *dune*. At this point, we can stop our deletion operation. It doesn't matter what happens beyond this point, for other word(s) rely on the preceding letters of *d* and *u* to be present.

Diving Deeper into Tries

When we started looking at tries in the previous section, we had the following definition:

A trie is a tree-based data structure that is ideal for retrieving strings or sequences of characters that is ideal for situations involving adding, deleting, or finding strings or sequences of characters.

Let's start with the obvious one. Our trie is a tree-based data structure. We can see that is the case (Figure 12-20).

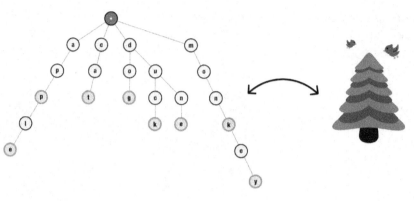

FIGURE 12-20

Tries are tree-based data structures

When we examine how our data is structured, the tree similarity still holds. We have a series of nodes where the value of each node is a singular part of a larger piece of data. In our example, the singular part is the letter. The larger piece is the word.

Now, let us get to the really big elephant in the room: What makes tries efficient for retrieving strings or sequences of characters? The answer has a lot to do with what we are trying to do. Where a trie is helpful is for a very particular set of use cases. **These cases involve searching for words given an incomplete input.** To go back to our example, we provide the character *d*, and our trie can quickly return *dog*, *duck*, and *dune* as possible destinations (Figure 12-21).

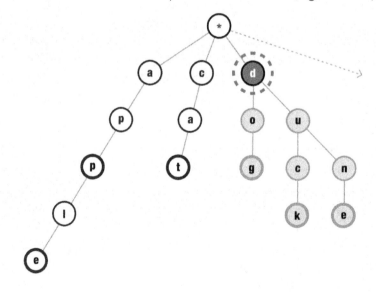

FIGURE 12-21

All values starting with the letter d are going to be fast

If instead what we are doing is checking whether or not our input characters (i.e., *d-o-g*) is a word, then the trie is the wrong data structure. We probably want something like a hashmap that can quickly tell us if our *complete* input is among a set of stored values, but a hashmap is less memory efficient compared to a trie. Just a pesky tradeoff to keep in mind!

Now, what are the situations where we may have incomplete input that may still have just enough detail to give us a shortcut to a final value? Let's take a look at a few of them:

- **Autocomplete and predictive text:** Reiterating a point we started off our look at tries with, when we start typing a word or a phrase in a search engine, email client, or messaging app, we often see suggestions that complete our input (Figure 12-22).

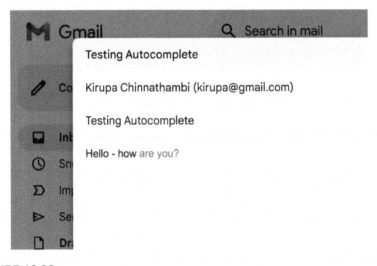

FIGURE 12-22

Another example of autocomplete

Tries are useful for implementing autocomplete functionality pretty efficiently. Each node in the trie represents a character, and each point leading from there represents the possible next characters. By traversing the trie on the basis of user input, we can quickly find and suggest the most likely completions, such as *monkey* and *monk* when our input is *m*.

- **Spell checking and correction:** Spell checkers rely on dictionaries to identify and correct misspelled words. Tries can be used to store a dictionary efficiently, allowing fast lookup and suggestions for alternative words (Figure 12-23).

FIGURE 12-23

Spellcheck at work

As we have seen a few times already, each node represents a character, and words are stored as paths from the root to the leaf nodes. When an incorrect (aka misspelled) character is entered, we can take a few steps back and see what a more likely path to reaching a complete word can be.

- **IP routing and network routing tables:** In computer networks, IP addresses are used to identify devices. Tries can be used to efficiently store and retrieve routing information for IP addresses (Figure 12-24).

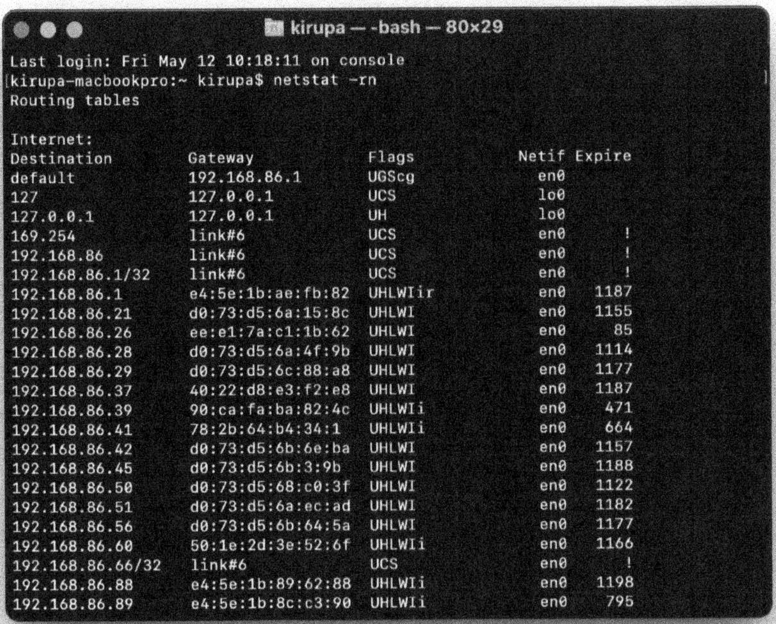

FIGURE 12-24

A routing table

Each node in the trie represents a part of the IP address, and the edges correspond to the possible values of that part. By traversing the trie on the basis of the IP address, routers can determine the next hop for routing packets in the network efficiently.

- **Word games and puzzles:** Tries can be handy for word games like Scrabble or Wordle where players need to quickly find valid words given a set of letters (Figure 12-25).

FIGURE 12-25

Word games commonly use tries under the hood

By constructing a trie that represents a dictionary, players can efficiently check whether a given sequence of letters forms a valid word by traversing the trie.

Many More Examples Abound!

These are just a few examples of the many use cases where tries can be super useful. The key idea is that tries allow us to efficiently store, retrieve, and manipulate words or sequences of characters, making them suitable for tasks that involve matching, searching, or suggesting based on prefixes.

NOTE Why Are Tries Sometimes Called Prefix Trees?

Tries are sometimes called prefix trees because their entire functionality revolves around prefixes! Tries store words in a tree-like structure that emphasizes common letters (aka a prefix). Each node in the trie represents a character, and the path from the root to a node forms a prefix. We can even go one step further and think of a complete word as just a prefix with the last character having a flag that designates it as a word. For these reasons and more, we'll often see tries referred to as prefix trees in various other books and online resources.

Implementation Time

Now that we can verbally describe how a trie works, let's turn all of the words and visuals into code. Our trie implementation will support the following operations:

- Inserting a word
- Searching for whether a word exists
- Checking whether words that match a given prefix exist
- Returning all words that match a given prefix

And . . . without further delay, here is our code:

```
class TrieNode {
  constructor() {
    // Each TrieNode has a map of children nodes,
    // where the key is the character and the value is the
    // child TrieNode
    this.children = new Map();

    // Flag to indicate if the current TrieNode represents the
    // end of a word
    this.isEndOfWord = false;
  }
}
```

```
class Trie {
  constructor() {
    // The root of the Trie is an empty TrieNode
    this.root = new TrieNode();
  }

  // Adds the word to trie
  insert(word) {
    let current = this.root;

    for (let i = 0; i < word.length; i++) {
      const char = word[i];

      // If the character doesn't exist as a child node,
      // create a new TrieNode for it
      if (!current.children.get(char)) {
        current.children.set(char, new TrieNode());
      }

      // Move to the next TrieNode.
      current = current.children.get(char);
    }

    // Mark the end of the word by setting isEndOfWord to true
    current.isEndOfWord = true;
  }

  // Returns true if the word exists in the trie
  search(word) {
    let current = this.root;

    for (let i = 0; i < word.length; i++) {
      const char = word[i];
      // If the character doesn't exist as a child node,
      // the word doesn't exist in the Trie
      if (!current.children.get(char)) {
```

```
      return false;
    }

    // Move to the next TrieNode.
    current = current.children.get(char);
  }

  // Return true if the last TrieNode represents the end of a word
  return current.isEndOfWord;
}

// Returns a true if the prefix exists in the trie
startsWith(prefix) {
  let current = this.root;

  for (let i = 0; i < prefix.length; i++) {
    const char = prefix[i];

    // If the character doesn't exist as a child node,
    // the prefix doesn't exist in the Trie
    if (!current.children.get(char)) {
      return false;
    }

    // Move to the next TrieNode.
    current = current.children.get(char);
  }

  // The prefix exists in the Trie.
  return true;
}

// Returns all words in the trie that match a prefix
getAllWords(prefix = '') {
  const words = [];
```

```
    // Find the node corresponding to the given prefix
    const current = this.#findNode(prefix);

    if (current) {
      // If the node exists, traverse the Trie starting from that node
      // to find all words and add them to the 'words' array
      this.#traverse(current, prefix, words);
    }

    return words;
}

delete(word) {
  let current = this.root;

  const stack = [];

  let index = 0;

  // Find the last node of the word in the Trie
  while (index < word.length) {
    const char = word[index];

    if (!current.children.get(char)) {
      // Word doesn't exist in the Trie, nothing to delete
      return;
    }

    stack.push({ node: current, char });

    current = current.children.get(char);
    index++;
  }

  if (!current.isEndOfWord) {
    // Word doesn't exist in the Trie, nothing to delete
```

```
    return;
  }


  // Mark the last node as not representing the end of a word
  current.isEndOfWord = false;


  // Remove nodes in reverse order until reaching a node
  // that has other children or is the end of another word
  while (stack.length > 0) {
    const { node, char } = stack.pop();

    if (current.children.size === 0 && !current.isEndOfWord) {
      node.children.delete(char);
      current = node;
    } else {
      break;
    }
  }
}


#findNode(prefix) {
  let current = this.root;
  for (let i = 0; i < prefix.length; i++) {
    const char = prefix[i];

    // If the character doesn't exist as a child node, the
    // prefix doesn't exist in the Trie
    if (!current.children.get(char)) {
      return null;
    }

    // Move to the next TrieNode
    current = current.children.get(char);
  }
```

```
    // Return the node corresponding to the given prefix
    return current;
  }


  #traverse(node, prefix, words) {
    const stack = [];

    stack.push({ node, prefix });

    while (stack.length > 0) {
      const { node, prefix } = stack.pop();

      // If the current node represents the end of a word,
      // add the word to the 'words' array
      if (node.isEndOfWord) {
        words.push(prefix);
      }

      // Push all child nodes to the stack to continue traversal
      for (const char of node.children.keys()) {
        const childNode = node.children.get(char);
        stack.push({ node: childNode, prefix: prefix + char });
      }
    }
  }
}
```

To see our trie code in action, add the following code:

```
const trie = new Trie();

trie.insert("apple");
trie.insert("app");
trie.insert("monkey");
trie.insert("monk");
trie.insert("cat");
```

```
trie.insert("dog");
trie.insert("duck");
trie.insert("dune");

console.log(trie.search("apple")); // true
console.log(trie.search("app")); // true
console.log(trie.search("monk")); // true
console.log(trie.search("elephant")); // false

console.log(trie.getAllWords("ap")); // ['apple', 'app']
console.log(trie.getAllWords("b")); // []
console.log(trie.getAllWords("c")); // ['cat']
console.log(trie.getAllWords("m")); // ['monk', 'monkey']

trie.delete("monkey");

console.log(trie.getAllWords("m")); // ['monk']
```

Our trie implementation performs all of the operations we walked through in detail earlier, and it does it by using a hashmap as its underlying data structure to help efficiently map characters at each node to its children. Many trie implementations may use arrays as well, and that is also a fine data structure to use.

Before we wrap up this section, do take a few moments to walk through the code and visualize how each line contributes to our overall trie design.

Performance

We are almost done here. Let's talk about the performance of our trie, focusing on a trie implementation that uses a hashmap under the covers. At a high level, all of our trie operations are impacted by two things:

1. How long the words or prefix we are dealing with are

2. How many child nodes exist for a given letter

Insertion, search, and deletion operations in a trie typically have a linear time complexity of $O(k)$ where k is the number of characters in our input word. For example, if we add the word duck to our trie, we process the *d*, the *u*, the *c*, and the *k* individually (Figure 12-26).

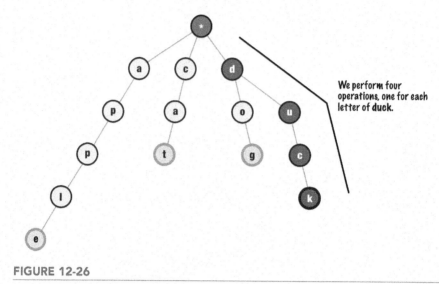

We perform four operations, one for each letter of *duck*.

FIGURE 12-26

Looking deeply at insertion behavior

For longer inputs involving large numbers of characters, more work needs to be done. Smaller inputs require less work. The amount of work is proportional to the size of our input, though. That makes this situation a perfect linear one.

Here is one more detail to keep in mind. Our trie implementation uses a hashtable, which we just learned about earlier, to keep track of character and node mappings. Checking whether a character exists as a child has an average time complexity of O(1). Putting it all together, in the worst case, the time complexity for seeing if a word (or phrase) exists in our trie will be O(N). This is especially true if any particular node in our trie has an abnormally large amount of children. Our hashing implementation uses JavaScript's built-in Map object, so the performance is well taken care of. If you are using your own hashing implementation or using an alternate data structure like an array, the performance can get degraded.

 NOTE   Why O(k) as opposed to O(n)?

Why did we not just use O(n) to describe the time complexity? There isn't a strong reason for this. The argument N typically refers to the total number of items we are dealing with and the number of operations relative to that. For our insert, search, and delete operations, the total size of N items in the trie doesn't matter. The only thing that matters is our input size, so it seemed reasonable to use a different notation.

Lastly, let's talk about memory. The memory usage of a trie is typically O(N). The amount of memory we take is related to the number of entries we have in our trie. Using a hashmap for tracking children adds a bit of overhead as well, but it isn't large enough to move us away from the O(N) upper boundary.

Long story short, the elevator pitch is this: Tries are very efficient data structures. That is something you can take to the bank!

Conclusion

The trie data structure, also known as a prefix tree, provides an efficient solution for working with words and their prefixes. Tries are like special trees that allow us to store and search for words on the basis of their common beginnings. By representing words as paths from the root to specific nodes, tries organize information in a way that makes it easy to find all words with a given prefix.

What makes tries totally sweet is how efficiently they work. As we highlighted in some of the earlier examples, there is a boatload of situations where we will be dealing with words. In those situations, the trie is going to end up becoming your best friend.

SOME ADDITIONAL RESOURCES

? Ask a question: **https://forum.kirupa.com**

⌨ Errors/Known issues: **https://bit.ly/algorithms_errata**

🖥 Source repository: **https://bit.ly/algorithms_source**

13

GRAPHS

It is time for us to learn about the graph data structure. This particular data structure is used in so many applications and has so much going for it, an entire field of study called graph theory exists for it. Smart people every year get advanced degrees in it. There are walls of books dedicated to just this topic. Famous musicians sing songs about . . . okay, maybe not.

The point to emphasize is that there is a lot to learn when it comes to graphs. We will certainly not cover everything in our time together, but cover the big topics that we will run into the most in our everyday programming life.

Onward!

What Is a Graph?

Graphs are a way to organize information and understand how different things are connected to each other. This *connected to each other* part is important. Graphs help us to find and analyze the relationships between things. Let's start with an example.

Meet Jerry, a fairly successful comedian who lives in New York City (Figure 13-1).

FIGURE 13-1

The first item in our graph

He has a handful of friends named Elaine, Kramer, and George. We can model Jerry's friendships as shown in Figure 13-2.

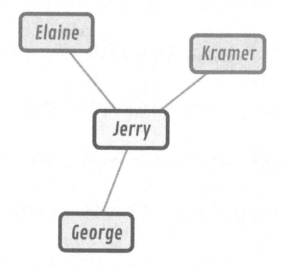

FIGURE 13-2

Connections in our graph

What we have here is a graph. The **nodes** (aka **vertexes** or **points**) are Jerry, Elaine, Kramer, and George. The connection between the nodes is known as an edge (Figure 13-3).

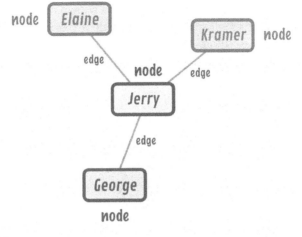

FIGURE 13-3

Nodes and edges

Right now, the edges don't have any direction to them. They are considered to be **bidirectional** where the relationship between the connected nodes is mutual. A graph made up of only bidirectional edges is known as an **undirected graph** (Figure 13-4).

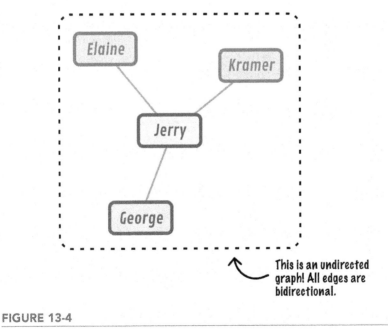

FIGURE 13-4

Our undirected graph

We can also visualize an undirected graph as shown in Figure 13-5, where the bidirectional property of the edges is more clearly evident and our ambiguous single path is separated into dedicated paths.

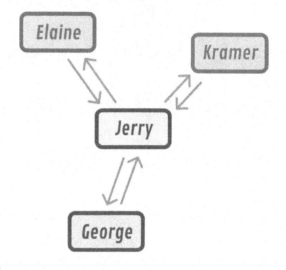

FIGURE 13-5

Another way to visualize an undirected graph

In many real-life cases, our graphs will rarely be undirected. They will have a specific order in the relationship where some connections may be one way. Continuing with our example, Jerry has an acquaintance named Newman. Newman considers Jerry a friend (Figure 13-6).

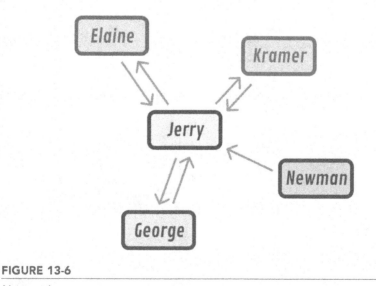

FIGURE 13-6

Newman!

This consideration isn't mutual. Jerry does not consider Newman a friend, so there won't be a reciprocating edge from Jerry pointing toward Newman. A graph where some of the edges have a direction, kind of like what we have right now, is known as a **directed graph**, or **digraph** for short.

Let's go ahead and detail more of the relationships between Jerry, Elaine, Kramer, George, and Newman (Figure 13-7).

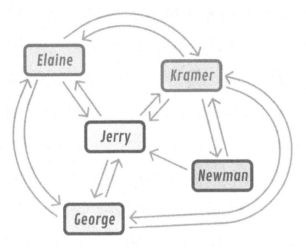

FIGURE 13-7

The various relationships modeled by our graph

We can now see that Jerry, Elaine, Kramer, and George are mutual friends with each other. Newman is a mutual friend of Kramer, and he has a one-way friendship with Jerry.

There is another detail of graphs that has to do with **cycles**. A cycle occurs when we have a path that starts and ends at the same node. For example, our graph highlighting Jerry's friends has many cycles with multiple paths that start and end with each node. If we had to list all the cycles for just Jerry, here are the paths that we can identify:

- Jerry to George to Elaine to Jerry
- Jerry to George to Elaine to Kramer to Jerry
- Jerry to George to Elaine to Kramer to Newman to Jerry
- Jerry to George to Kramer to Jerry
- Jerry to Elaine to George to Jerry
- Jerry to Elaine to Kramer to George to Jerry

- Jerry to Elaine to Kramer to Newman to Jerry
- Jerry to Kramer to Elaine to Jerry
- Jerry to Kramer to Elaine to George to Jerry
- Jerry to Kramer to Newman to Jerry

Graphs with cycles are commonly known as **cyclic graphs**. We will also encounter graphs that contain no cycles whatsoever (Figure 13-8).

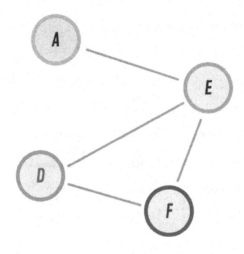

FIGURE 13-8

An acylic graph

These graphs are known as **acyclic graphs**, and what we see in the figure is a more specific variation known as a **directed acyclic graph** (aka **dag**) because the edges have a direction to them. We also have acyclic graphs that are undirected. Can you guess what these types of graphs are also more commonly known as? Spoiler alert! Look at Figure 13-9.

They are known as **trees**, a data structure we spent a fair amount of time looking into earlier. Yes, trees are a very specific type of graph. They are acyclic in that there aren't multiple paths that start from and end at the same node. They are undirected in that the edges are bidirectional. There is one more detail: the graphs that represent a tree are **connected**. Connected means that there is a path between every pair of nodes.

The best way to visualize a connected graph is to look at one that is **unconnected** (Figure 13-10).

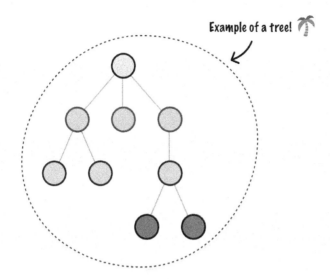

FIGURE 13-9

Is this a tree I see?

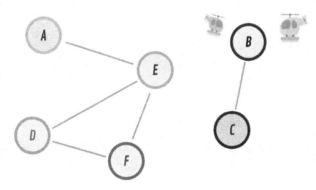

FIGURE 13-10

A graph that isn't very connected

Notice that nodes B and C are floating on an island with no way to get to either B or C from any of the other nodes. For example, is there a path from F to either B or C? Nope. A connected graph will not have this problem (Figure 13-11).

The path created by A and B brings B and C back into connectedness. Now, every pair of nodes in our graph can be reached by some path.

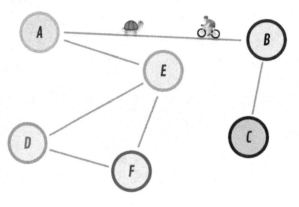

FIGURE 13-11

A graph that is totally connected

Graph Implementation

Now that we have a good overview of what graphs are and the variations they come in, it's time to shift gears and look at how we can actually implement one. If we take many steps back, the most common operations we'll do with a graph are:

- Add nodes

- Define edges between nodes

- Identify neighbors:

  - If our graph is directional, make sure we respect the direction of the edge

  - If our graph is nondirectional, all immediate nodes connected from a particular node will qualify as a neighbor

- Remove nodes

Representing Nodes

Before we dive into the implementation, an interesting detail here has to do with how exactly we will represent our node and its relationship with its neighbors. Let's say that we have a graph and a node called A that has the connections shown in Figure 13-12.

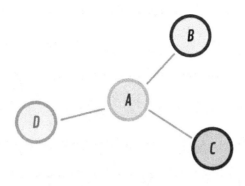

FIGURE 13-12

Another example of a graph

The nodes are A, B, C, and D. We have edges that connect A-B, A-C, and A-D. Because our graph is undirected, the direction of the edges is bidirectional. This means we also have edges that connect B-A, C-A, and D-A.

Getting back to our A node, its neighbors are the nodes B, C, and D. Some nodes will have fewer neighbors, and some nodes can have significantly more. It all boils down to both the type and volume of data our graph represents. So, how would we represent a node's neighbors? One really popular way is by using what is known as an **adjacency list**.

When using an adjacency list, each node is associated with a list of adjacent nodes. A rough visualization using our current example can look as follows:

```
A: [B, C, D]
B: [A]
C: [A]
D: [A]
```

This list can take many forms in a potential graph implementation. Our list can be an array, map, hashtable, or host of other data structures. Because we mentioned earlier that a node can have a large number of neighbors, we will want to go with a data structure that makes finding a node lightning fast. This is why, in a few moments, you'll see us representing our adjacency list using a map (aka hashtable) data structure (see www.kirupa.com/data_structures_algorithms/hashtable_hashmap_dictionary.htm).

By using a map, we can have the *key* be a node. The *value* will be a set data structure whose contents will be all of the neighboring nodes. Sets are great because they don't allow duplicate values. This ensures we avoid a situation where we are going in a loop and adding the same node repeatedly.

The Code

With the background out of the way, let's dive right in and look at our implementation for the graph data structure:

```
class Graph {
  constructor() {
    // Map to store nodes and their adjacent nodes
    this.nodes = new Map();

    // Flag to indicate if the graph is directed or undirected
    this.isDirected = false;
  }

  // Add a new node to the graph
  addNode(node) {
    if (!this.nodes.has(node)) {
      this.nodes.set(node, new Set());
    }
  }

  // Add an edge between two nodes
  addEdge(node1, node2) {
    // Check if the nodes exist
    if (!this.nodes.has(node1) || !this.nodes.has(node2)) {
      throw new Error('Nodes do not exist in the graph.');
    }

    // Add edge between node1 and node2
    this.nodes.get(node1).add(node2);

    // If the graph is undirected, add edge in
    // the opposite direction as well
    if (!this.isDirected) {
      this.nodes.get(node2).add(node1);
    }
  }
}
```

```
// Remove a node and all its incident edges from the graph
removeNode(node) {
  if (this.nodes.has(node)) {
    // Remove the node and its edges from the graph
    this.nodes.delete(node);
    // Remove any incident edges in other nodes
    for (const [node, adjacentNodes] of this.nodes) {
      adjacentNodes.delete(node);
    }
  }
}


// Remove an edge between two nodes
removeEdge(node1, node2) {
  if (this.nodes.has(node1) && this.nodes.has(node2)) {
    // Remove edge between node1 and node2
    this.nodes.get(node1).delete(node2);

    // If the graph is undirected, remove edge
    // in the opposite direction as well
    if (!this.isDirected) {
      this.nodes.get(node2).delete(node1);
    }
  }
}


// Check if an edge exists between two nodes
hasEdge(node1, node2) {
  if (this.nodes.has(node1) && this.nodes.has(node2)) {
    return this.nodes.get(node1).has(node2);
  }
  return false;
}


// Get the adjacent nodes of a given node
getNeighbors(node) {
```

```
    if (this.nodes.has(node)) {
      return Array.from(this.nodes.get(node));
    }
    return [];
  }

  // Get all nodes in the graph
  getAllNodes() {
    return Array.from(this.nodes.keys());
  }

  // Set the graph as directed
  setDirected() {
    this.isDirected = true;
  }

  // Set the graph as undirected
  setUndirected() {
    this.isDirected = false;
  }
  // Check if the graph is directed
  isGraphDirected() {
    return this.isDirected;
  }
}
```

Following is an example of how we can use the preceding graph implementation to perform common graph operations:

```
// Create a new graph
const characters = new Graph();
characters.setDirected();

// Add nodes
characters.addNode('Jerry');
characters.addNode('Elaine');
characters.addNode('Kramer');
```

```
characters.addNode('George');
characters.addNode('Newman');

// Add edges
characters.addEdge('Jerry', 'Elaine');
characters.addEdge('Jerry', 'George');
characters.addEdge('Jerry', 'Kramer');
characters.addEdge('Elaine', 'Jerry');
characters.addEdge('Elaine', 'George');
characters.addEdge('Elaine', 'Kramer');
characters.addEdge('George', 'Elaine');
characters.addEdge('George', 'Jerry');
characters.addEdge('George', 'Kramer');
characters.addEdge('Kramer', 'Elaine');
characters.addEdge('Kramer', 'George');
characters.addEdge('Kramer', 'Jerry');
characters.addEdge('Kramer', 'Newman');
characters.addEdge('Newman', 'Kramer');
characters.addEdge('Newman', 'Jerry');

// Get the adjacent nodes of a node
console.log("Jerry's neighbors: ");
console.log(characters.getNeighbors('Jerry'));
      // ['Elaine', 'George', 'Kramer']

console.log("Newman's neighbors: ");
console.log(characters.getNeighbors('Newman')); // ['Kramer',
'Jerry']

// Check if an edge exists between two nodes
console.log("Does edge exist between Jerry to Newman? ");
console.log(characters.hasEdge('Jerry', 'Newman')); // false

console.log("Does edge exist between Newman to Jerry? ");
console.log(characters.hasEdge('Jerry', 'Newman')); // true
```

```
console.log("Does edge exist between Elaine to George? ");
console.log(characters.hasEdge('Elaine', 'George')); // true


// Get all nodes in the graph
console.log("All the nodes: ");
console.log(characters.getAllNodes());
    // ['Jerry', 'Elaine', 'Kramer', 'George', 'Newman']


// Remove a node
console.log("Remove the node, Newman: ")
characters.removeNode("Newman");
console.log(characters.getAllNodes());
    // ['Jerry', 'Elaine', 'Kramer', 'George']


console.log("Does edge exist between Kramer to Newman: ");
console.log(characters.hasEdge('Kramer', 'Newman')); // false
```

Take a moment to walk through the code, especially the comments. As we can see, this implementation of the graph data structure very closely matches the type of graph we have been describing. That's good and bad. It's good because there should be no surprises in our code. It's bad because a more complete graph implementation will contain a few more bells and whistles . . . which our implementation does not contain. Rest assured that we'll touch upon those missing pieces when we go deeper into looking at graphs in subsequent tutorials.

Conclusion

The graph data structure is one of those fundamental concepts in computer science that you and I can't avoid running into. Because graphs provide a powerful way to model relationships between things, their usefulness is through the roof. So many activities we take for granted, such as navigating using an online map, joining a multiplayer game, analyzing data, navigating to anywhere on the Internet, following friends on social media, and doing a billion other activities, all rely on the core capabilities the graph data structure provides. We've only scratched the surface of what graphs are capable of, so we are going to cover more graph-related things in this book.

SOME ADDITIONAL RESOURCES

? Ask a question: **https://forum.kirupa.com**

Errors/Known issues: **https://bit.ly/algorithms_errata**

Source repository: **https://bit.ly/algorithms_source**

14

INTRODUCTION TO RECURSION

Recursion is a powerful programming technique that allows us to break down large, complicated problems into smaller, more manageable pieces. Not only is it a valuable tool in our coding toolkit, but understanding recursion will also help us improve our logical thinking and problem-solving skills. So why wait? In this chapter, we get a good overview on what recursion is and why knowing more about it will kick our coding skills up a bunch of notches!

Onward!

Our Giant Cookie Problem

One way to think about recursion is as follows: we start with a large problem, and we break this large problem down into ever-smaller pieces until we reach a point where the problem is simple enough to solve directly. This will make more sense with an example, so let's imagine our job is to eat a gigantic cookie (Figure 14-1).

FIGURE 14-1

A giant cookie!

Because of its size, most people will have no way to eat this entire cookie in one bite. What we can do is break it into smaller pieces (Figure 14-2).

As we can see, these smaller pieces are still too big to eat in one bite. What we need to do is keep breaking our pieces down into even smaller pieces. Eventually, we will have broken our cookie down into a bite-sized piece that we can easily eat (Figure 14-3).

The part to notice is that we now have *many* bite-sized cookies that we need to eat. We don't have just one big cookie, nor do we have just one small cookie. The quantity of cookies we eat remains the same. The only difference is that the quantity is now spread across many cookies. This process of taking something large and breaking it into ever-smaller pieces is very similar to how recursion works in the context of our programming problems.

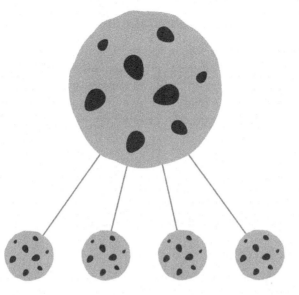

FIGURE 14-2

Breaking our cookie into smaller pieces

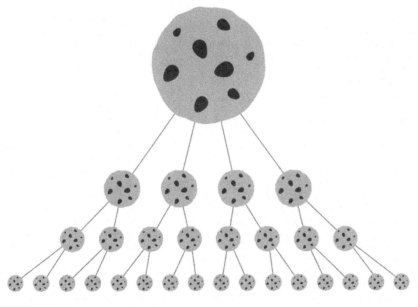

FIGURE 14-3

Breaking our cookie down further into even smaller pieces

Recursion in Programming

While thinking about recursion in the form of a cookie is all good and great—and delicious—we'll find the biggest bang when we throw recursion at thorny programming problems. Echoing what we started off with, the textbook definition of recursion involves two parts: a function that calls itself repeatedly and a condition that stops our function from calling itself. Let's go into more detail on what these two parts do.

Recursive Function Call

The first part involves what is known as a **recursive function call** where a function calls itself repeatedly. Taken literally, it would look a little bit like this:

```
function hello() {
  console.log("I'm a little function, short and stout!");

  hello();
}
```

We have a function called `hello`, and inside the function body, we are calling `hello` again. Now, this code won't actually run if we try it. It will cause an infinite loop because the code will never stop running. More specifically, our code will cause a stack overflow error (Figure 14-4).

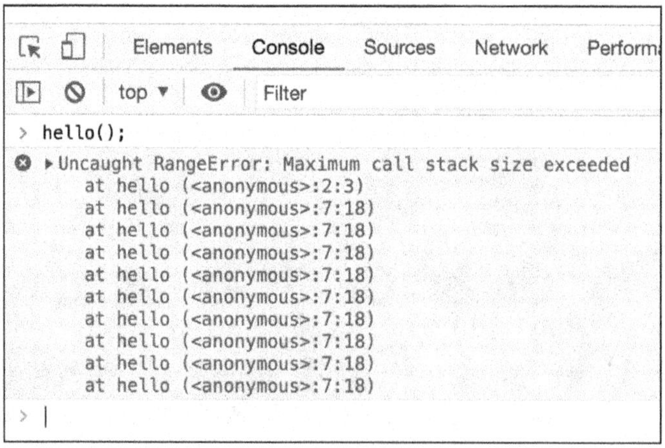

FIGURE 14-4

Example of what a stack overflow can look like

The way we avoid this problem brings us to the second part of our discussion.

Terminating Condition

The second part is a condition that stops our function from calling itself forever, the scary-sounding **terminating condition**. Leaning on our cookie example, we kept dividing our cookie into smaller pieces until it became bite-sized. The terminating condition is to check whether the size of the cookie is bite-sized. If the size is bite-sized, then eat the cookie. If the size isn't bite-sized, then divide the cookie further into smaller pieces.

Turning all of those words into code, let's say we want our `hello` function to act as an accumulator where we pass in a number, and it returns the sum of all the numbers leading up to the number we passed in. For example, if we pass in the number 5, our code will add up all numbers leading up to it, where it will calculate 5 + 4 + 3 + 2 + 1 and return a final value of 15. Following is what our revised `hello` function will look like if we do all of this:

```
function hello(num) {
  if (num <= 1) {
    // terminating condition
    return num;
  } else {
    // recursive function call
    return num + hello(num - 1);
  }
}


console.log(hello(5)); // 15
```

Take a moment to look at what our code is doing. If we had to visualize how this code runs, it would look as Figure 14-5 where we have our initial `hello(5)` call at the top and the results of our `return` statements following it.

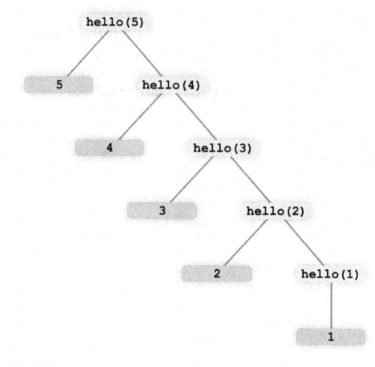

FIGURE 14-5

Visualizing our code

At each row where our num argument is greater than 1, we show the result of `num + hello(num - 1)` (Figure 14-6).

We keep repeating this until our num value hits 1. When this happens, we hit our terminating condition (num `<=` 1) and return the value of num itself, which is just 1 in our case (Figure 14-7).

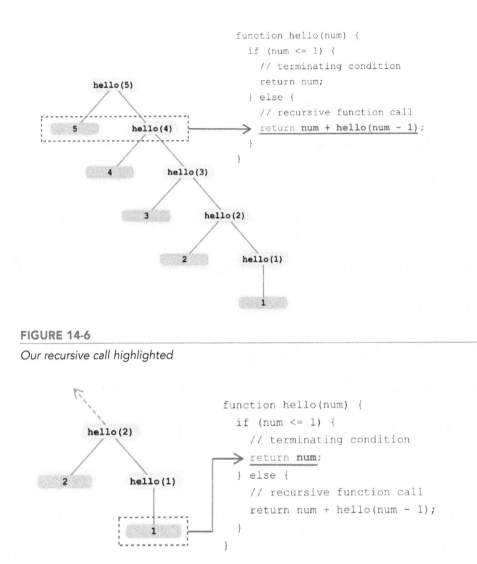

```
function hello(num) {
  if (num <= 1) {
    // terminating condition
    return num;
  } else {
    // recursive function call
    return num + hello(num - 1);
  }
}
```

FIGURE 14-6

Our recursive call highlighted

```
function hello(num) {
  if (num <= 1) {
    // terminating condition
    return num;
  } else {
    // recursive function call
    return num + hello(num - 1);
  }
}
```

FIGURE 14-7

When our code stops running

Taking a step back, for just one more time, we can see how we started with a large problem and, with each recursive call, broke the problem down into much smaller steps. We continued until we hit our terminating condition and were left with an easily digestible nugget, a plain old number. Really cool, right?

Conclusion

As we can see, recursion is the gift that keeps on giving . . . and giving . . . and giving! Jokes aside, while our `hello` accumulator function is a bit contrived, it does do a good job of highlighting the two basic ingredients needed to solve a problem using recursion:

- Recursive function call
- Terminating condition

We go a bit deeper in future chapters where we apply recursive techniques to solve more realistic and more complicated problems. Also, as with any problem-solving tool, recursion is the cure only for some things. There are situations (quite a bunch, as it turns out) where we need to look beyond recursion to solve problems in a more efficient way, and we'll cross that bridge shortly as well.

SOME ADDITIONAL RESOURCES

? Ask a question: **https://forum.kirupa.com**

Errors/Known issues: **https://bit.ly/algorithms_errata**

Source repository: **https://bit.ly/algorithms_source**

15

FIBONACCI AND GOING BEYOND RECURSION

If there was a Greatest Hits list of popular algorithms, the **Fibonacci sequence** would be right at the top. It would be the Beatles or the Rolling Stones of its generation. The Fibonacci sequence is a series of numbers in which each number is the sum of the previous two numbers. The sequence starts with 0 and 1, and then each subsequent number is the sum of the previous two. So, the sequence goes 0, 1, 1, 2, 3, 5, 8, 13, 21, 34, and so on.

To dive into that a bit deeper, here is how the sequence is calculated:

```
fibonacci(0) = 0
fibonacci(1) = 1
fibonacci(2) = 1 // Sum of fibonacci(1) + fibonacci(0)
fibonacci(3) = 2 // Sum of fibonacci(2) + fibonacci(1)
fibonacci(4) = 3 // Sum of fibonacci(3) + fibonacci(2)
   .

   .

   .

fibonacci(n) = fibonacci(n-1) + fibonacci(n-2)
```

This is cool . . . sort of. Why do we care about it? Besides its many practical uses, the Fibonacci sequence is a great example of an algorithm that can be solved recursively (Figure 15-1).

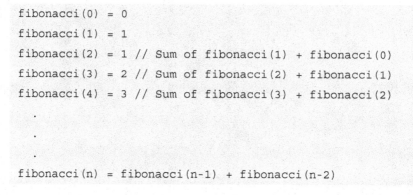

FIGURE 15-1

Somebody here likes recursion!

The Fibonacci sequence is also a great example of an algorithm that highlights the limitations of using recursion (Figure 15-2).

It provides the perfect jumping-off point for us to learn about alternate (nonrecursive!) ways to calculate the Fibonacci sequence and apply what we know to other types of computation problems that we'll encounter in the future.

Onward!

FIGURE 15-2

Recursion isn't for everyone

Recursively Solving the Fibonacci Sequence

As we saw earlier, a number in the Fibonacci sequence is the sum of the two preceding numbers. We know the first two numbers are always 0 and 1. All subsequent numbers can be calculated by using the following formula:

```
fibonacci(n) = fibonacci(n-1) + fibonacci(n-2)
```

If we turn all of this into JavaScript, here is a recursive way to identify any number in the Fibonacci sequence:

```javascript
function fibonacci(n) {
  if (n == 0) {
    return 0;
  } else if (n == 1) {
    return 1;
  } else {
    return fibonacci(n - 1) + fibonacci(n - 2);
  }
}

console.log('Result is', fibonacci(10));
```

This function takes a number n and returns the nth number in the Fibonacci sequence. The function works recursively by calling itself repeatedly with smaller and smaller values of n until it reaches one of the terminating conditions (where n is 0 or 1).

For example, if we call `fibonacci(3)`, the function will first call itself with n equal to 2, and then with n equal to 1 (Figure 15-3).

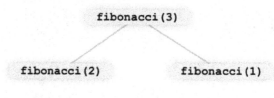

FIGURE 15-3

Our initial Fibonacci sequence call

This leads to the next step, where `fibonacci(1)` hits our terminating condition and returns a 1. The `fibonacci(2)` call will expand further (Figure 15-4).

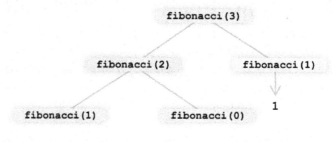

FIGURE 15-4

Going deeper into Fibonacci

At this stage, both `fibonacci(1)` and `fibonacci(0)` will hit their respective terminating conditions and return 0 and 1, respectively (Figure 15-5).

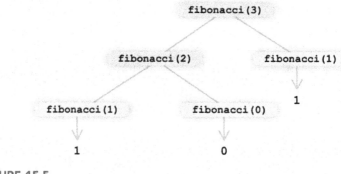

FIGURE 15-5

Our terminating conditions

In our code, we are adding the result of each recursive call:

```
function fibonacci(n) {
  if (n == 0) {
    return 0;
  } else if (n == 1) {
    return 1;
  } else {
    return fibonacci(n - 1) + fibonacci(n - 2);
  }
}
```

This means that we end up adding 1 + 0 + 1, which is 2. The third number in the fibonacci sequence is indeed 2, so we did good here!

Now, we went a little lengthy in our visual explanation here, but let's speed things up and look at one more example of calculating the Fibonacci sequence recursively. This time, let's calculate what the fifth number in the Fibonacci sequence will look like (Figure 15-6).

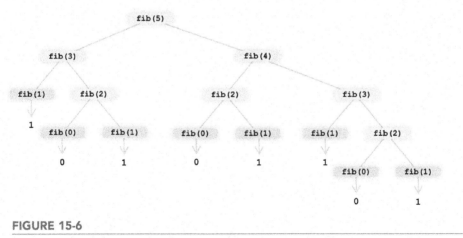

FIGURE 15-6

A more involved Fibonacci example

If we add up the final numbers that appear, we get a value of 5—which is exactly what the fifth number in the Fibonacci sequence is.

One thing to notice is the sheer number of recursive calls we are dealing with here. We aren't even dealing with large numbers. The jump in recursive calls between calculating the third number to calculating the fifth number in the Fibonacci sequence is huge. To see how many recursive function calls our favorite Fibonacci number requires, take a look at the chart in Figure 15-7.

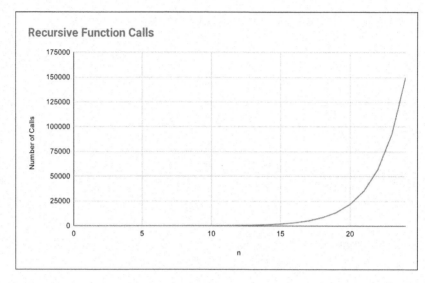

FIGURE 15-7

Visualizing the number of recursive calls

Your eyes aren't deceiving you. To calculate, for example, the 20th number in the Fibonacci sequence, there are 21,891 function calls. Just four numbers later, the 24th number in the Fibonacci sequence is a whopping 150,049 function calls.

That's a lot of calls, and each function call is an expensive operation. The running time here is $O(2^n)$, which puts it toward the high end in terms of operation cost. There are faster ways that improve upon the recursive approach we are taking, and we look into them next.

 NOTE   Why Are Function Calls Expensive?

Function calls, especially in long-running recursive operations, can be expensive (take a long time to run, take up a lot of memory, or both) for a few reasons:

- **Function calls require additional memory:** When a function is called, the interpreter needs to store the current state of the program (including the values of all the variables) on the call stack. This can consume a lot of memory, especially if the recursion goes deep.

- **Function calls require additional processing time:** Each function call requires the interpreter to push the current state onto the call stack and then pop it off again when the function returns. This can be time-consuming, especially if the function calls itself multiple times.

- **Function calls can cause stack overflow errors:** If the recursion goes too deep (e.g., if the function calls itself a whole bunch of times in short succession), it can cause the call stack to overflow, which can lead to a runtime error.

The more we can reduce the number of function calls, the faster our code will run. In the next few sections, we take our recursive-only approach for calculating the Fibonacci sequence and look at ways we can greatly reduce the number of recursive function calls we need to make!

Recursion with Memoization

One of the big reasons our current recursive approach is expensive is that it does a lot of duplicate work. In many of the paths our recursive call takes, we are recalculating the result for an operation even though we may have already calculated it earlier. The visual of the function call tree for fib(5) in Figure 15-8 calls out the number of duplicate calculations we perform.

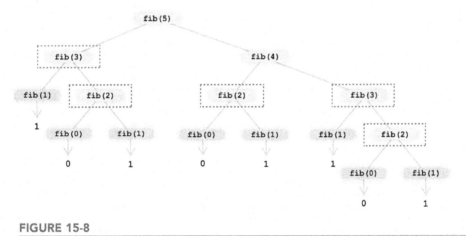

FIGURE 15-8

There are some duplicate calculations

Ignoring the numerous fib(1) and fib(0) calls, if we had a way of remembering the result of fib(3) or fib(2) from earlier calculations, we could eliminate entire branches of duplicated work.

The technique we can use here is known as **memoization**. Boring definition time: memoization is a programming technique that involves storing the results of expensive function calls so that they can be reused later. To put it differently, it's a way of optimizing a function by reducing the number of times it needs to be called.

If we apply memoization to our Fibonacci sequence problem, our code can be modified as follows:

```
function fibonacci(index, cache = []) {
  if (cache[index]) {
    return cache[index];
  }
  else {
    if (index <= 2) {
      return 1;
    } else {
      cache[index] = fibonacci(index - 1, cache) +
                     fibonacci(index - 2, cache);
    }
  }
  return cache[index];
}


console.log('Result is', fibonacci(10));
```

Notice that we have an array called cache that stores the result of each calculation we make. Each time we are about to make a recursive call, we check to see if we already have a result stored in our cache array:

```
function fibonacci(index, cache = []) {
  if (cache[index]) {
    return cache[index];
  }
  else {
    if (index <= 2) {
      return 1;
    } else {
      cache[index] = fibonacci(index - 1, cache) +
                     fibonacci(index - 2, cache);
    }
  }
}
```

```
      return cache[index];
}


console.log('Result is', fibonacci(10));
```

If we don't have the result stored, we do the full recursive call but store the result for future use:

```
function fibonacci(index, cache = []) {
  if (cache[index]) {
    return cache[index];
  }
  else {
    if (index <= 2) {
      return 1;
    } else {
      cache[index] = fibonacci(index - 1, cache) +
                       fibonacci(index - 2, cache);
    }
  }
  return cache[index];
}


console.log('Result is', fibonacci(10));
```

By relying on memoization, where we store the result of calculations we have already made, we greatly reduce the number of unnecessary work our code does. We saw earlier that calculating the 20th Fibonacci sequence resulted in 21,891 calls in the purely recursive approach. By combining the recursive approach with memoization, we made a total of just 37 calls. **That's a whopping 99.8% reduction in the amount of work we are doing.**

Taking an Iteration-Based Approach

The final (and fastest!) approach we look at is one where we wave goodbye to recursion completely and take an iteration-based approach. In an iteration-based approach, we typically use a loop, such as a for loop or a while loop. Applying it to our Fibonacci sequence problem, there are a few reasons why we might choose to use an iterative approach:

- **Fast:** Iterative approaches are generally faster than recursive approaches with a running time of O(n), especially for large values of *n*, because an iterative approach doesn't have to build up a stack of function calls, which can consume a lot of memory and slow down the program.

- **Simple:** Iterative approaches are often simpler to understand and implement than recursive approaches, especially for beginners.

- **Clear:** Iterative approaches can be easier to read and understand than recursive approaches, especially for complex problems.

Following is an example of how we could write an iterative version of the Fibonacci function we have been seeing so far:

```
function fibonacci(n) {
  if (n == 0) {
    return 0;
  } else if (n == 1) {
    return 1;
  } else {
    let a = 0;
    let b = 1;
    for (let i = 2; i <= n; i++) {
      let c = a + b;
      a = b;
      b = c;
    }
    return b;
  }
}

console.log('Result is', fibonacci(10));
```

As we can see, this version of the function uses a loop to iterate through the numbers in the sequence and compute the next number in the series using the previous two. It doesn't use recursion at all, and the `fibonacci` function is called just once.

Going Deeper on the Speed

From what we have seen so far, the fastest approach for calculating the Fibonacci sequences is the iterative approach. The second-fastest is recursion with memoization. The slowest approach is the recursive-only one that we started this discussion with. Let's get more precise. How fast is each of the approaches? Take a look at the graph in Figure 15-9 that plots the time (in milliseconds) it takes to calculate the Fibonacci sequence from 0 to 30.

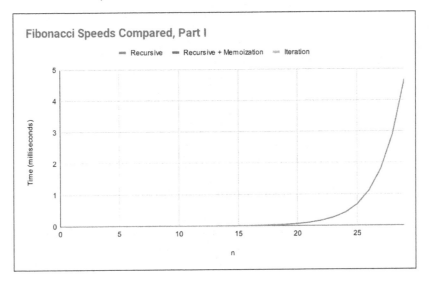

FIGURE 15-9

There (really!) are three different lines shown in this graph. We only "see" two, for the iteration and recursive + memorization values are nearly identical and overlapping.

What you are seeing here isn't a glitch. The time for calculating the Fibonacci sequence for the first 30 numbers is almost 0 in the recursive + memoization and iteration-based approaches. The purely recursive approach starts to take increasing amounts of time at around the 17th Fibonacci number, and it grows exponentially from there on out. There is a reason why the chart includes only the first 30 numbers of the Fibonacci sequence. **The recursive-only approach couldn't handle larger numbers without massive delays and, ultimately, a stack overflow error.**

If we ignore the recursive-only approach and focus our attention on the memoization and iteration approaches, Figure 15-10 shows the time for calculating the Fibonacci sequence for the first 300 (!!!) numbers.

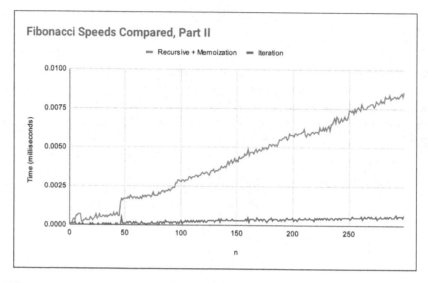

FIGURE 15-10

Iteration is much more efficient!

Here, we can see our iteration-based approach being a much faster solution when we compare it to the recursive approach with memoization. The reason is that, no matter how effective our memoization strategy is, recursive function calls are expensive operations. If we can avoid them entirely, as we do in the iteration-based approach, we will get the best results.

Conclusion

We covered a huge boatload of ground here. The Fibonacci sequence is an important concept in computer science (and family dinner conversations involving algorithms!) because it illustrates the basic idea of recursion, which is a technique where a function calls itself to solve a problem. The problem with recursion is that it can be slow. This is especially true when we are dealing with large inputs or complex calculations that result in many recursive function calls. To address this shortcoming, we looked at two additional approaches that greatly sped up our Fibonacci calculations:

- **Recursive with memoization:** This involves storing the results of expensive function calls so that they can be reused later.

- **Iterative:** This involves using a loop to iterate through the numbers in the sequence and compute the next number in the series using the previous two.

While we looked at all of this in the context of calculating a number in the Fibonacci sequence, the concepts we saw in this chapter will continue to carry over into other problems we'll see in later chapters. It's going to be a fun ride!

SOME ADDITIONAL RESOURCES

? Ask a question: **https://forum.kirupa.com**

Errors/Known issues: **https://bit.ly/algorithms_errata**

Source repository: **https://bit.ly/algorithms_source**

16

TOWERS OF HANOI

As puzzles go, nobody really did it better than the monks who came up with the one we are going to learn about, the **Towers of Hanoi**. Besides being a really cool puzzle, it has a lot of practical (and historical!) significance as we learn about recursion.

Onward!

How Towers of Hanoi Is Played

Before we get to the programming side of things, let's first get a good idea of what the monks were trying to do. The objective of this puzzle is pretty simple. You have a series of disks and three pillars (Figure 16-1).

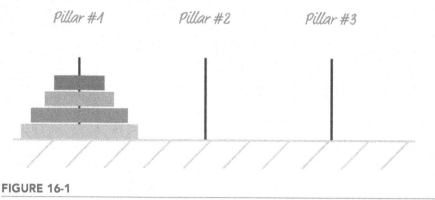

FIGURE 16-1

The start of our puzzle

At the beginning, all of the disks are stacked on top of each other and start off in the first pillar. At the end, the stack of disks is shifted over to the last pillar (Figure 16-2).

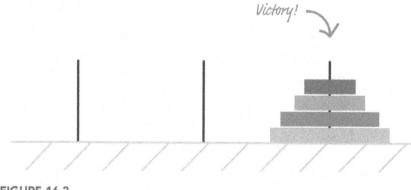

FIGURE 16-2

How the puzzle will end

This seems pretty straightforward, but there are a few conditions that make things frustratingly complex:

- You can move only one disk at a time.
- At each move, you take the disk from the top of any of the stacks and place it on another tower.

- You can place only a smaller disk on top of a larger disk.

- Victory is achieved when all of the starting disks are arranged in their same starting order on a destination tower. You can use any tower other than the one you started from as your destination. We'll use tower 3.

These conditions probably don't make a whole lot of sense. To fix that, let's walk through a handful of examples and see how a typical game with these conditions is played.

The Single Disk Case

The easiest way to play the game is to use a single disk (Figure 16-3).

FIGURE 16-3

Starting with a single disk

We have one disk at the beginning. Because there are no other disks to worry about, we can win in just one single move (Figure 16-4).

FIGURE 16-4

We can win in a single move

We can move our single disk directly to the destination without doing anything extra. With just a single disk, the puzzle isn't challenging at all. To see what is really going on, we need more disks.

It's Two Disk Time

This time, let's start with two disks (Figure 16-5).

FIGURE 16-5

We now start with two disks

Our goal is still the same. We want to shift these disks to our destination, the third tower, while maintaining the same stacking order *and* ensuring that a smaller disk is always placed on top of a larger disk at every move along the way.

The first thing we need to do is clear a path for our larger disk to reach its destination. We do that by first shifting our topmost disk to our temporary second tower (Figure 16-6).

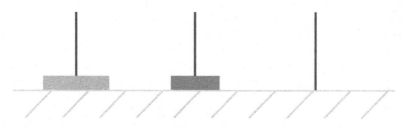

FIGURE 16-6

Going through our puzzle

Once we've made this move, our larger disk has a direct path to the destination. Our next move is to shift that disk to tower 3 (Figure 16-7).

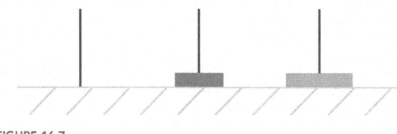

FIGURE 16-7

Our larger disk reaches its destination

The final step is to move our smaller disk from the temporary tower to the destination as well (Figure 16-8).

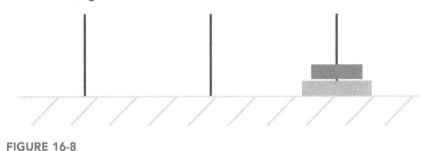

FIGURE 16-8

Game is over

At this point, we've successfully shifted all of the disks from our starting point to the destination while respecting the various conditions. Now, with two disks we can see a little bit more about what makes this puzzle challenging. To see how challenging the Towers of Hanoi can be, we look at one more example in great detail. We are going to throw another disk into the mix!

Three Disks

All right. With three disks, the training wheels come off and we really see what the monks who inspired this puzzle were up against. We start off with all of our disks at the starting point (Figure 16-9).

FIGURE 16-9

Repeating the puzzle with three disks

The first thing we do is move our largest disk to the destination. To do so, we must first move our smallest disk out of the way (Figure 16-10).

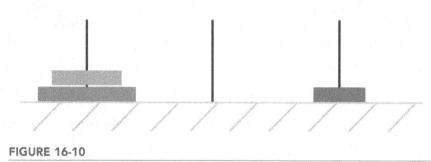

FIGURE 16-10

Moving the topmost item to the end

Wait, why is our smallest disk at our destination as opposed to our temporary tower? There is a technical reason for that. For now, let's just say that if you start with an **even number of disks**, your smallest disk will move to the temporary tower first. If you start with an **odd number of disks**, your smallest disk will move to the destination tower first.

Next, let's move our second disk to the empty spot in our temporary tower (Figure 16-11).

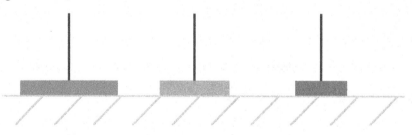

FIGURE 16-11

Our middle disk moves to the middle tower

This leaves our third and largest disk almost ready to be moved to the destination tower. Our smallest disk currently stands in the way, but we can move that to our temporary tower (Figure 16-12).

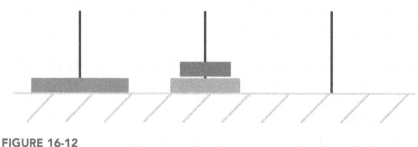

FIGURE 16-12

Clearing a path for our largest disk

With the decks cleared, we move our third disk to the destination (Figure 16-13).

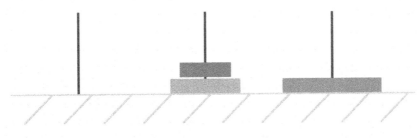

FIGURE 16-13

Our largest disk reaches its destination

At this point, we have only two disks in play. They are both in our temporary tower. What we do now is no different than what we started out doing earlier. We need to move our largest disk to the destination tower. This time around, that disk is our second one because our third disk is already safe at home in the destination tower. You may start to see a pattern emerging.

To make progress, let's move our topmost (and first . . . and smallest!) disk from our temporary tower to our starting tower (Figure 16-14).

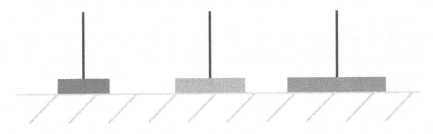

FIGURE 16-14

Each disk is now in its own tower

Next, let's move our second disk to the destination tower (Figure 16-15).

FIGURE 16-15

The end is near for our puzzle

The remaining step is easy. Our first disk is patiently waiting at the starting tower. Let's move it to the destination (Figure 16-16).

FIGURE 16-16

All disks have been moved over!

We are now done moving three disks from our starting tower to the destination tower. We can repeat all of these steps for more disks, but we've seen all the interesting details to note about this puzzle by now. Now let's look more formally at all that this puzzle has going on and figure out how we can get our computers to solve it.

The Algorithm

As humans, talking out loud and visually solving the problem totally works for us. Our computers are far less evolved. For them, we need to simplify our solution in terms that they understand. We can do that by restating what we know about how to solve this problem:

- The goal is to get the largest, bottommost disk to the destination tower.
- We do that by moving all of the disks (except the largest) from the starting tower to our temporary tower.
- Once that has been done, we move our largest disk to the destination tower.
- We then move all of the disks (except the new largest) from our temporary tower to the destination tower.

To state this a bit more formally, it will look like this:

1. Move the top N-1 disks from the starting tower to the temporary tower.

2. Move the bottom most (aka Nth) disk from the starting tower to the destination tower.

3. Move the remaining N-1 disks from the temporary tower to the destination tower.

There is one additional detail that is subtle but important to call out. The role our towers play while solving this puzzle is fluid. While we have given our towers strict names like *starting*, *temporary*, and *destination*, these names are really just helpful for us to understand what is going on. As part of moving the disks around, each tower plays an *interim* role as the temporary location, the destination location, or the starting location. For example, let's say you have a disk moving from the temporary tower to the destination (Figure 16-17).

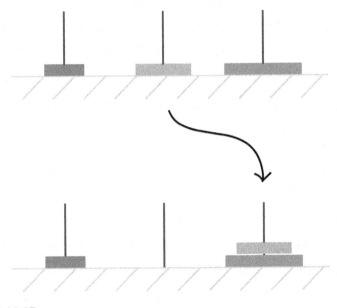

FIGURE 16-17

Algorithm explained

In this case, for just this move, our starting tower is really the temporary tower. The destination tower remains the same, but you can imagine the destination might be our starting tower in some intermediate step. It is this fluidity in our tower roles that makes it difficult for us to mentally make sense of this puzzle! But it is exactly this fluidity that makes solving it using code much easier as well.

The Code Solution

If we had to solve what we outlined in the three formal steps earlier, here is what one solution would look like:

```
var numberOfDisks = 3;

var hanoi = function(n, a, b, c) {
```

```
if (n > 0) {
  hanoi(n - 1, a, c, b);
  console.log("Move disk " + n + " from " + a + " to " + c + "!");
  hanoi(n - 1, b, a, c);
  }
}
hanoi(numberOfDisks,"starting", "temporary", "destination");
```

If you run this code for the three disks, your console will look like Figure 16-18.

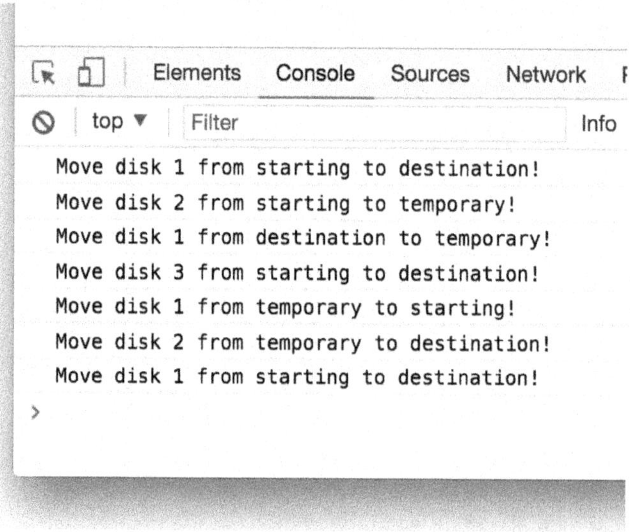

FIGURE 16-18

Example of the output for three disks

If you follow the path the output displays, you'll see what our code does to ultimately solve the puzzle for three disks. If you change the value for numberOfDisks
from 3 to another (larger) number, you'll see a lot more stuff getting printed to your
console. If you plot the path shown in the console, you'll again see what the solution looks like and the path each disk took in getting there. What we've just done
is looked at the full code needed to solve our monks' Towers of Hanoi puzzle.
We aren't done yet, though. Let's look at this solution in greater detail for a few
moments.

Check Out the Recursiveness!

If you take a quick glance at the code, you can tell that our solution is a recursive one:

```
var numberOfDisks = 3;

var hanoi = function(n, a, b, c) {
  if (n > 0) {
    hanoi(n - 1, a, c, b);
    console.log("Move disk " + n + " from " + a + " to " + c + "!");
    hanoi(n - 1, b, a, c);
  }
}
hanoi(numberOfDisks,"starting", "temporary", "destination");
```

Our hanoi function is really solving the sub-problem of moving N-1 disks from one location to another. This function keeps getting called until you are on your last disk (aka n > 0).

If we had to draw out the full recursive call for three disks, it would look as follows:

```
hanoi(3, starting, temporary, destination)
    hanoi(2, starting, destination, temporary)
        hanoi(1, starting, temporary, destination)
            hanoi(0, starting, destination, temporary)
            // Move disk 1 from starting to destination!
            hanoi(0, temporary, starting, destination)

        // Move disk 2 from starting to temporary!

        hanoi(1, destination, starting, temporary)
            hanoi(0, destination, temporary, starting)
            // Move disk 1 from destination to temporary!
            hanoi(0, starting, destination, temporary)

    // Move disk 3 from starting to destination!
```

```
hanoi(2, temporary, starting, destination)
    hanoi(1, temporary, destination, starting)
        hanoi(0, temporary, starting, destination)
        // Move disk 1 from temporary to starting!
        hanoi(0, destination, temporary, starting)

    // Move disk 2 from temporary to destination!

    hanoi(1, starting, temporary, destination)
        hanoi(0, starting, destination, temporary)
        // Move disk 1 from starting to destination!
        hanoi(0, temporary, starting, destination)
```

I get that this doesn't look very nice, but take a moment to follow through with what is going on. Pay special attention to how we swapped the values for where a disk needs to end up by jumping between the starting, temporary, and destination towers. The end result of all of this is still the same: our disks move from their starting point to the destination without breaking those annoying rules.

It's Math Time

According to the legend, the monks were not moving a handful of disks. They were moving 64, and it took them one second to make a single move. I'm guessing those monks were pretty buff. Now, let's figure out how many moves it would take for a team of modern-day (and somewhat geeky) monks to move all 64 disks. To figure that out, we must throw some math into the mix.

For one disk, the number of moves to complete the puzzle was 1. For two disks, the number of moves was 3. For three disks, the number of moves was 7. For zero disks, the answer is of course, 0. If you tested with four disks, the number of moves (if you count the output in your console perhaps) to complete moving all the disks is 15.

You should start to see a pattern for the number of moves needed to complete the puzzle for a given number of disks:

0 disks: 0 moves

1 disk: 1 move

2 disks: 3 moves

3 disks: 7 moves

4 disks: 15 moves

To figure out the number of moves for any arbitrary number of disks, after experimenting with a few guesses, the formula would be 2n − 1. We can go into more detail in our analysis if you don't like coming up with the formula by finding patterns in the output.

From our code (and our rules), we know that there are three distinct steps:

1. Move the top N-1 disks from the starting tower to the temporary tower.

2. Move the bottom most (aka Nth) disk from the starting tower to the destination tower.

3. Move the remaining N-1 disks from the temporary tower to the destination tower.

Steps 1 and 3 take T_{n-1} moves each. Step 2 takes just 1 move. We can state all of this as:

$$T_n = 2T_{n-1} + 1$$

This is the number of total moves involved in solving the puzzle, where *n* stands for the number of disks. For T_0, we know the number of moves is 0. For T_1, we know the number of moves is 1. Extending this to our formula, we can do something like the following:

$$T_0 = 0$$
$$T_1 = 2T_0 + 1 = 2(0) + 1 = 1$$
$$T_2 = 2T_1 + 1 = 2(1) + 1 = 3$$
$$T_3 = 2T_2 + 1 = 2(3) + 1 = 7$$

This seems to check out, so let's prove that this form maps to the $T_n = 2n − 1$ equation figured out earlier. Let's assume that this formula holds for n − 1. This would mean that our equation could be rewritten as $T_{n-1} = 2n − 1 − 1$.

Let's combine this with what we looked at earlier:

$$T_n = 2T_{n-1} + 1$$
$$T_n = 2(2^{n-1} − 1) + 1$$
$$T_n = 2(2^{n-1}) − 2 + 1$$
$$T_n = 2(2^{n-1}) − 2 + 1$$
$$T_n = 2^{n-1+1} − 1$$
$$\mathbf{T_n = 2^n − 1}$$

This proves out that the answer we came up with earlier holds for all ranges *n* where *n* is 1 or greater. This is a less rigorous form of an induction proof that doesn't dot all the i's and cross the t's, so don't use it as the proof if you are asked to formally prove it.

Conclusion

Do you know why the monks were moving 64 disks in the first place? They believed that the world would end once the last disk was placed in its rightful location. If that were true, how long do we all have? Using the formula we have for the number of moves, and knowing from legend that each move takes one second, how long will our monks take to complete the puzzle? Unfortunately for them, using the $2^{64} - 1$ formula, the amount of time it will take them is somewhere around 585 billion years. That's good for us, though! To learn more about the history of this puzzle and the French mathematician Édouard Lucas who actually introduced it to everyone, visit https://en.wikipedia.org/wiki/Towers_of_Hanoi.

17

SEARCH ALGORITHMS AND LINEAR SEARCH

In the real world, when we talk about search or searching, we are trying to find something. We might be looking for a sock in a pile of clothes, a needle in a haystack, a matching fork to go with a knife, Waldo (and possibly his dog companion Woof), car keys, a particular star in our solar system, or a billion other things (Figure 17-1).

FIGURE 17-1

Maybe they are real!

In our algorithmic digital world, when we talk about **search** or **searching**, we are still trying to find something. The key difference is that what we are trying to find will live in a collection of data, such as an array, a list, or a tree. Depending on what we are looking for and what the collection of data looks like, we will employ a variety of approaches to help us find something efficiently. These *varieties of approaches* have a more formal name: **search algorithms**.

Together, we're going to look at some really popular search algorithms, each with its own unique twist that makes it special. In this chapter, we start our journey by looking at one of the most approachable search algorithms, the **linear search** (sometimes called a **sequential search**).

Onward!

Linear Search

As search algorithms go, linear search is easy to explain. It works by iterating through each item in a collection of data and checking whether the item you are on matches the item you are looking for. This search continues until either we find the item or we reach the end of our collection and end up not finding the item. Let's look at an example.

Linear Search at Work

Here is our setup. We have a collection of items stored in an array (Figure 17-2).

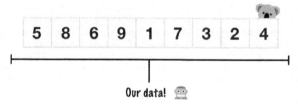

FIGURE 17-2

Our starting data

What we want to do is find the item whose value is 3 (Figure 17-3).

FIGURE 17-3

We are looking for the 3

With linear search, we start at the beginning with the first item (aka array index position 0) and ask ourselves this question: **Is the value at this location the same as what I am looking for?** For our example, we check whether our first item, 5, is the same as 3—which we know isn't the case (Figure 17-4).

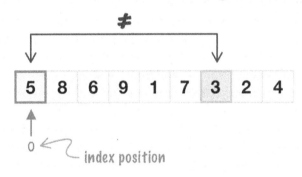

FIGURE 17-4

Let's start our search at the beginning

Because we don't have a match, we move to the next item in our array and repeat the same process. We ask: **Is the value at this location the same as what we are looking for?** We know that our second item's value is 8, and 8 isn't equal to 3 either (Figure 17-5).

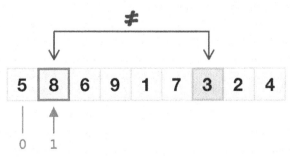

FIGURE 17-5

We continue going down our list

This pattern keeps repeating. We continue going down each item in our array until we eventually get to the item storing our 3 value (Figure 17-6).

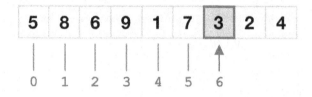

FIGURE 17-6

We found our result

At this point, we have a match. We found what we were looking for, and it was at array index position 6.

If our array never contained the item we were looking for, we would have examined every item in our array and returned the equivalent of a "Not found" result upon reaching our last item.

JavaScript Implementation

If we turn all of our words and diagrams into code, following is what one implementation of our linear search algorithm can look like:

```
function linear_search(collection, item) {
  for (let i = 0; i < collection.length; i++) {
    if (collection[i] === item) {
      // Return index position of found item
      return i;
    }
  }
  // Item not found
  return -1;
}
```

We have a function called `linear_search`, and it takes two arguments. The first argument is our array, and the second argument is for the item we are looking for.

If the item we are looking for is found, our code returns the index position of the found item:

```
let data = [5, 8, 6, 9, 1, 7, 3, 2, 4];

let result = linear_search(data, 3);
console.log(result) // 6
```

If the item we are looking for is not found, our code returns a -1:

```
let data = [5, 8, 6, 9, 1, 7, 3, 2, 4];

let result = linear_search(data, "koala");
console.log(result) // -1
```

The -1 answer is a popular convention in JavaScript and other programming languages for signaling that something we are looking for can't be found. You are certainly welcome to change it to something such as the string "Not found" if that is more to your liking.

 NOTE **Beware of Duplicates**

If we have duplicates of a value, the linear search we implemented will return the very first occurrence.

Runtime Characteristics

Our linear search algorithm runs in O(*n*) linear time. The best-case scenario is when the item we are looking for happens to be the first item in our collection of data. In this case, we can just stop after reaching the first item. The worst-case scenario happens in one of two cases:

- The item we are looking for happens to be in the last spot in our collection of data.

- The item we are looking for doesn't exist in our collection of data at all.

In both of these cases, we had to go and examine every item in our array until we reached the end. The number of operations this takes is directly related to the number of items in our collection. There are no shortcuts here. If we have a bunch of items, our linear search will start at the beginning and go through each item to find what we are looking for.

NOTE   The Global Linear Search

There is a variation of our linear search algorithm that we should be aware of, and that is the **global linear search**. When finding something in a linear search, the moment we find a match we stop everything and return the position of the found item. If another item is also a match elsewhere in our collection, we will never find it, for we stop searching after finding the first match.

What happens in a global linear search is that every matching item in our collection of data is returned. This means what we return is not a single position value. Nope. What we return is an array of position values where the position of every matching item is returned. The code for a global linear search will look as follows:

```
function global_linear_search(collection, item) {
  let foundPositions = [];

  for (let i = 0; i < collection.length; i++) {
    if (collection[i] === item) {
      // Store position of found item
      foundPositions.push(i);
    }
  }

  if (foundPositions.length > 0) {
    return foundPositions;
  } else {
    // No items found
    return -1;
  }
}
```

The way we use our `global_linear_search` function is identical to our `linear_search` function from earlier:

```
let data = [5, 8, 3, 9, 1, 7, 3, 2, 4, 3, 6];

let result = global_linear_search(data, 3);
console.log(result) // [2, 6, 9];
```

The major difference is that our result when items are found is an array of index positions as opposed to a single index position returned as a number.

Conclusion

The linear search algorithm is a simple and straightforward approach for finding an item within a collection of data. Because we iterate through each item in our collection, linear search isn't considered to be a fast algorithm. It is quite inefficient for large collections of data. This doesn't mean that we won't ever have a practical use for it, though. Linear search is useful in situations where our collection of data is small, our data is unsorted, we have to perform a one time search on the collection (ie: not repeatedly have to search inside it), or the item we are looking for is going to be stashed somewhere near the beginning of our collection.

SOME ADDITIONAL RESOURCES

? Ask a question: **https://forum.kirupa.com**

Errors/Known issues: **https://bit.ly/algorithms_errata**

Source repository: **https://bit.ly/algorithms_source**

18

FASTER SEARCHING WITH BINARY SEARCH

In Chapter 17, we looked at linear search, a simple algorithm that works by scanning every item in a collection until it finds what it is looking for. While simple is good, the linear approach is slow. The more items you have, the longer it will take to find something. Its running time is $O(n)$. There is a faster way to search, and that is the star of this chapter: the **binary search**.

In the following sections, we learn all about binary search, how it is implemented, its performance characteristics, and a whole lot more.

Onward!

Binary Search in Action

A binary search starts the same way as many great search algorithms do: with a collection of items (Figure 18-1).

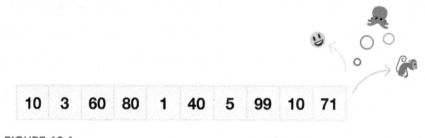

FIGURE 18-1

Our collection of items

In this collection, we want to find the number 60 and return its index position. The rest of our steps walk through how we can use binary search to accomplish this.

Sorted Items Only, Please

Before we take our first step, there is an important prerequisite that we need to meet. Our collection of items must already be sorted, so let's go ahead and do that (Figure 18-2).

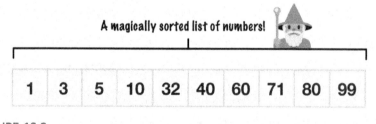

FIGURE 18-2

A sorted list of items

Later, we'll look into the various ways we have to properly take an unsorted collection and sort the items inside it. For now, let's keep it simple and ensure that the items we throw into our binary search algorithm are already sorted.

Dealing with the Middle Element

With the paperwork out of the way, the first real thing we do is find the **middle element** of our entire collection and check whether its value is the target we are looking for. For our collection, the middle element is 32 (Figure 18-3).

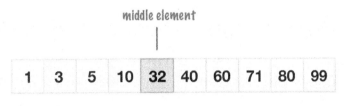

FIGURE 18-3

Finding the middle element

How did we get 32? This is especially confusing when we have an even number of items, as we do in this example. Let's talk about this for a brief moment.

When dealing with a collection of *odd* numbers of elements, we have a clear middle element we can pick (Figure 18-4).

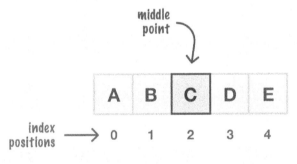

FIGURE 18-4

The middle element is easy to spot when we have an odd number of items

As we see here, we have five elements. The third element would be the middle.

For arrays with *even* numbers of elements, there is a trick we need to use. The middle element will be one that is to the *left* of the ideal midpoint. This can be visualized as in Figure 18-5.

We have to do something like this because when we have six elements, as in this example, there is no clear middle element. Either we will be heavy on the left or we will be heavy on the right. There is no way around that, so the general consensus is that we want to lean left toward the start of our collection when we are in a tie-breaking situation. When we apply this trick to our larger example that has an even number of items, we can see how we chose the number 32 (Figure 18-6).

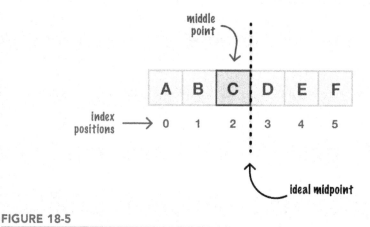

FIGURE 18-5

For an even number of elements, keep left of the ideal midpoint

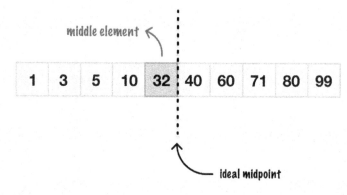

FIGURE 18-6

For even numbers of items, the middle item is left of the midpoint

Later on, we'll look at a more formal way of finding the middle element that takes our hand-wavy explanation into something more concrete. For now, we are good!

OK, where were we? Yes! We need to check whether our middle element contains the target value of 60 that we are looking for. We can tell that 32 is not equal to 60. What we do next is the famed division operation that binary search is known for.

Dividing FTW!

With our middle element not matching our target value, our next step is to figure out where to go and continue our search. We put our finger on the middle element and mentally *divide our list into a left half and a right half* (Figure 18-7).

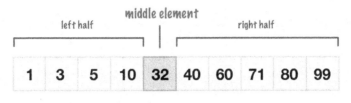

FIGURE 18-7

Setting up for a divide operation

For this next step, we ask ourselves whether the value we are looking for (60) is greater than or less than the value in our current middle element (32):

- If the value we are looking for is greater than our middle element value, the value we are looking for must be in the right half.

- If the value we are looking for is less than our middle element value, the value we are looking for must be in the left half.

In our case, 60 is greater than 32 (and all elements to the left of 32 are lesser than 32 and can never be 60!), so it must mean that we need to continue our search by looking in the right half (Figure 18-8).

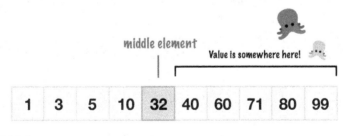

FIGURE 18-8

Looking at the right half

At this moment, we only care about what is contained in the right half of our collection. We can safely ignore all other items. To be specific, this means our earlier midpoint and all items left of it are no longer relevant for our future search activities (Figure 18-9).

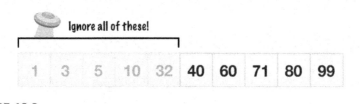

FIGURE 18-9

We ignore the left half

With only the right half of our collection in play, we repeat our earlier steps. We find the middle element, check whether the middle element's value matches the target value we are looking for, and if the value doesn't match, divide and decide whether to go deeper into the remaining left half or right half of our collection.

If we apply these steps to the right half, the first thing we do is find our middle element (Figure 18-10).

FIGURE 18-10

We look for the middle element in the right half of the array

The middle element value is 71, and it isn't the 60 value we are looking for. Next, we check whether 71 is greater than or less than our target 60 value. Because 71 is greater than 60, it means the half of the collection we want to focus on is the left half (Figure 18-11).

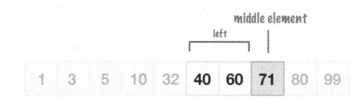

FIGURE 18-11

Let's repeat our steps

When we look at our left half, we have only two items. It doesn't matter how many items we have; we must still follow our binary search algorithm step by step. We must rinse and repeat what we've done a few times already. The value of our middle element will be 40 (Figure 18-12).

middle element

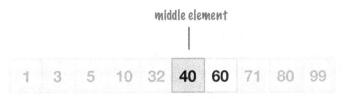

FIGURE 18-12

We continue to work with smaller regions of numbers

Our 40 value is not the same as 60. Because our current middle point value of 40 is less than 60, we focus on the right half (Figure 18-13).

middle element

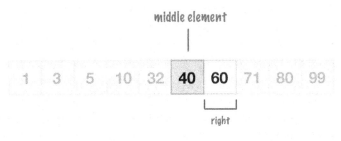

right

FIGURE 18-13

We are almost at the end

We only have one item at this point, and this item will also be our middle element for the next step (Figure 18-14).

middle element

FIGURE 18-14

We found our answer!

The value of our middle element is going to be 60. When we ask ourselves if the middle element value of 60 is what we are looking for, the answer will be a ginormous YES. This is exactly what we have been looking for, and we will return the index position of where our 60 value is located.

The JavaScript Implementation

If we take all of our many words and visuals from the previous section and simplify how binary search works, we can land on these steps:

1. Look at the middle value in a sorted collection.

    a. If our middle value is the target value we are looking for, stop searching and return its index position

    b. If it is greater than the value we are looking for, ignore the right half of the collection and repeat step 1 on the left half

    c. If it is less than the value we are looking for, ignore the left half of the collection and repeat step 1 on the right half

2. Keep repeating steps 1 to 4 until we find the number we are looking for or determine that it is not in the collection.

All that remains is to turn these steps into code.

Iterative Approach

The efficient iterative approach looks as follows:

```
// Iterative Approach
function binarySearch(arr, val) {
  let start = 0;
  let end = arr.length - 1;

  while (start <= end) {
    let middleIndex = Math.floor((start + end) / 2);

    if (arr[middleIndex] === val) {
      return middleIndex;
    } else if (arr[middleIndex] < val) {
      start = middleIndex + 1;
    } else {
```

```
        end = middleIndex - 1;
    }
  }


  return -1;
}
```

For reasons we saw in Chapter 15, this approach doesn't inflate the function call stack. We keep a lot of the heavy lifting localized to the loop itself.

Recursive Approach

For completeness, a less efficient recursive approach is provided as well:

```
// Recursive Approach
function binarySearch(arr, val, start = 0, end = arr.length - 1)
{
  const middleIndex = Math.floor((start + end) / 2);

  if (val === arr[middleIndex]) {
    return middleIndex;
  }

  if (start >= end) {
    return -1;
  }

  if (val < arr[middleIndex]) {
    binarySearch(arr, val, start, middleIndex - 1);
  } else {
    binarySearch(arr, val, middleIndex + 1, end);
  }
}
```

With this approach, when we are about to do a division, we recursively call `binarySearch` again. The number of times we will call `binarySearch` and inflate our call stack is directly related to how deep we will have to search. This is where the efficiency of the iterative approach really shines.

Example of the Code at Work

The way we would use our `binarySearch` function is by calling it with two arguments:

- Our presorted array of items
- The target value we are looking for

Here is an example of how we can call `binarySearch`:

```
let numbers = [1, 3, 5, 10, 32, 40, 60, 71, 80, 99];


let foundIndex = binarySearch(numbers, 60);
console.log(foundIndex) // 6
```

In our example, the `numbers` array is the same collection we spent much of this chapter deconstructing, so it should look welcomingly familiar. The value that gets returned by our `binarySearch` function is the index position of the found item or `-1` if the item isn't found. In our case, 60 exists and is located at index position 6. Also, outside of the runtime behavior we briefly talked about, the values that get returned are the same across both the iterative and recursive binary search implementations.

Finding the Middle Element

Much earlier, we looked at a very hand-wavy approach to finding the middle element. For the full enchilada, the article at www.kirupa.com/javascript/finding_middle_element_array.htm goes into great detail on this topic. We briefly summarize that article and shine some light on how our code works for finding the middle element, especially as part of a subset of our array.

The expression for calculating the index position of our middle element looks as follows:

```
let middleIndex = Math.floor((left + right) / 2);
```

We take the average of the starting and ending index positions, and then round the result down (via `Math.floor`) to ensure we always end on a whole number. If we had to visualize this, Figure 18-15 shows how we would calculate the middle point for the highlighted region taken from an intermediate step from the walkthrough we looked at earlier.

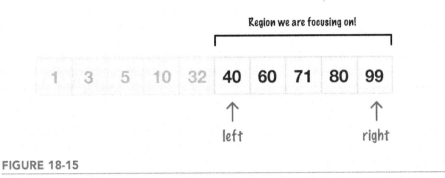

FIGURE 18-15

Focusing on one region

The values for **left** and **right** are the corresponding **5** and **9** index positions of our array, so if we substitute in those values and calculate the middle point, the earlier expression will look like Figure 18-16.

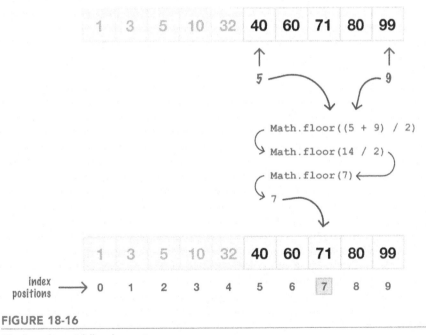

FIGURE 18-16

Finding the middle element

Our middle index position for this region is 7, and the value here is 71. A trippy detail to note is that, even though we are examining only a subset of our collection, our index positions are relative to the entire collection itself.

Runtime Performance

We started off by talking about how fast binary search is, especially when we compare it to the slower linear search. Binary search runs at a scorching $O(\log n)$, and it is able to pull this off because it follows a **divide and discard** approach. As we saw in the walkthrough, at each stage of trying to hone in on our target value, our binary search algorithm ignores half of the remaining items.

If we had to talk about this generally, let's say we start with a sorted collection of n items (Figure 18-17).

n items

FIGURE 18-17

Our array has n items

In the first step, we work with the full n items. At the next step, we work with $n/2$ items (Figure 18-18).

FIGURE 18-18

Working with n/2 items

Assuming we never find the value we are looking for (or the value we are looking for is the very last item), this pattern will keep going where each step discards another half of the items from the previous step (Figure 18-19).

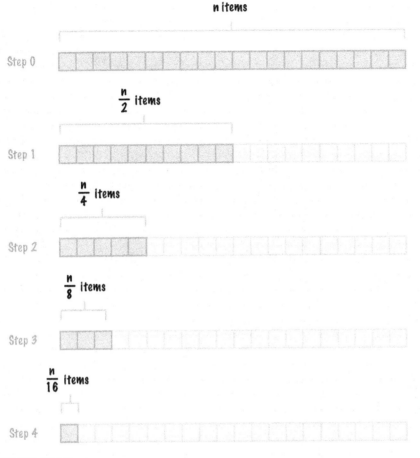

FIGURE 18-19

We keep whittling down our problem space

We keep going until we reach the last step, where all we are left with is a single element. There is a pattern here. We can see this pattern by observing the number of elements in play at each step (Figure 18-20).

If each *divide* step in our binary search is represented by k, the total number of steps we take can be represented by n/2k. How does all of this lead to the statement that binary search runs in log(n) time? After k iterations, when we reach the last item in our collection, the number of elements we have left are . . . well, just 1. This means we can solve for k as shown in Figure 18-21.

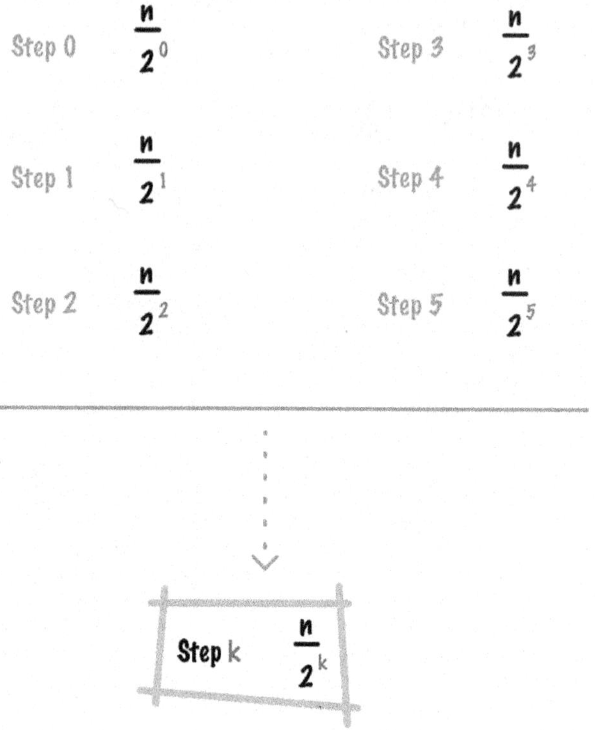

Step 0 $\dfrac{n}{2^0}$ Step 3 $\dfrac{n}{2^3}$

Step 1 $\dfrac{n}{2^1}$ Step 4 $\dfrac{n}{2^4}$

Step 2 $\dfrac{n}{2^2}$ Step 5 $\dfrac{n}{2^5}$

Step k $\dfrac{n}{2^k}$

FIGURE 18-20

Number of elements at each step

$$\dfrac{n}{2^k} = 1 \quad \text{// last item}$$

$$n = 2^k$$

$$\log_2 n = \log_2 2^k$$

$$\log_2(n) = k$$

FIGURE 18-21

How we solve for k and get the running time

The way to read this in the context of binary search is that if we have *n* items, in the worst case, we need to run through the various stages of our algorithm log(*n*) times before we reach the end!

Conclusion

We just covered a lot of ground here. We learned how binary search works, how we can use it in our code, what its runtime behavior looks like, and a whole lot more. What makes binary search interesting is that its core approach of dividing the problem space into something smaller is a common pattern that we'll repeatedly see, especially in algorithms that classify themselves as divide and conquer. We will get to those algorithms shortly, but you should kick back and relax for now. You've earned it!

SOME ADDITIONAL RESOURCES

? Ask a question: **https://forum.kirupa.com**

Errors/Known issues: **https://bit.ly/algorithms_errata**

Source repository: **https://bit.ly/algorithms_source**

19

BINARY TREE TRAVERSAL

With linear data structures like our array or linked list, navigating (aka traversing) through all of the items is fairly straightforward. We start at the beginning and just keep going to the next item until we hit the end, where there are no more items left (Figure 19-1).

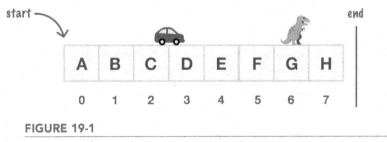

FIGURE 19-1

Working with a linear data structure is pleasant

This nice and easy approach doesn't work with trees (Figure 19-2).

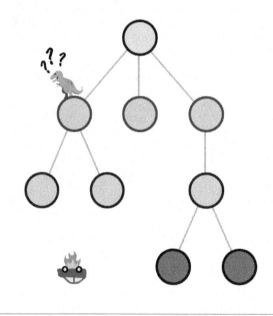

FIGURE 19-2

Working with a nonlinear data structure like a tree can be stressful

Trees are hierarchical data structures, so the way we traverse through them must be different. There are two types of traversal approaches we can use. One approach is **breadth-first**, and another approach is **depth-first**. In the following sections, we go both broader and deeper (ha!) into what all of this means.

Onward!

Breadth-First Traversal

Echoing a detail from when we first looked at trees, our trees have a **depth** or a **level** to them that indicates how far away they are from the root (Figure 19-3).

Level 0 (or Depth 0) is always going to be the root. All of the children nodes from there will find themselves on their own level depending on how far from the root they are.

In a breadth-first approach, these levels play an important role in how we traverse our tree. We traverse the tree *level by level*, starting from the root node and visiting all the nodes at each level before moving on to the next level.

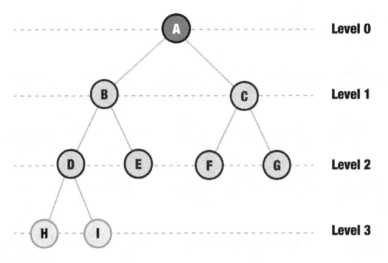

FIGURE 19-3

Tree levels

This process will be clearer with an example. So, we start with our root node, A (Figure 19-4).

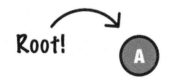

FIGURE 19-4

Our root node

At this point, we don't know much about our tree or what it looks like. The only thing we know is that we have a root node, so we explore it. We discover that our root node has two children, B and C (Figure 19-5).

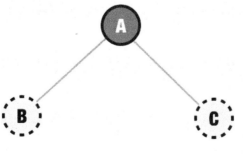

FIGURE 19-5

Exploring our root node

Here lies a subtle but important detail: **Discovering is not the same thing as exploring.** When we discover nodes, we are aware that they exist. When we explore them, we actively inspect them and see if they have any children. In the figures that follow, when a node has simply been discovered, it's displayed in a dotted outline. Once a node has been explored, it's displayed in a solid outline.

From our discovered nodes B and C, we explore B first. It has two children (Figure 19-6).

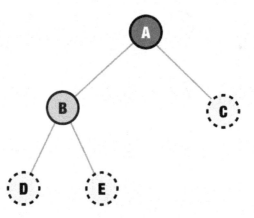

FIGURE 19-6

We continue exploring

We ignore these newly discovered children for now. Instead, we continue on to explore C and find out that it has two children as well (Figure 19-7).

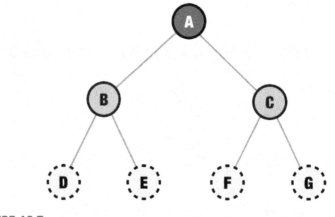

FIGURE 19-7

We explore C next

We are done with the current row made up of our B and C nodes, and we now repeat the process for the next row of nodes. We start on the left with the D node and explore it to see if it has any children. The D node does have two children (Figure 19-8).

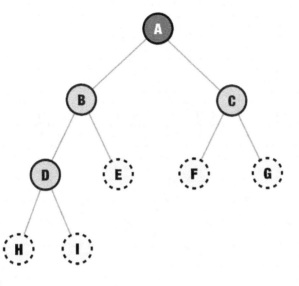

FIGURE 19-8

We are exploring by going row by row first

We then move to the E node, the F node, and the G node and explore them to see if they have any children. They don't have any children (Figure 19-9).

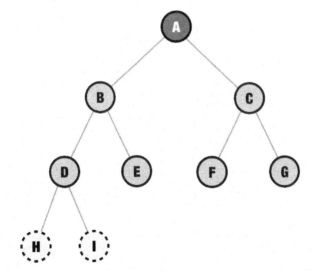

FIGURE 19-9

Nodes E, F, and G have no children

At this point, we are done exploring one more row. Now, it's time to go into the next row and see what is going on with the H and I nodes. We find that neither H nor I contains children. There are no more nodes to discover and explore, so we have reached the end of the line and have fully explored (aka traversed) our tree (Figure 19-10).

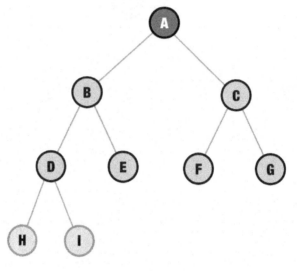

FIGURE 19-10

Our tree is now fully explored

The order in which we explored our nodes is highlighted by the numbers in the visualization in Figure 19-11.

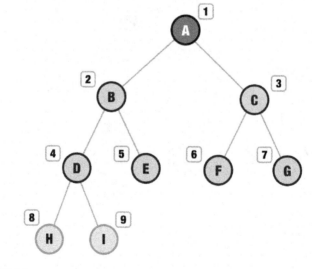

FIGURE 19-11

The order we explored our tree in

The order our nodes have been explored in is A-B-C-D-E-F-G-H-I. The breadth-first traversal approach is a bit like exploring a tree in a very organized and methodical way. This is quite a bit different than our next traversal approach.

Depth-First Traversal

The other popular way to traverse through our tree is the depth-first approach. Instead of exploring the tree level by level as we did with our breadth-first approach, in this depth-first world, **we follow the leftmost path as deeply as possible** before backtracking and exploring another path.

Let's walk through what this looks like. At the top, we have our root node (Figure 19-12).

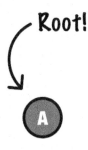

FIGURE 19-12

Starting with our root again

We explore it to see how many children it has, and we find that it has two children, B and C (Figure 19-13).

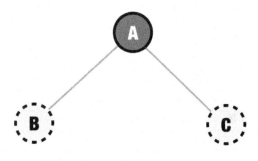

FIGURE 19-13

We discover two children

Next, we explore the B node and see if it has any children. As it turns out, we discover that it has two children (Figure 19-14).

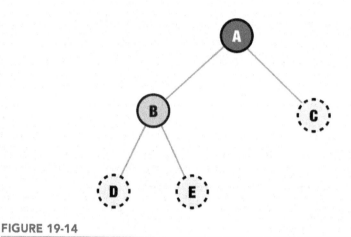

FIGURE 19-14

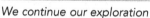

We continue our exploration

Up until this point, what we have seen is consistent with the first few steps we took in our breadth-first approach earlier. Now, here is where things get different. Instead of exploring the C node next, we go deeper into exploring B's children, starting with the first leftmost node. That would be the D node, so we explore it next (Figure 19-15).

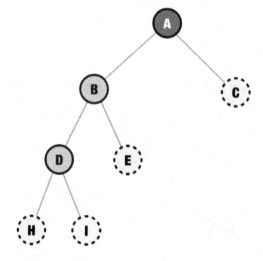

FIGURE 19-15

We explore deep first

D's children are H and I, but (under depth-first rules) we explore H next because it is the leftmost first child node (Figure 19-16).

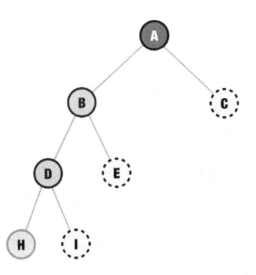

FIGURE 19-16

We explored the left branch fully

H does not have any children, so we then **backtrack to the nearest unexplored node**. As Figure 19-17 shows, that would be our I node.

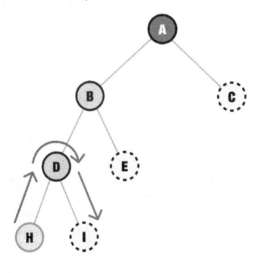

FIGURE 19-17

Backtracking

Our I node has no children either, so we backtrack even further to the next spot that has any unexplored children: the E node (Figure 19-18).

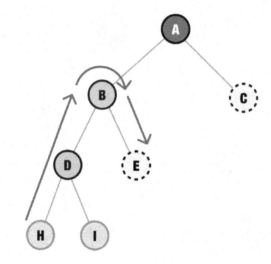

FIGURE 19-18

Continue backtracking to the next node with unexplored children

As it turns out, E has no child nodes, so we continue on to our next nearest destination where we have unexplored children. That would be the C node near the top. When we explore the C node, we find it has two children: F and G (Figure 19-19).

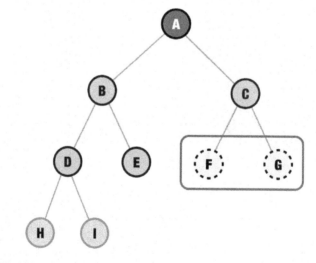

FIGURE 19-19

We have almost fully explored this tree

In classic depth-first fashion, we explore the F child node first. It has no children. We then backtrack to the next nearest unexplored node, which happens to be G. It has no children either, so we are now done exploring our tree (Figure 19-20).

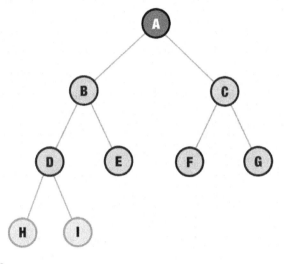

FIGURE 19-20

Our tree is fully explored

If we trace our steps, we did a lot of jumping around here. The order in which we explored our nodes is A-B-D-H-I-E-C-F-G. We can visualize the order as shown in Figure 19-21.

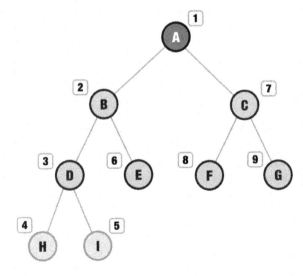

FIGURE 19-21

The order in which we explored our tree using DFS

To summarize the behavior we walked through in our depth-first approach, we explored:

1. Our root node first

2. The left subtree fully

3. The right subtree fully

There are several depth-first variations, and the three steps we saw here are referred to, collectively, as a **preorder traversal**. This is a popular variation we'll be using for searching our tree later on, but other variations include **postorder traversal** and **inorder traversal**. We will talk about those much later.

Implementing Our Traversal Approaches

In the past few sections, we learned how both breadth-first and depth-first traversals work. It is now time for us to turn all of our knowledge into working code. As we will see in a few moments, the code for both breadth-first and depth-first traversals looks very similar. There is a very good reason for this!

Backing up a bit, there are two steps to how a node gets explored:

1. **Node is discovered.** This is where we simply recognize that a node exists.

2. **Node is explored.** This is where we examine the node and discover any children that we need to . . . um . . . discover.

Where both our traversal approaches vary is in how exactly our nodes get discovered, explored, and inserted. This is worth diving into, and we do that next.

Node Exploration in the Breadth-First Approach

Let's say that we have a partially explored tree that looks as shown in Figure 19-22.

If we explicitly call out what we have explored and discovered, we'll see that our explored nodes are A and B. Our discovered nodes are C, D, and E. It's time to go exploring! In a breadth-first approach, the next node we explore is going to be the *first* item in our discovered collection of nodes. That would be node C, so let's explore it next (Figure 19-23).

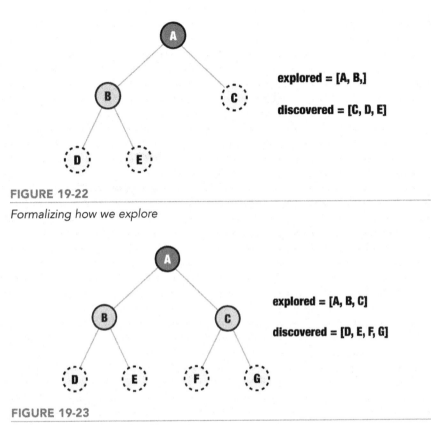

FIGURE 19-22

Formalizing how we explore

FIGURE 19-23

Exploring by rows, BFS style!

Notice what happened when we decided to explore node C. We removed C from our *discovered* collection and added it to the end of our *explored* collection. Node C has two children, F and G, so we added those to the *end* of our discovered collection for processing eventually. The rest of what happens follows this pattern. For our next step, we take the D node from the beginning of our *discovered* collection and add it to the end of our *explored* collection. If D happens to have any children that we discover, we add those to the end of our *discovered* collection. And so on and so on.

If we had to describe everything that we've done in a bite-sized nugget, in a breadth-first traversal approach, we would add newly discovered nodes to the end of a discovered collection. The nodes we explore next are taken from the beginning of our discovered nodes collection. **The behavior we just described is essentially a queue.** Items are removed from the front. Items are added at the back.

Node Exploration in the Depth-First Approach

To see what happens in a depth-first traversal approach, let's look at another example of a partially explored tree (Figure 19-24).

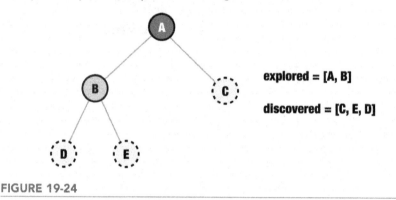

explored = [A, B]

discovered = [C, E, D]

FIGURE 19-24

Partially explored tree

Notice the order of our discovered nodes in the collection. They are not left to right, as the nodes appear visually in the tree. They are the opposite. They go from right to left. There is a reason for this. The next node we explore is taken from the **end of our discovered nodes**. This would be node D (Figure 19-25).

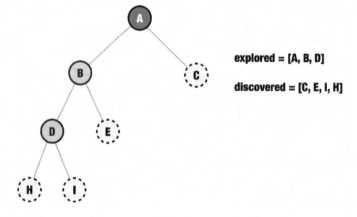

explored = [A, B, D]

discovered = [C, E, I, H]

FIGURE 19-25

With DFS, the order in which we explore is different and is reflected in our general approach

Our D node goes into the explored collection at the end, and we discover it has two child nodes: H and I. Because we add the children from right to left, we add our I node to the end of our discovered collection first. We next add the H node to the end of our discovered collection, which ends this step of our traversal. Our next step is to continue exploring, and (you guessed it) we pick the last item in our discovered collection. This process keeps repeating until we have no more nodes to discover.

If we had to summarize the behavior for our depth-first approach, we would add newly discovered nodes *to the end* of our discovered collection. The next node we explore will also come *from the end* of our discovered collection. **This is the behavior of a stack.** Items are removed from the back. Items are added to the back as well.

Looking at the Code

Now that we have taken a deeper look at how our breadth-first and depth-first approaches differ, we can start looking at the code.

Building Our Tree

The first thing we do is build an example tree whose nodes are arranged identically to the example we have been seeing throughout this chapter:

```
class Node {
  constructor(data) {
    this.data = data;
    this.left = null;
    this.right = null;
  }
}

const rootNodeA = new Node("A");
const nodeB = new Node("B");
const nodeC = new Node("C");
const nodeD = new Node("D");
const nodeE = new Node("E");
const nodeF = new Node("F");
const nodeG = new Node("G");
const nodeH = new Node("H");
const nodeI = new Node("I");
```

```
rootNodeA.left = nodeB;
rootNodeA.right = nodeC;

nodeB.left = nodeD;
nodeB.right = nodeE;

nodeC.left = nodeF;
nodeC.right = nodeG;

nodeD.left = nodeH;
nodeD.right = nodeI;
```

We use this tree for both our examples when testing our breadth-first and depth-first traversal implementations. The most important thing to note is that the root node for our tree is referenced by the `rootNodeA` variable. All of the child nodes will follow from there.

Breadth-First Traversal Implementation

The code for our breadth-first implementation looks as follows:

```
function breadthFirstTraversal(root) {
  if (!root) {
    return;
  }

  let explored = [];

  // Create a queue and add the root to it
  const discovered = new Queue();
  observed.enqueue(root);

  while (discovered.length > 0) {
    // Remove (dequeue) the first item from our
    // queue of observed nodes
    const current = discovered.dequeue();
```

```
  // Process the current node
  explored.push(current);

  // Store all unvisited children of the current node
  if (current.left) {
    discovered.enqueue(current.left);
  }

  if (current.right) {
    discovered.enqueue(current.right);
  }
}

return explored;
}
```

This code uses an implementation of a queue from Chapter 6. You can either copy/paste the implementation from that chapter or reference it directly via the following `script` tag:

```
<script src="https://www.kirupa.com/js/queue_v1.js"></script>
```

We can see our `breadthFirstTraversal` function in action by having it run against the tree we created a few moments ago:

```
let fullTree = breadthFirstTraversal(rootNodeA);
console.log(fullTree);
```

Can you guess what we'll see when we examine the output of this code? It will be all of our tree's nodes listed in the order it was explored when using our breadth-first traversal (Figure 19-26).

The output will be the nodes A, B, C, D, E, F, G, H, and I. This matches what we saw when we walked through this example visually and with words a few sections earlier.

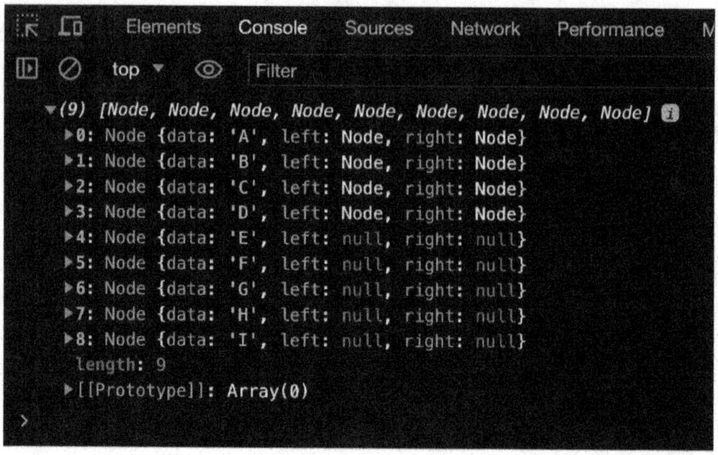

FIGURE 19-26

Our code output

Now, you may be wondering why we are using a queue for dealing with our observed nodes. The reason has to do with performance. To repeat what we looked at earlier about how a breadth-first traversal works, at each stage, we **explore and remove the very first item** in our collection of discovered nodes. Removing the first item is an expensive operation for arrays, but it is a fast operation for our queue, which is internally built on a linked list.

Depth-First Traversal Implementation

The code for our depth-first implementation looks as follows:

```
function depthFirstTraversal(root) {
  if (!root) {
    return;
  }

  let explored = [];

  // Create a stack and add the root to it
  const discovered = new Stack();
  discovered.push(root);

  while (discovered.length > 0) {
```

```
  // Remove the last item from our list of observed nodes
  const current = discovered.pop();

  // Process the current node
  explored.push(current);

  // Store all unvisited children of the current
  // node in reverse order
  if (current.right) {
    discovered.push(current.right);
  }

  if (current.left) {
    discovered.push(current.left);
  }
}


  return explored;
}
```

Our depth-first traversal uses an implementation of a stack from Chapter 5. You can either copy/paste the implementation from that chapter or reference it directly via the following `script` tag:

```
<script src="https://www.kirupa.com/js/stack_v1.js"></script>
```

To see our `depthFirstTraversal` function in action, let's pass in the same tree we created—represented by `rootNodeA`:

```
let fullTreeTwo = depthFirstTraversal(rootNodeA);
console.log(fullTreeTwo);
```

The output we see in our console when running this example is shown in Figure 19-27.

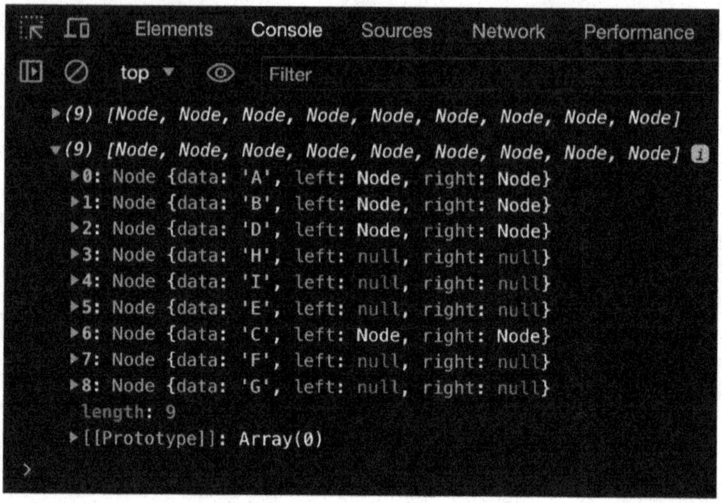

FIGURE 19-27

Our DFS output

This, as totally expected, matches the output we saw earlier when we walked through a visual representation of our tree.

The implementation of our depth-first traversal uses a stack for dealing with our discovered nodes. The reason is that, as we saw earlier, for depth-first traversals, **we examine and remove the last node** in our collection of discovered nodes. Removing the last item from a stack is a fast operation, so that is why we use them. Now, you can also use an array instead of a stack if you want, but our stack implementation uses arrays under the covers anyway.

Performance of Our Traversal Approaches

As we get closer to wrapping up our look at the breadth-first and depth-first traversals, let's talk about runtime and memory consumption. The goal of our traversal approaches is to provide a representation of every node that exists in our tree. The runtime performance is $O(n)$ where n is the total number of nodes in our tree. The memory/space consumption is also going to be $O(n)$. There isn't much we can differentiate between by looking at the best-case, average-case, and worst-case scenarios. The result is the same. It's $O(n)$ all around.

Conclusion

Okay, that's it. We've covered a lot of ground in our look at traversing a tree using both breadth-first and depth-first approaches. There is a lot more we need to cover here, but we'll get to those points later as we look into searching. For now, here are the main things to keep in mind:

1. With breadth-first traversal, we visit all nodes at each level of the tree before moving on to the next level.

2. With depth-first traversal, we visit nodes along a branch until we reach a leaf node, then backtrack to visit other branches.

SOME ADDITIONAL RESOURCES

? Ask a question: **https://forum.kirupa.com**

Errors/Known issues: **https://bit.ly/algorithms_errata**

Source repository: **https://bit.ly/algorithms_source**

20

DEPTH-FIRST SEARCH (DFS) AND BREADTH-FIRST SEARCH (BFS)

When we look at graphs (or trees), we often see this nice collection of nodes with the entire structure fully mapped out (Figure 20-1).

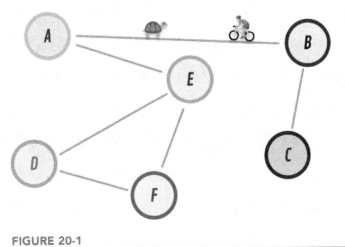

FIGURE 20-1

Our example graph

In real-world scenarios, this fully mapped-out view is the final result of our code having fully explored the graph. When we encounter a graph for the first time, Figure 20-2 is what our computers see.

FIGURE 20-2

Exploring a graph at the beginning

It is an unknown, blank slate. We have to actively explore our graph node by node to create the final picture of what all the nodes and edges look like. There is an art and a science to how we perform this exploration. That's where the stars of this chapter, depth-first search (DFS) and breadth-first search (BFS), come in. In the following sections, we'll learn how they work to help us fully explore a graph.

Onward!

A Tale of Two Exploration Approaches

DFS and BFS are two approaches used to explore a graph. We get into the nitty-gritty details of how they work, but let's keep it high-level right now. Imagine we have a map with different locations, as shown in Figure 20-3.

Start here!

FIGURE 20-3

Our map

Our goal is to start from our starting point and explore all of the places in the graph. At first, this will look a bit like the traversal examples we saw earlier. We'll start here and shift to how it applies to search as the chapter goes on. We'll use both a DFS approach and a BFS approach for our exploration. By the time we're done, we'll be able to clearly see how these two approaches differ!

Depth-First Search Overview

DFS is like exploring the map by picking one location and going as far as possible along a single path before backtracking and trying another path (Figure 20-4).

It's like taking one road and following it until we can't go any further, then going back and trying a different road. We keep doing this until we have explored all possible paths.

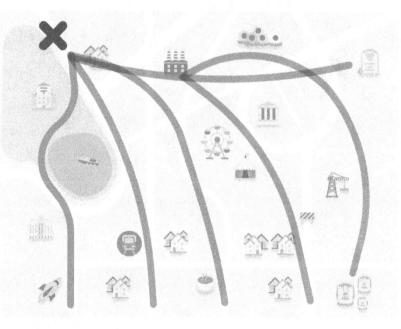

FIGURE 20-4

How DFS explores a map

Breadth-First Search Overview

In contrast, BFS is like exploring the map by starting at one location and gradually moving outward (Figure 20-5).

It's similar to how we might search for something by checking all the places in our immediate neighborhood first before expanding our search to other places.

Yes, They Are Different!

As you can see, the end result of using either DFS or BFS is that we explore all the interesting landmarks. The gigantic detail lies in how we do this exploration. Both DFS and BFS are quite different here, and we go beyond the generalities and get more specific about how they work in the next section.

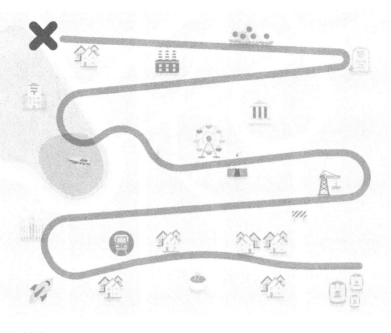

FIGURE 20-5

How BFS explores a map

It's Example Time

To more deeply understand how DFS and BFS work, let's work with a more realistic graph example. Our example graph looks like Figure 20-6.

This graph is fairly plain. It is undirected, cyclic, and contains a bunch of nodes. In the following sections, we walk through how we're going to explore all of the nodes contained here.

Exploring with DFS

DFS works by starting at a chosen node and then exploring as far as possible along each branch before hitting a dead end, backing up (aka *backtracking*), and trying again with the next unexplored node. It's example time.

With graphs, we can start exploring from any arbitrary node. To keep things simple, we start with node A (Figure 20-7).

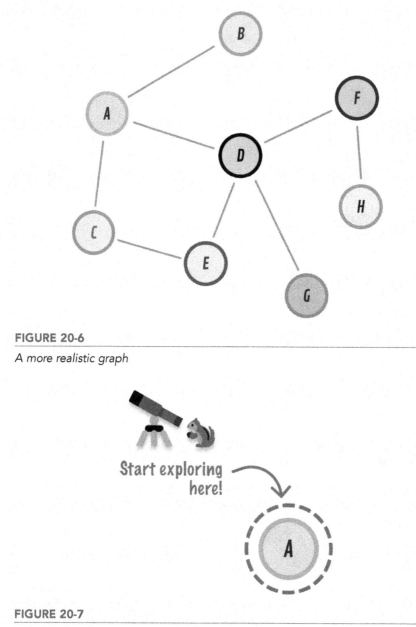

FIGURE 20-6

A more realistic graph

Start exploring here!

FIGURE 20-7

Starting with node A

Let's take a quick timeout and call out two things here:

- What exactly does *exploring* mean? It is a fancy way of saying that we are discovering any immediate neighbor nodes that can be reached from the node we are at.

- When we start our exploration, our code has no prior knowledge of what the rest of the graph looks like. We use DFS and BFS to help us paint the full landscape. This is why, as highlighted in Figure 20-7, we see only node A with all other nodes hidden.

Getting back to it, we are at node A, and we are going to explore it. This exploration leads us to discover nodes B, C, and D (Figure 20-8).

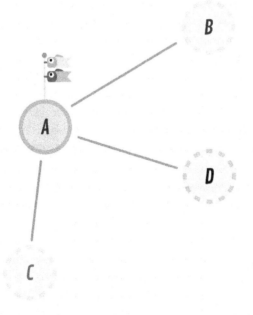

FIGURE 20-8

We discover unexplored children

We can keep track of our findings by using the same *explored* and *discovered* terminology we used earlier when looking at how to traverse binary trees (Figure 20-9).

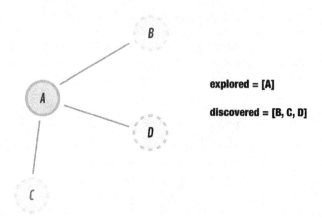

explored = [A]

discovered = [B, C, D]

FIGURE 20-9

Keeping track of what we explored

As of right now, our explored list contains only node A. The discovered list contains nodes B, C, and D.

Next, we explore the first item in our discovered list, node B. When we explore node B, we find that it has node A as a neighbor. Because we have already explored node A, **we don't consider it to be a new node that we have discovered**.

Node B, then, has no new neighbors. We remove node B from our discovered list and move it over to our explored list (Figure 20-10).

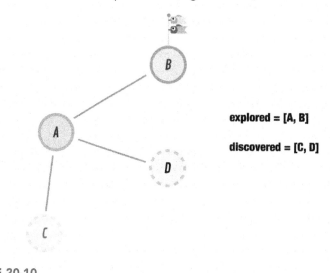

explored = [A, B]

discovered = [C, D]

FIGURE 20-10

Continuing our exploration

Because we reached a dead end with B, we *backtrack* by retracing our steps and exploring the next nearest unexplored node, which is represented in our discovered list as node C. When we explore node C, we find that it has nodes A and E as its neighbors. Because node A has already been explored, the only new addition to our discovered list is node E. We move node C from our discovered list to our explored list, and we add node E to the *front* of our discovered list (Figure 20-11).

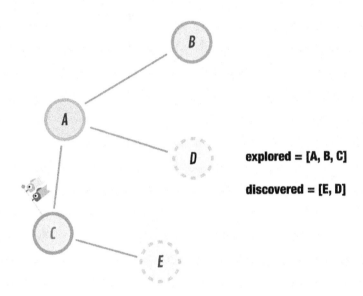

explored = [A, B, C]

discovered = [E, D]

FIGURE 20-11

More nodes to explore!

Note that we didn't add node E to the end of our discovered list. We added it to the front, and this ensures that this is the node we explore next. This is an important implementation detail of the DFS approach that we should keep in mind.

When we explore node E, nodes D and C show up as neighbors. Node C is one we have already explored, and node D is already in our list to be discovered next. This puts us in the state shown in Figure 20-12.

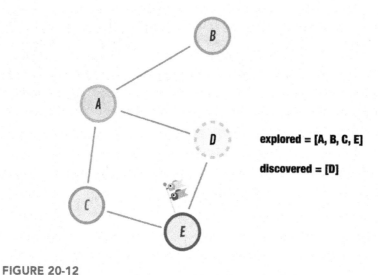

FIGURE 20-12

We finished exploring node E

Because we don't have any new nodes to discover, we go ahead and explore node D next. When we explore node D, we discover nodes F and G as new nodes to explore in the future. Node E, since we already explored it, is happily ignored (Figure 20-13).

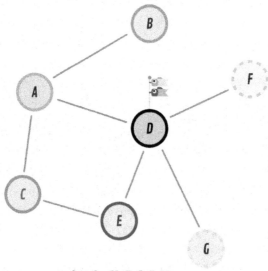

explored = [A, B, C, E, D]

discovered = [F, G]

FIGURE 20-13

Exploring node D and seeing what details it has hiding!

If we speed things up a bit and continue the logic we have employed so far, we explore node F next. Node F has one unexplored node: node H (Figure 20-14).

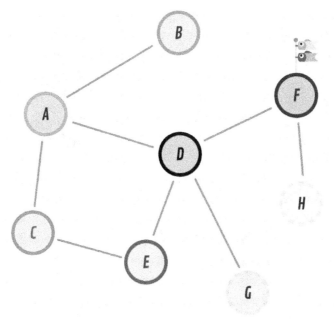

explored = [A, B, C, E, D, F]

discovered = [H, G]

FIGURE 20-14

We continue to have some nodes we haven't explored

After moving node F to our explored list, we add node H to the beginning of our discovered list and go exploring it next (Figure 20-15).

Node H has no neighbors, so we backtrack to the next unexplored node, which is . . . lucky node G (Figure 20-16).

Node G has no neighbors. At this point, we have no more nodes to explore further. Our discovered list is empty. When we run into this situation, we can safely say that we have fully explored the reachable parts of our graph. The path our DFS approach took to discover all of our nodes is captured by our explored list: A-B-C-E-D-F-H-G.

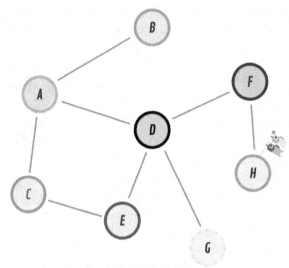

explored = [A, B, C, E, D, F, H]

discovered = [G]

FIGURE 20-15

Only node G remains

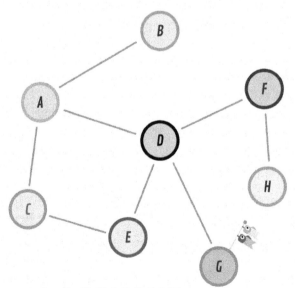

explored = [A, B, C, E, D, F, H, G]

discovered = [ ]

FIGURE 20-16

Fully explored graph!

Exploring with BFS

In a BFS approach, we start at a given node, explore all of this node's neighbors, and then move on to the next level of nodes. It's very different than what we saw with DFS, and these differences will be clear as we walk through our example.

We start our exploration from node A (Figure 20-17).

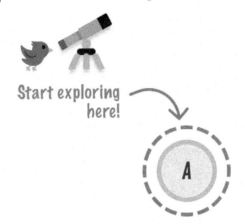

FIGURE 20-17

Starting with node A again

The first thing we do is discover whether node A has any neighbors. As it turns out, it does (Figure 20-18).

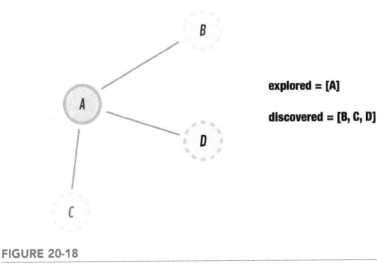

explored = [A]

discovered = [B, C, D]

FIGURE 20-18

Exploring neighbors

Node A has three neighbors, and we catalog them in our discovered list for exploration later. The next node we explore is the first node under our discovered list: node B. Node B has no neighbors, so we move it from our discovered list to our explored list (Figure 20-19).

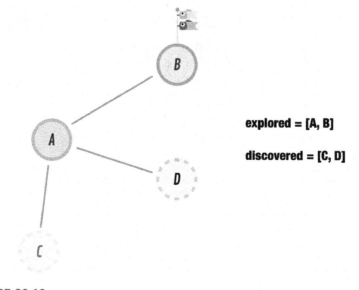

explored = [A, B]

discovered = [C, D]

FIGURE 20-19

Exploring node B

So far, what we've seen that our early exploration closely mimics what we saw with DFS earlier. That all changes momentarily.

The next node we explore is node C. Node C has one neighbor: node E (Figure 20-20).

Because we have explored node C, we move it from the discovered list to the explored list. We then add our newly discovered node E to our discovered list. Notice where we add it. We don't add it to the front of our list as we did with DFS. Nope. **We add it to the end of our discovered list.** Any newly discovered nodes in a BFS approach will always be appended at the end. This ensures that nodes we had discovered earlier remain at a higher priority for being explored next.

This leads us to the next node we are about to explore: node D. Node D has two neighbors, nodes F and G (Figure 20-21).

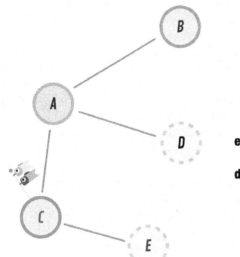

explored = [A, B, C]

discovered = [D, E]

FIGURE 20-20

Exploring node C

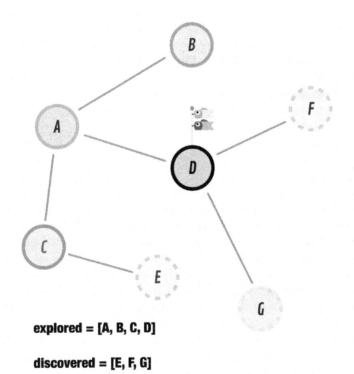

explored = [A, B, C, D]

discovered = [E, F, G]

FIGURE 20-21

We are taking a different path here than what we did with DFS earlier

At this point, node D moves into the explored list, and our discovered list now contains nodes E, F, and G.

The next node we explore is node E (Figure 20-22).

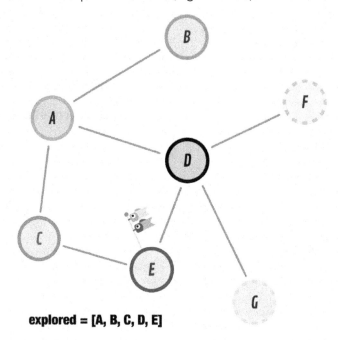

explored = [A, B, C, D, E]

discovered = [F, G]

FIGURE 20-22

Time to explore node E

Node E has no new unexplored neighbors, so we just move it to our explored list and move on. Let's go a bit faster here.

The next node to explore is node F, and it has nodes D and H as its neighbors (Figure 20-23).

Node D has already been explored, but node H is new. Let's add it to the end of our discovered list and move on to node G (Figure 20-24).

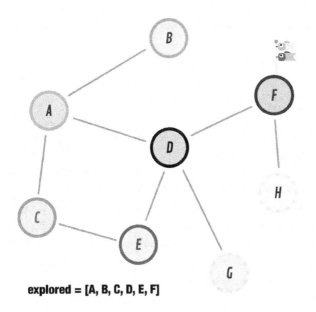

explored = [A, B, C, D, E, F]

discovered = [G, H]

FIGURE 20-23

Exploring node F next

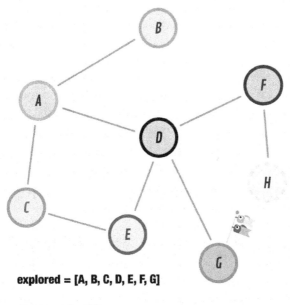

explored = [A, B, C, D, E, F, G]

discovered = [H]

FIGURE 20-24

Our graph is getting to be fully explored!

Node G has no unexplored neighbors, so we tag it as explored and move on to node H (Figure 20-25).

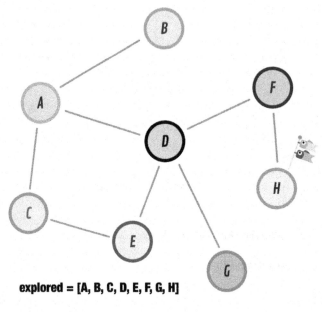

explored = [A, B, C, D, E, F, G, H]

discovered = [ ]

FIGURE 20-25

We explore node H last

Node H has no new unexplored neighbors, so we move it to our explored list. At this point, our discovered list is empty, and we have no more nodes left to discover. The explored list tracks the order our BFS approach took for exploring all of our nodes: A-B-C-D-E-F-G-H. You may have noticed that this is very similar to the traversal algorithms we saw earlier in the order of nodes discovered and explored.

When to Use DFS? When to Use BFS?

We have seen two approaches for exploring all the connected nodes in a graph. We started by looking at DFS and its way of exploring nodes by going as deep as possible along each branch before backtracking (Figure 20-26).

The second approach, BFS, explores nodes level by level, starting from the initial node and moving outward, visiting all the neighbors before moving to the next level (Figure 20-27).

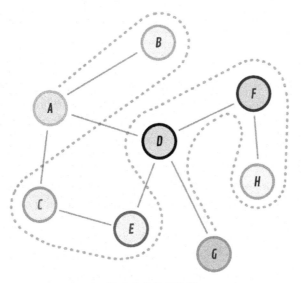

explored = [A, B, C, E, D, F, H, G]

FIGURE 20-26

The path we took with DFS

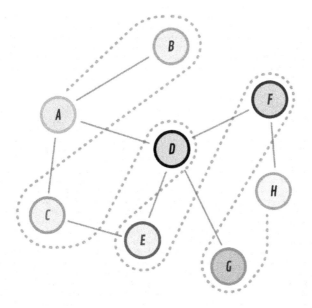

explored = [A, B, C, D, E, F, G, H]

FIGURE 20-27

The path we took with BFS

These two approaches for exploring nodes lead to the following state:

- BFS, with its measured approach toward checking immediate neighbors, helps us efficiently explore a graph level by level.

- DFS is more suited for tasks such as finding a path between two nodes, detecting cycles, or searching for a specific condition in a graph, as it may exhaustively explore a single branch before backtracking, potentially going deeper and exploring more nodes overall.

Depending what our purpose is for exploring our graph, we'll use either DFS or BFS. If we are looking for just a way to explore all the nodes in a graph, then pick between DFS or BFS randomly. You can't go wrong with either.

A JavaScript Implementation

Now that we have seen in great detail how DFS and BFS work to explore the nodes in a graph, let's shift gears and look at how both of these exploration approaches are implemented. We are going to build on top of the `Graph` class we looked at earlier when looking specifically at the graph data structure, so there is a lot of code that is familiar. Some new code (which is highlighted) implements what we need to have DFS and BFS working:

```
class Graph {
  constructor() {
    // Map to store nodes and their adjacent nodes
    this.nodes = new Map();

    // Flag to indicate if the graph is directed or undirected
    this.isDirected = false;
  }

  // Add a new node to the graph
  addNode(node) {
    if (!this.nodes.has(node)) {
      this.nodes.set(node, new Set());
    }
  }
```

```
// Add an edge between two nodes
addEdge(node1, node2) {
  // Check if the nodes exist
  if (!this.nodes.has(node1) || !this.nodes.has(node2)) {
    throw new Error('Nodes do not exist in the graph.');
  }

  // Add edge between node1 and node2
  this.nodes.get(node1).add(node2);

  // If the graph is undirected, add edge in the opposite
  // direction as well
  if (!this.isDirected) {
    this.nodes.get(node2).add(node1);
  }
}

// Remove a node and all its incident edges from the graph
removeNode(node) {
  if (this.nodes.has(node)) {
    // Remove the node and its edges from the graph
    this.nodes.delete(node);

    // Remove any incident edges in other nodes
    for (const [node, adjacentNodes] of this.nodes) {
      adjacentNodes.delete(node);
    }
  }
}

// Remove an edge between two nodes
removeEdge(node1, node2) {
  if (this.nodes.has(node1) && this.nodes.has(node2)) {
    // Remove edge between node1 and node2
    this.nodes.get(node1).delete(node2);
```

```
      // If the graph is undirected, remove edge in the opposite
      // direction as well
      if (!this.isDirected) {
        this.nodes.get(node2).delete(node1);
      }
    }
  }


  // Check if an edge exists between two nodes
  hasEdge(node1, node2) {
    if (this.nodes.has(node1) && this.nodes.has(node2)) {
      return this.nodes.get(node1).has(node2);
    }
    return false;
  }


  // Get the adjacent nodes of a given node
  getNeighbors(node) {
    if (this.nodes.has(node)) {
      return Array.from(this.nodes.get(node));
    }
    return [];
  }


  // Get all nodes in the graph
  getAllNodes() {
    return Array.from(this.nodes.keys());
  }


  // Set the graph as directed
  setDirected() {
    this.isDirected = true;
  }


  // Set the graph as undirected
  setUndirected() {
```

```
      this.isDirected = false;
   }


   // Check if the graph is directed
   isGraphDirected() {
      return this.isDirected;
   }


   // Class variable for storing explored nodes
   #explored = new Set();


   getExploredNodes() {
      return this.#explored;
   }


   //
   // Depth First Search (DFS)
   //
   dfs(startingNode) {
      // Reset to keep track of explored nodes
      this.#explored = new Set();


      // Call the recursive helper function to start DFS
      this.#dfsHelper(startingNode);
   }


   #dfsHelper(node) {
      // Mark the current node as explored
      this.#explored.add(node);


      // Get neighbors to explore in the future
      const neighbors = this.getNeighbors(node);


      for (const neighbor of neighbors) {
         if (!this.#explored.has(neighbor)) {
            // Recursively call the helper function for unexplored
neighbors
```

```
        this.#dfsHelper(neighbor);
      }
    }
  }
}


//
// Breadth First Search (BFS)
//
bfs(startingNode) {
  // Reset to keep track of explored nodes
  this.#explored = new Set();

  // Queue to store nodes to be explored
  const queue = new Queue();

  // Mark the starting node as explored
  this.#explored.add(startingNode);

  // Enqueue the starting node
  queue.enqueue(startingNode);

  while (queue.length > 0) {
    // Dequeue a node from the queue
    const node = queue.dequeue();

    const neighbors = this.getNeighbors(node);

    for (const neighbor of neighbors) {
      if (!this.#explored.has(neighbor)) {
        // Mark the neighbor as explored
        this.#explored.add(neighbor);

        // Enqueue the neighbor to be explored
        queue.enqueue(neighbor);
      }
```

```
        }
     }
   }
 }
```

This code uses an implementation of a queue from Chapter 6. You can either copy/paste the implementation from that chapter or reference it directly via the following `script` tag:

```
<script src="https://www.kirupa.com/js/queue_v1.js"></script>
```

We can certainly modify this code to avoid using a queue and work with arrays directly, but the performance penalties may be quite high—especially if we are dealing with a lot of nodes.

Using the Code

The new additions to our earlier `Graph` implementation are the `dfs`, `#dfsHelper`, `getExploredNodes`, and `bfs` methods along with a few private variables. To perform an exploration, we need to call the appropriate `dfs` or `bfs` method with a starting node provided as the argument. Take a look at the following code, where we re-created the graph we looked at in the previous sections, and perform both a DFS and BFS operation on it:

```
// Our graph from earlier!
const graph = new Graph();

graph.addNode("A");
graph.addNode("B");
graph.addNode("C");
graph.addNode("D");
graph.addNode("E");
graph.addNode("F");
graph.addNode("G");
graph.addNode("H");

graph.addEdge("A", "B");
graph.addEdge("A", "C");
graph.addEdge("A", "D");
```

```
graph.addEdge("C", "E");
graph.addEdge("D", "E");
graph.addEdge("D", "F");
graph.addEdge("D", "G");
graph.addEdge("F", "H");

console.log("DFS:");
graph.dfs("A"); // Perform DFS starting from node "A"
console.log(graph.getExploredNodes());

console.log("BFS:");
graph.bfs("A"); // Perform BFS starting from node "A"
console.log(graph.getExploredNodes());
```

When you run this code, pay attention to the console output where we print the final explored node for both our DFS and BFS approaches. Notice that the output matches what we manually walked through in the previous sections.

Implementation Detail

A key distinction between DFS and BFS is in where newly discovered nodes get added to our discovered list.

For DFS, newly discovered items are added to the beginning of our discovered list. This ensures DFS maintains its behavior of exploring deep into a path. For BFS, newly discovered items are added to the end of our discovered list. This behavior ensures BFS fully explores its immediate neighbors before going to the next level.

Our implementations of DFS and BFS reflect the difference in how discovered items are added to our discovered list. For DFS, we perform a recursive call on the newly discovered node:

```
for (const neighbor of neighbors) {
  if (!explored.has(neighbor)) {
    // Recursively call the helper function for unexplored neighbors
    this.#dfsHelper(neighbor, explored);
  }
}
```

This allows us to mimic a stack-like behavior by relying on our underlying runtime's call stack to preserve the order of nodes to explore.

With BFS, we implement a queue to keep track of our discovered nodes:

```
for (const neighbor of neighbors) {
  if (!explored.has(neighbor)) {
    // Mark the neighbor as explored
    explored.add(neighbor);

    // Enqueue the neighbor to be explored
    queue.enqueue(neighbor);
  }
}
```

This allows us to efficiently add items to the end and remove items from the beginning to explore more deeply.

Performance Details

There is one more thing before we wrap up here, and that has to do with how efficient both DFS and BFS are when it comes to exploring a graph.

- **DFS:**
  - **Runtime Complexity:** The runtime complexity of DFS depends on the representation of the graph and the implementation. In the worst-case scenario, where every node and edge is visited, DFS has a time complexity of $O(|N| + |E|)$, where $|N|$ represents the number of nodes and $|E|$ represents the number of edges in the graph.
  - **Memory Complexity:** The memory complexity of DFS is determined by the maximum depth of recursion, which is the approach our implementation here takes. In the worst-case scenario, where the graph forms a long path, DFS may require $O(|N|)$ space for the call stack.

- **BFS:**
  - **Runtime Complexity:** The runtime complexity of BFS, just like with DFS, is also influenced by the graph representation and the implementation. In the worst-case scenario, where every node and edge is explored, BFS has a time complexity of $O(|N| + |E|)$.

- **Memory Complexity:** The memory complexity of BFS primarily depends on the space required to store the visited nodes and the queue used for traversal. In the worst-case scenario, where the entire graph needs to be explored, BFS may require $O(|N|)$ space.

In the grand scheme of things, if we had to summarize the performance, it is safe to say that both DFS and BFS run in linear time and take up a linear amount of space. That's not too shabby.

Conclusion

Well, this was quite a blast! In the many preceding sections, we learned how to explore all the nodes in a graph using both DFS and BFS! On the surface, DFS and BFS are similar. You throw a starting node at them and a graph to start exploring. Both approaches explore all the nodes that they encounter. What sets them apart is how they go about doing their exploration. DFS goes deep down the first path it finds and doesn't stop until it reaches a dead end, at which point it goes back to the last unexplored node and continues diving deep again. BFS goes broad. It explores all its immediate nodes first and then goes to the next level and explores all of those nodes next. It takes a gradual outward approach.

In the end, by learning DFS and BFS, we gain valuable tools to tackle a wide range of graph problems. As we find out shortly, DFS and BFS are one of the more foundational pieces of path-finding algorithms and other more interesting things we will want to do with graphs. Happy exploring!

SOME ADDITIONAL RESOURCES

? Ask a question: **https://forum.kirupa.com**

Errors/Known issues: **https://bit.ly/algorithms_errata**

Source repository: **https://bit.ly/algorithms_source**

21

QUICKSORT

When it comes to sorting stuff, one of the most popular algorithms we have is **quicksort**. It is popular because it is fast—really fast—when compared to other algorithms for similar types of workloads. Key to its speed is that quicksort is a **divide-and-conquer algorithm**. It is called that because of how it breaks up its work. Instead of eating a giant chunk of data in one bite and chewing it over a long period of time (kinda like an anaconda), quicksort breaks up its data into smaller pieces and chews on each smaller piece quickly.

In this in-depth chapter, we go a tad more precise and really understand how quicksort works. By the end of the chapter, you'll be able to regale your friends and family (over dinner, preferably) with all the cool things quicksort does. You may even improve your code with this knowledge.

Onward!

A Look at How Quicksort Works

Quicksort works by dividing the input into several smaller pieces. On these smaller pieces, it does its magic by a combination of further dividing the input and sorting the leftovers. This is a pretty complex thing to explain in one attempt, so let's start with a simple overview of how quicksort works before diving into a more detailed, fully working quicksort implementation that puts into code all of the text and diagrams that you are about to see.

A Simple Look

To start things off, imagine that the grid of squares in Figure 21-1 represents the numbers we want to sort.

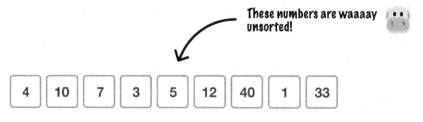

FIGURE 21-1

Our unsorted list of numbers

We want to use quicksort to sort these numbers, and this is what quicksort does:

1. Picks a midpoint value called the *pivot*

2. Reorders items based on how large they are relative to the pivot:

   a. Items smaller than the pivot are moved to the left of the pivot

   b. Items larger than the pivot are moved to the right of the pivot

3. Repeats steps 1 and 2 on the partially sorted values

At first glance, how these three steps help us sort some data may seem bizarre, but we see shortly how all of this ties together.

Starting at the top, because this is our first step, the region of values we are looking to sort is everything. The first thing we do is pick our pivot, the value at the middle position, as shown in Figure 21-2.

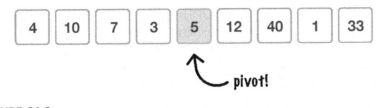

FIGURE 21-2

Choosing a pivot

We can pick our pivot from anywhere, but all the cool kids pick (for various good reasons) the pivot from the midpoint. Since we want to be cool as well, that's what we'll do. Quicksort uses the pivot value to order items in a very crude and basic way. From quicksort's point of view, all items to the left of the pivot value should be smaller, and all items to the right of the pivot value should be larger, as highlighted by Figure 21-3.

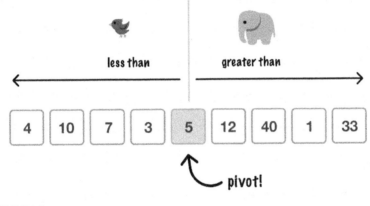

FIGURE 21-3

Looking at the two halves our pivot divides

This is the equivalent of throwing things over the fence to the other side where the pivot value is the fence. When we do this rearranging, Figure 21-4 shows what we will see.

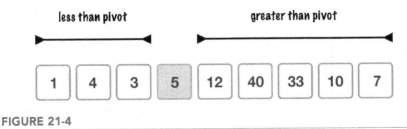

FIGURE 21-4

Items less than our pivot and items greater than our pivot

There are a few things to note here. First, notice that all items to the left of the pivot are smaller than the pivot. All items to the right of the pivot are larger than the pivot. Second, these items also aren't ordered. They are just smaller or larger relative to the pivot value, but they aren't placed in any ordered fashion. Once all of the values to the left and right of the pivot have been properly placed, our pivot value is considered to be sorted. What we just did is identify a single pivot and rearrange values to the left or right of it. The end result is that we have one sorted value. There are many more values to sort, so we repeat the steps we just saw on the unsorted regions.

At this point, we now have two sections of data on either side of our initial pivot value that are partially sorted by whether they are less than or greater than our pivot value. What we do next is repeat all of this pivot picking and rearranging on each of these two unsorted sections, as illustrated by Figure 21-5.

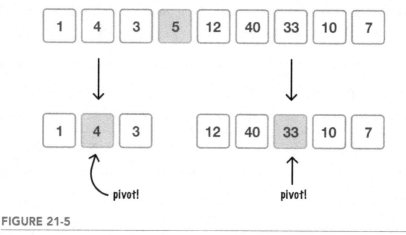

FIGURE 21-5

Two pivots!

In each unsorted section, we pick our pivot value first. This will be the value at the midpoint of the values in the section. Once we have picked our pivot, it is time to do some rearranging, as shown in Figure 21-6.

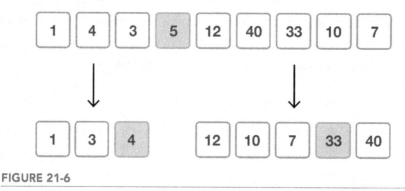

FIGURE 21-6

Rearranging values

Notice that we moved values smaller than our pivot value to the left. Values greater than our pivot were thrown over the fence to the right. We now have a few more pivot values that are in their final sorted section, and we have a few more unsorted regions that need the good old quicksort treatment applied to them. If we speed things up a bit, Figure 21-7 shows how each step will ultimately play out.

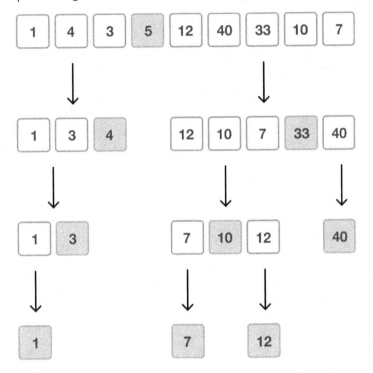

FIGURE 21-7

Each step of our sorting approach

We keep repeating all of this pivoting and sorting on each of the sections until we get to the point where we don't have enough values to pick a pivot and divide from. Once we reach that point and can divide no further, guess what? We are done! Our initial collection of unordered data is now sorted from small to large, and we can see that if we read our pivot items from left to right, as shown in Figure 21-8.

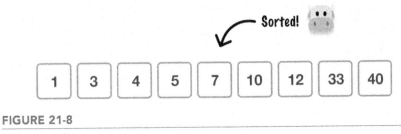

FIGURE 21-8

Fully sorted list

If we take many steps back, what we did here was pick a pivot and arrange items around it based on whether the item is less than or greater than our current pivot value. We repeated this process for every unsorted section that came up, and we didn't stop until we ran out of items to process.

Another Simple Look

Before we jump into the code and related implementation details, let's look at one more example that explains how quicksort works by taking a different angle. Unlike earlier, when we had a collection of numbers, the major change is that we are going to be using bar height to indicate the size of the value that we wish to sort (Figure 21-9).

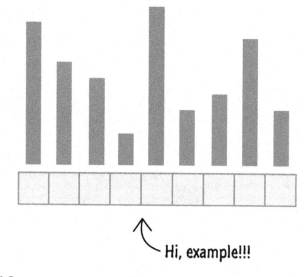

Hi, example!!!

FIGURE 21-9

Another example

The size (or magnitude) of the value is represented by the height of the bar. A taller bar indicates a larger value. A smaller bar indicates a smaller value. Let's take what we learned in the previous section and see how quicksort helps us sort this. Hopefully, much of this will be a review.

As always, the first thing is for us to pick a pivot value, and we pick one in the middle (Figure 21-10).

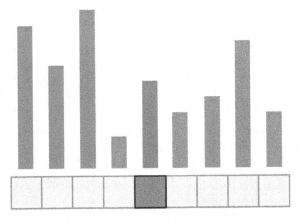

FIGURE 21-10

Picking the pivot

Once the pivot has been picked, the next step is to move smaller items to the left and larger items to the right of the pivot (Figure 21-11).

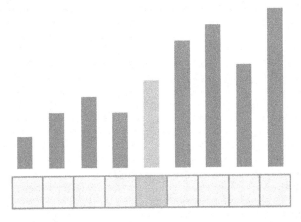

FIGURE 21-11

Rearranging between the two halves created by our pivot

At this point, your pivot value is considered to be sorted and in the proper location. After all, it is right in the middle of all the items that will appear before or after it. The next step is to sort the left half of the newly arranged items (Figure 21-12).

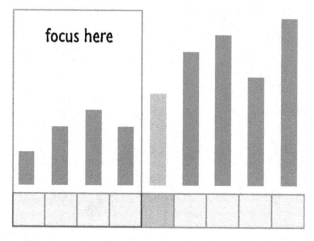

FIGURE 21-12

Focusing on the smaller items

This is done by recursively calling quicksort on just the left region. Everything that you saw before, such as picking a pivot and throwing values around, will happen again (Figure 21-13).

pick pivot   re-order

FIGURE 21-13

Rinse and repeat

The end result is that our left half is now semi-ordered and we have a smaller range of values left to arrange. Let's jump over to the right half that we left alone after the first round of reorderings and go mess with it (Figure 21-14).

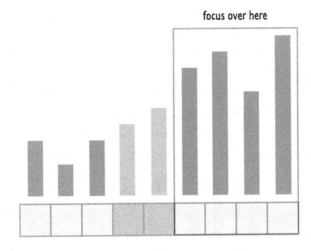

focus over here

FIGURE 21-14

Rinse and repeat on the right now

Let's rinse and repeat our pivot and reordering steps on this side of our input (Figure 21-15).

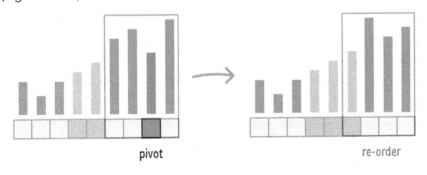

pivot   re-order

FIGURE 21-15

Continuing to rearrange items

By now, we should be able to see the pattern more clearly. To save some time (and ink!), let's speed through the remaining steps for getting our entire input properly ordered (Figure 21-16).

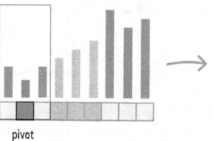
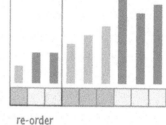
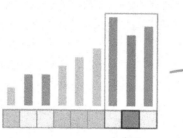
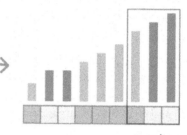

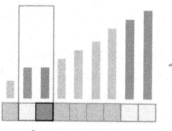
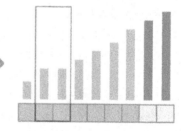
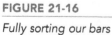
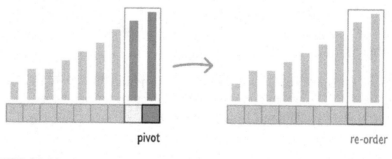

FIGURE 21-16

Fully sorting our bars

Yet again, the end result of the various pivotings and reorderings is that we get a fully ordered set of numbers. Let's now look at another example . . . no, just kidding! We are good on examples for now. Instead, it's time to look at the coding implementation.

It's Implementation Time

All of these words and diagrams are only helpful for people like you and me. Our computers have no idea what to do with all of this, so that means we need to convert everything we know into a form that computers understand. Before we go all out on that quest, let's meet everyone halfway by looking at some pseudocode (not quite real code, not quite real English) first.

The pseudocode for quicksort is shown in Figure 21-17.

```
quickSort(array, left, right) {
    i = left;
    j = right;
    pivot = middle(array);

    loop while (i <= j) {
        loop while (array[i] < pivot) {
            i++;
        }

        loop while (array[j] > pivot) {
            j--;
        }

        if (i <= j) {
            temp = array[i];
            array[i] = array[j];
            array[j] = temp;
            i++;
            j--:
        }
    }

    if (left < j) {
        quickSort(array, left, j);
    }

    if (i < right) {
        quickSort(array, i, right);
    }
}
```

FIGURE 21-17

High-level overview of our code

Each of the colored regions represents an important step in what quicksort does. Not to give too much away, but here is a super-quick guide to what each chunk of code does (Figure 21-18).

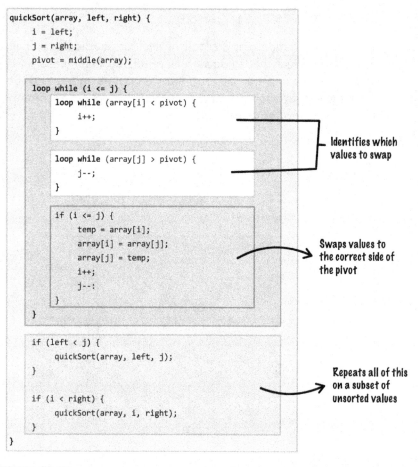

```
quickSort(array, left, right) {
    i = left;
    j = right;
    pivot = middle(array);

    loop while (i <= j) {
        loop while (array[i] < pivot) {
            i++;
        }

        loop while (array[j] > pivot) {
            j--;
        }

        if (i <= j) {
            temp = array[i];
            array[i] = array[j];
            array[j] = temp;
            i++;
            j--:
        }
    }

    if (left < j) {
        quickSort(array, left, j);
    }

    if (i < right) {
        quickSort(array, i, right);
    }
}
```

Identifies which values to swap

Swaps values to the correct side of the pivot

Repeats all of this on a subset of unsorted values

FIGURE 21-18

Interesting sections in our code

Take a few moments to walk through how this code might work and how it might help you to sort an unsorted list of data. Turning all of this pseudocode into real code, we have the following:

```
function quickSortHelper(arrayInput, left, right) {
    let i = left;
    let j = right;
```

```
let pivotPoint = arrayInput[Math.round((left + right) * .5)];

// Loop
while (i <= j) {

  while (arrayInput[i] < pivotPoint) {
    i++;
  }

  while (arrayInput[j] > pivotPoint) {
    j--;
  }

  if (i <= j) {
    let tempStore = arrayInput[i];

    arrayInput[i] = arrayInput[j];
    i++;

    arrayInput[j] = tempStore;
    j--;
  }

}

// Swap
if (left < j) {
  quickSortHelper(arrayInput, left, j);
}

if (i < right) {
  quickSortHelper(arrayInput, i, right);
}

return arrayInput;
}
```

```
function quickSort(input) {
    return quickSortHelper(input, 0, input.length - 1);
}
```

The code we see here is largely identical to the pseudocode we saw earlier. The biggest change is that we have a `quickSortHelper` function to deal with specifying the array, left, and right values. This makes the call to the `quickSort` function very clean. You just specify the array.

Here is an example of how to use this code:

```
let myData = [24, 10, 17, 9, 5, 9, 1, 23, 300];
quickSort(myData);


alert(myData);
```

If everything is set up correctly (and why wouldn't it be?!!), you'll see a dialog displaying a sorted list of numbers.

Performance Characteristics

We have said a few times already that quicksort is really good at sorting numbers quickly—hence its name. It is a divide-and-conquer sorting algorithm that works by repeatedly partitioning the array into two smaller subarrays, each of which is then sorted recursively. The performance of quicksort is typically O(n log n), which is the best possible time complexity for a sorting algorithm. Nothing faster has been invented/discovered yet. However, the worst-case time complexity of quicksort is O(n^2), which can occur if the array is already sorted or nearly sorted.

Table 21-1 highlights quicksort's performance characteristics.

TABLE 21-1   Quicksort's Performance Characteristics

Scenario	Time Complexity	Memory Complexity
Best case	O(n log n)	O(log n)
Worst case	O(n^2)	O(1)
Average case	O(n log n)	O(log n)

To expand on the performance characteristics a bit further, the following sections provide some additional talking points.

Time Complexity

- **Best Case:** In the best-case scenario, the pivot chosen divides the array into two roughly equal halves. Each recursive call partitions the array into two halves, and there will be log(n) levels of recursion, where n is the number of elements in the input array. At each level of recursion, all n elements are compared once. Therefore, the best-case time complexity is O(n log n).

- **Average Case:** Quicksort's average case performance is also O(n log n). It occurs when the pivot selection is done randomly or in a way that avoids consistently unbalanced partitions.

- **Worst Case:** The worst-case scenario happens when the pivot chosen is always the smallest or largest element, leading to highly unbalanced partitions. In this case, the recursion depth reaches its maximum, and the algorithm exhibits poor performance. The worst-case time complexity is O(n^2).

Famed computer scientiest Donald Knuth recommends that we jumble our array's contents intentionally to reduce the odds of this ever happening.

Space Complexity

Quicksort is generally an in-place sorting algorithm, meaning it does not require additional memory proportional to the input size. The space complexity is O(log n) due to the recursion stack space required to maintain the call stack during the sorting process.

Stability

Quicksort is not a stable sorting algorithm, which means the relative order of equal elements might not be preserved after sorting. Stability isn't something we talked about in the past, but given the importance (and popularity!) of quicksort, it is worth calling out here so that you have all the details.

Conclusion

Well, you have reached the end of this dive into one of the fastest sort algorithms. Will all of this knowledge help you out in real (nonacademic) life? I highly doubt it. Almost all popular programming languages have their own built-in sort mechanism that you can use. Many are already based on quicksort (or a highly optimized and specialized version of it), so the performance gains you will see by using your own version of quicksort compared to using a built-in sort approach will be zero.

In that case, why did we spend so much time on this? Besides the obvious reasons of entertaining people with your newfound knowledge, one of the reasons is that the built-in sort mechanisms will fail you at some point. You may find yourself needing to sort a more complex set of data that goes beyond what the built-in sorts support. At times like that, you may have to implement your own sort algorithm. What you implement may be based on quicksort or it may be something completely unrelated. Speaking of unrelated, Table 21-2 compares various popular sorting algorithms on their performance and memory characteristics.

TABLE 21-2 Sorting Algorithms and Their Performance and Memory Characteristics

Name	Best	Average	Worst	Memory
Quicksort	$n \log n$	$n \log n$	n^2	$\log n$ (average)
Mergesort	$n \log n$	$n \log n$	$n \log n$	n (worst case)
Heapsort	$n \log n$	$n \log n$	$n \log n$	1
Timsort	n	$n \log n$	$n \log n$	n
Bubblesort	n	n^2	n^2	1
Selection sort	n^2	n^2	n^2	1
Insertion sort	n	n^2	n^2	1

And with that, you are free to go and use your newfound knowledge to sort all sorts of things really, REALLY quickly.

SOME ADDITIONAL RESOURCES

? Ask a question: **https://forum.kirupa.com**

Errors/Known issues: **https://bit.ly/algorithms_errata**

Source repository: **https://bit.ly/algorithms_source**

22

BUBBLESORT

When it comes to sorting stuff, one of the worst algorithms you can use is known affectionately as **bubblesort**. It is sooo terrible that people have stopped naming kids after it. Despite its terribleness, it is important for you to learn how bubblesort works. The main reason is to understand what it does and avoid doing anything in your code that even remotely resembles it. The other reason is purely for trivial purposes. You'll never know when this is belted out as a *Final Jeopardy* answer one day.

Onward!

How Bubblesort Works

Let's say you have a collection of numbers that are currently unsorted (Figure 22-1).

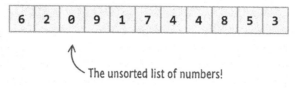

The unsorted list of numbers!

FIGURE 22-1

Our unsorted list of numbers

The way bubblesort works is a bit unremarkable, as terribly slow sorting algorithms go. It starts at the beginning and slowly moves through each number until it hits the end. At each number, it compares the size of the number it is at with the number directly next to it. That probably makes little sense, so take a look at the diagram in Figure 22-2.

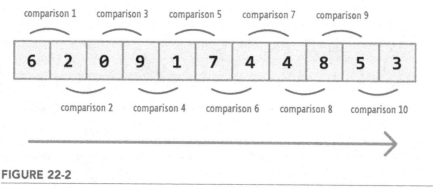

FIGURE 22-2

Comparison ftw!

The first two numbers are compared. Then the next two numbers are compared. Then the next two, and the next two, and so on. You get the picture. The comparison it performs is to see if the first number is smaller than the second number. If the first number happens to be bigger, then the first and second numbers are swapped. Let's walk through this briefly.

In our example, the first comparison will be between the 6 and the 2 (Figure 22-3).

FIGURE 22-3

The first comparison

The first number is not smaller than the second one—that is, 6 is not less than 2. What you do in this situation is swap the numbers so that your first number is always smaller than the second number (Figure 22-4).

FIGURE 22-4

Getting the first two numbers sorted

Yay! You just completed one step as a human being role-playing as bubblesort. Next, you move one number to the right and compare the new two numbers that you are standing in front of (Figure 22-5).

FIGURE 22-5

Comparing the next two numbers

The 6 is not less than 0, so another swap takes place (Figure 22-6).

FIGURE 22-6

Swapping to ensure the correct order

You repeat this process of sliding over by one, comparing the two numbers in front of you, and swapping them if you need to until you have no more numbers left (Figure 22-7).

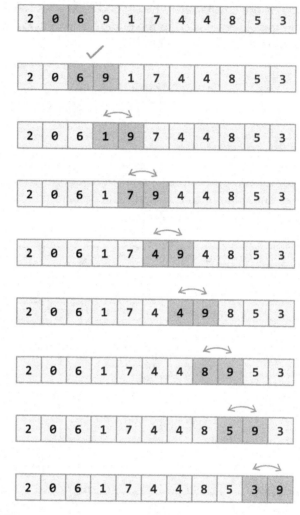

FIGURE 22-7

The process for checking each pair of numbers

When you reach the last number, you go back to the beginning and repeat this whole process again. This is because, as you can see, your numbers are still not fully sorted. You repeat this painfully time-consuming process over and over and over again until you get to the point where all of your numbers are sorted perfectly (Figure 22-8).

Ze numbers...they are sorted!!!

FIGURE 22-8

The numbers are finally sorted

From bubblesort's point of view, your numbers are considered to be perfectly sorted when you make a pass through your numbers without having to swap any of them around. To put it differently, it means that every two consecutive numbers you looked at were properly arranged from small to large.

Walkthrough

In the previous section, you learned a bit about how bubblesort works. In this section, let's clarify everything you've seen so far by doing a full walkthrough. To avoid boring you to tears, I'm going to trim our example to only four numbers (Figure 22-9).

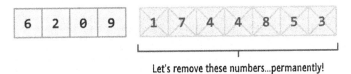

Let's remove these numbers...permanently!

FIGURE 22-9

Simplifying our example

Don't worry. Because we are dealing with bubblesort, these four numbers will ensure you do a lot of scrolling (or page turning or hand gesturing) to get to the fully sorted version of things. You've already sorta (ha!) seen the first few numbers, but we'll go through them again with a little more detail for the sake of completeness.

The first run of bubblesort through our four numbers looks as shown in Figure 22-10.

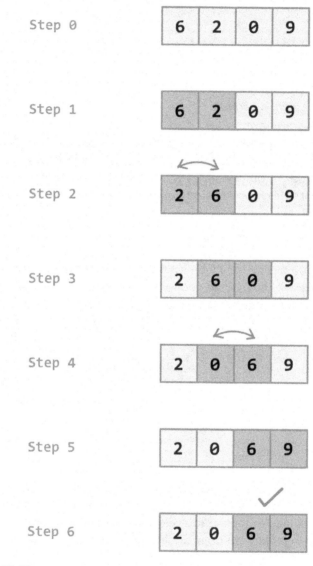

FIGURE 22-10

The first round of sorting

Now, we start at the beginning and do our old song and dance again (Figure 22-11).

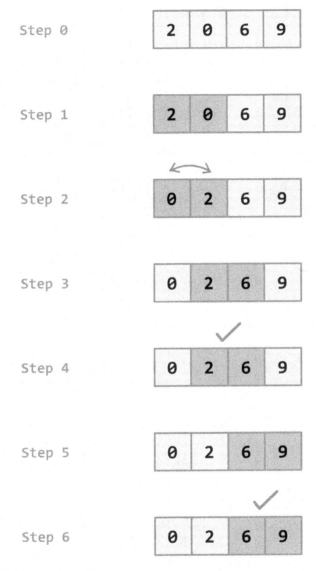

FIGURE 22-11

The second round of sorting

At this point, if you look at the results of the last step, our numbers are fully sorted. To us humans, we would call it a night and take a break. Bubblesort doesn't know that the numbers are sorted just yet. It needs to run through the numbers one more time to realize, when no swaps take place, that its job is done (Figure 22-12).

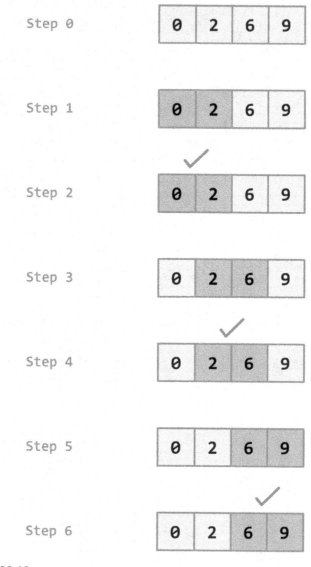

FIGURE 22-12

Running through the remaining numbers

When no swaps happen, it means that every number is properly arranged. That signals to bubblesort to stop bothering these poor numbers and to go home.

The Code

Now that you've seen how bubblesort operates, let's take a look at one implementation of it:

```
function bubbleSort(input) {
  let swapSignal = true;
  while (swapSignal) {
    swapSignal = false;
    for (let i = 0; i < input.length - 1; i++) {
      if (input[i] > input[i + 1]) {
        let temp = input[i];
        input[i] = input[i + 1];
        input[i + 1] = temp;
        swapSignal = true;
      }
    }
  }
}
let myData = [6, 2, 0, 9, 1, 7, 4, 4, 8, 5, 3];
bubbleSort(myData);
console.log(myData);
```

If you walk through this code, everything you see should map to what we looked at in the previous sections. The main thing to call out is the swapSignal variable that is used to indicate whether bubblesort has gone through these numbers without swapping any values. Besides that one thing of note, everything else is just simple array and for loop tomfoolery.

Conclusion

As you've seen from the walkthrough, bubblesort is not very efficient. For sorting four numbers, it took about 18 steps if you count the shifting and comparison as two individual operations. This was despite several numbers requiring no further sorting.

Bubblesort is fastest when you are already dealing with a fully sorted list of numbers. It goes through the numbers once, realizes that no numbers were swapped, and then heads over to the local discotheque and does some . . . discothequeing with all of the other cool kids. If you are dealing with a list of numbers that are sorted in reverse, bubblesort takes the longest amount of time. Every single number needs to be swapped and moved over to the end. I feel bad for whatever computing device has to deal with that reversed situation.

Before we call it a night (and join bubblesort at the local discotheque), Table 22-1, repeated from Chapter 21 for convenience, compares various popular sorting algorithms and their performance and memory characteristics.

TABLE 22-1   Sorting Algorithms and Performance and Memory Characteristics

Name	Best	Average	Worst	Memory
Quicksort	$n \log n$	$n \log n$	n^2	$\log n$ (average)
Mergesort	$n \log n$	$n \log n$	$n \log n$	n (worst case)
Heapsort	$n \log n$	$n \log n$	$n \log n$	1
Timsort	n	$n \log n$	$n \log n$	n
Bubblesort	n	n^2	n^2	1
Selection sort	n^2	n^2	n^2	1
Insertion sort	n	n^2	n^2	1

And with that, you are free to go and use your newfound knowledge to sort all sorts of things really, REALLY slowly. If you want to learn about a fast sorting algorithm that leaves bubblesort behind in the dust, you should become friends with quicksort.

SOME ADDITIONAL RESOURCES

? Ask a question: **https://forum.kirupa.com**

Errors/Known issues: **https://bit.ly/algorithms_errata**

Source repository: **https://bit.ly/algorithms_source**

23

INSERTION SORT

A fun sorting algorithm is insertion sort. Have you ever played cards and needed to sort the cards in your hand (Figure 23-1)?

↑
I think that one with the pointed
ears is counting cards!

FIGURE 23-1

Sorting cards . . . a classic canine tradition!

The approach you (or your canine friend) use to sort a playing card from one part of your hand and move it to the other part is nearly identical to how insertion sort works. It is actually a tad more exciting than that sounds, so let's look at how insertion sort works.

Onward!

How Insertion Sort Works

The way insertion sort works is sorta kinda really cool. The best way to understand it is by working through an example. We formally describe the algorithm's behavior a bit later. For our example, as shown in Figure 23-2, our goal is to sort these bars (aka our values) from shortest to tallest.

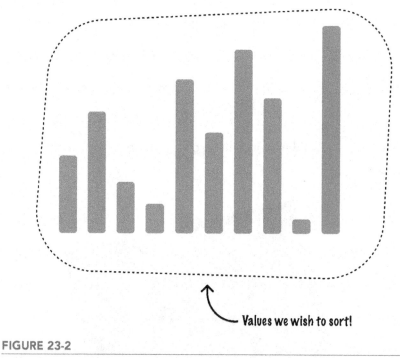

Values we wish to sort!

FIGURE 23-2

Our example

At the very beginning before anything happens, what we have right now is a collection of unsorted values (Figure 23-3).

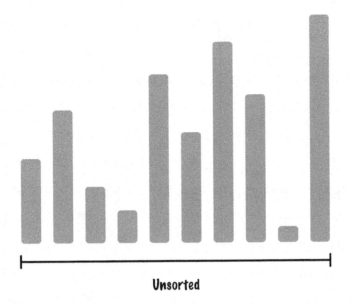

FIGURE 23-3

A collection of unsorted values

Our goal is to turn these unsorted values into sorted ones. We start with our first item, and if we think of these bars as values in an array (or similar collection), we start at the very left. We select our first item for processing. When we select an item, it becomes known as the **active item** or **value** (Figure 23-4).

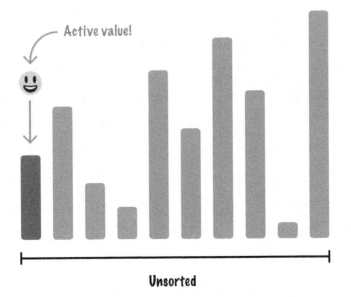

FIGURE 23-4

Starting with our first item

When we have our active value, we ask ourselves the following question: **When I look at the sorted items, am I in the right spot?**

For the very first item in our collection, this question doesn't apply. There are no items that are already sorted, so we go ahead and claim our first item as already being sorted (Figure 23-5).

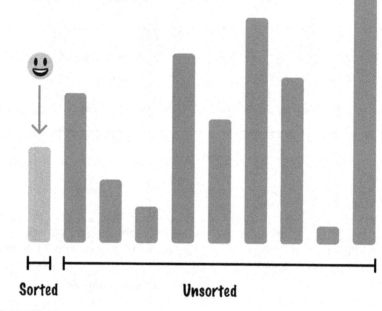

Sorted   **Unsorted**

FIGURE 23-5

Our first item is assumed to be sorted . . . for now!

It's time for us to go to our next item, so move one item to the right and mark it as active (Figure 23-6). This also happens to be our first item in our unsorted region, so that's another way to refer to it.

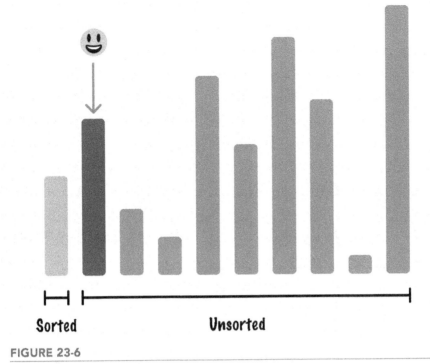

Sorted   **Unsorted**

FIGURE 23-6

Moving to the next item

We repeat the question we asked earlier: **When I look at the sorted items, am I in the right spot?** When we look at our region of sorted items, we have just a single entry. When we compare its size to our active item, our active item is larger. That meets our goal of sorting from short to tall, so we can answer yes to this question and mark our active item as sorted (Figure 23-7).

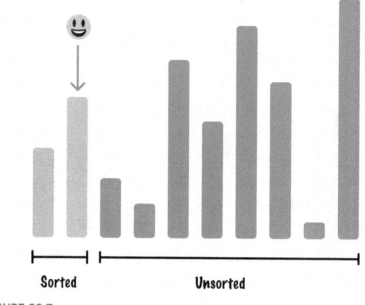

FIGURE 23-7

We have two (temporarily) sorted items

We move on to our next item and repeat the steps we have been following so far. We mark our third item (or the current first unsorted item) as active (Figure 23-8).

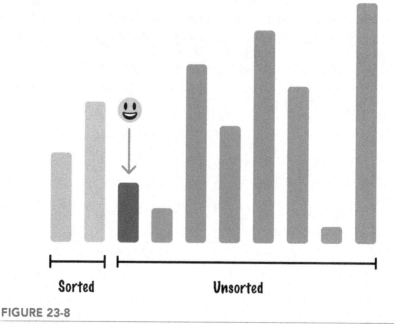

FIGURE 23-8

Moving on to the third item

When we look at our sorted items, where should this active item go? This requires that we go through each sorted item, compare heights, and continue onward until we are at the right spot (Figure 23-9).

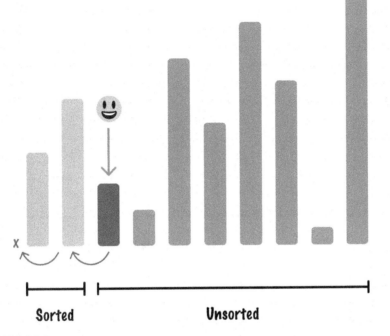

FIGURE 23-9

Moving it to the right location

In the case of this active item, we move it all the way to the beginning of our sorted items region (Figure 23-10).

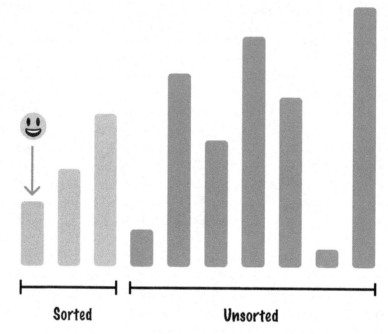

Sorted   Unsorted

FIGURE 23-10

We have three sorta sorted items

By now, we should see a pattern starting to emerge where we:

1. Pick the first item from our unsorted region.

2. Mark this item as active.

3. Compare its value with the items in our sorted region to identify where to place it.

4. Place our active item in the right spot within the sorted region.

Continuing this trend and speeding things up, Figure 23-11 shows our next active item and where it belongs when we sort by height.

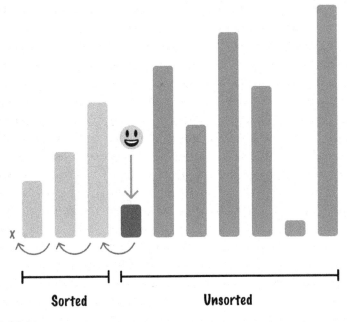

FIGURE 23-11

Ensuring our fourth item is placed into the right location

The number of items in our sorted region is gradually growing (Figure 23-12).

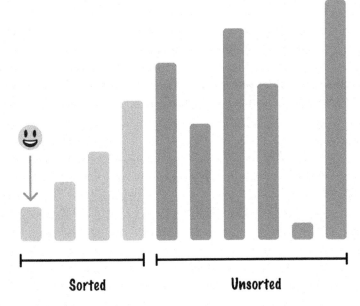

FIGURE 23-12

Our sorted region is getting larger

Moving on to our next active item and skipping a few steps, this is a straightforward comparison where this active item is already in the right spot given that it is now the largest sorted item (Figure 23-13).

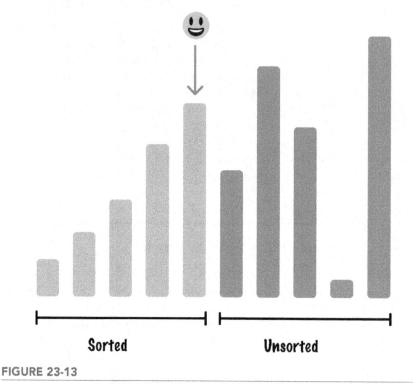

FIGURE 23-13

Our next item happens to already be sorted

We are going to look at one more item before closing the book on this example. Our next active item is shown in Figure 23-14.

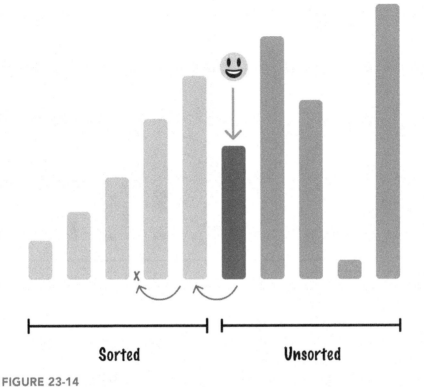

FIGURE 23-14

Moving the next item into the appropriate order

When we compare it with our other sorted items, as the previous image also highlights, we'll need to move it to the left by two spots to ensure it is in the appropriate sorted location (Figure 23-15).

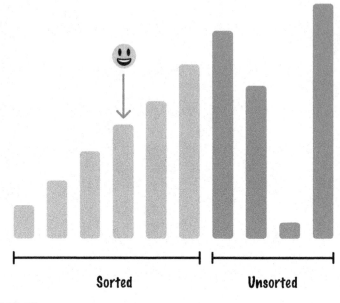

FIGURE 23-15

Our sorted region is starting to better take shape

At this point, we aren't going to continue this example further. The steps to sort the remaining items are identical to the ones we've taken so far. At the end, we'll have a nicely sorted array, as shown in Figure 23-16.

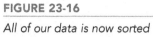

FIGURE 23-16

All of our data is now sorted

The approach we've seen here with our **sorted region**, **unsorted region**, and **active number** are all core to how insertion sort works. Now that we've seen all of this, let's look into one more example that shows in greater detail how insertion sort works.

One More Example

In real life, we'll probably not be sorting bars. We'll be sorting values like numbers, so let's take what we've learned so far and fully sort some numbers using insertion sort (Figure 23-17).

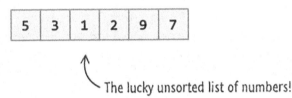

The lucky unsorted list of numbers!

FIGURE 23-17

Another example

Because you have a good understanding of how insertion sort works, we move through this example at a brisk pace. To start with, we skip the first number (which is by default considered to be sorted) and focus on the second number. This **active number** (the number we are currently trying to sort) is the number 3 (Figure 23-18).

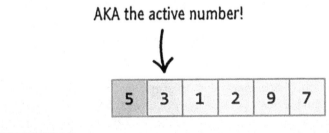

AKA the active number!

FIGURE 23-18

Starting with our active number

Once we have our active number, we follow the "look left" approach that insertion sort operates under. In this approach, it compares the active number against each number to the left of it until it hits a number that is smaller than itself.

We have only one number to the left, so let's compare the 3 against the 5. Is the active number (3) greater than 5? The answer is no, so we move left. Because there is nothing more to the left, the active number gets inserted in to its new home at the beginning (Figure 23-19).

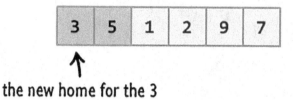

the new home for the 3

FIGURE 23-19

Swapping to ensure the order is maintained

Next, we move right and pick a new active number (Figure 23-20).

FIGURE 23-20

Moving to our next item

That new active number is 1. Repeating the earlier process, let's look left. The 1 is not greater than 5. The 1 is not greater than 3. There is no other number to the left, so the 1 now gets inserted as the first item in the list (Figure 23-21).

FIGURE 23-21

We sorted our active items correctly

So far, so good, right? Let's speed this up even more by skipping a lot of the explanations and just showing the results of our active number reaching its new destination for the remaining numbers (Figure 23-22).

And . . . we are done! All that remains now is to analyze how insertion works, present a JavaScript implementation, and look at insertion sort's performance characteristics.

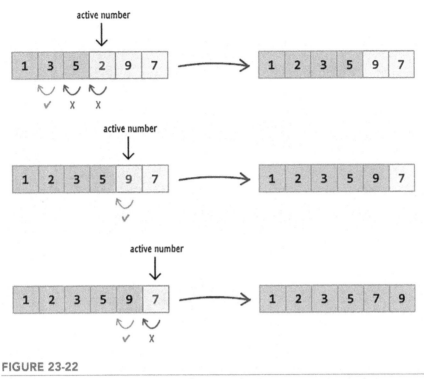

FIGURE 23-22

Going through and sorting the remaining items

Algorithm Overview and Implementation

If we had to formally describe insertion sort using words instead of diagrams, the description would be as follows:

1. Start at the beginning and assume the first number is already sorted. The number we are going to focus on (aka the active number) is the second item.

2. With our active number in our grasp, see if it is less than or greater than the number that is before it:

    a. If the active number is greater than the number to its left, do nothing. The ordering is correct, for now. Jump to step 3.

    b. If the active number is less than the number to its left, keep moving left. Keep moving over until our active number hits another number whose value is less than it. When that joyous moment happens, stay put and wedge the active number just next to that number.

3. It's time to repeat the whole process with a new active number. Pick the next unsorted number and start all over from step 2.

If we turn this algorithm into code, what we'll see will look as follows:

```javascript
function insertionSort(input) {
    // Variable to store the current element being compared
    let activeNumber;

    // Loop through the array starting from the second element (index 1)
    for (let i = 1; i < input.length; i++) {
        // Store the current element in the activeNumber variable
        activeNumber = input[i];

        // Inner loop to compare activeNumber with the elements before it
        for (let j = i - 1; j >= 0; j--) {
            if (input[j] > activeNumber) {
                // Move the greater element one position ahead to make space
                // for the activeNumber
                input[j + 1] = input[j];
            } else {
                // If we find an element that is smaller than or
                // equal to the activeNumber, exit the inner loop
                break;
            }
        }
        // Place the activeNumber in its correct sorted position
        input[j + 1] = activeNumber;
    }
}

let myinput = [24, 10, 17, 9, 5, 9, 1, 23, 300];
insertionSort(myinput);

alert(myinput);
```

This implementation is a near-direct translation of the English explanations and diagrams we saw earlier. The main thing to note is that we have two loops working in parallel. First, there is the outer loop that is responsible for traveling through our entire data. Second, we have the inner loop that is responsible for taking each active number, looking left at the already sorted data, and specifying the spot that the active number will be inserted into.

Performance Analysis

The performance characteristics of insertion sort are nothing to write home about. It's not very efficient for large data sets, and Table 23-1 highlights its performance characteristics.

TABLE 23-1   Insertion Sort's Performance Characteristics

Scenario	Time Complexity	Memory Complexity
Best case	$O(n)$	$O(1)$
Worst case	$O(n^2)$	$O(1)$
Average case	$O(n^2)$	$O(1)$

Digging into this deeper, at a bare minimum, it takes *n* operations just to go from one end of our data to the other (Figure 23-23).

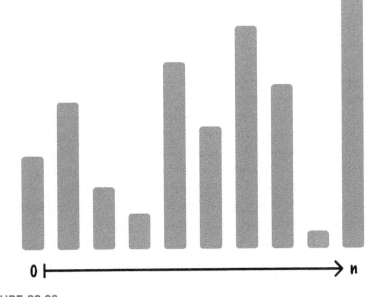

FIGURE 23-23

There are n items

As we move from left to right, we take our active number and try to find the correct place in our sorted region to move it to. This too takes up around *n* operations on average (Figure 23-24).

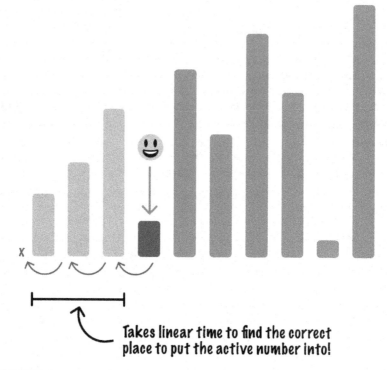

Takes linear time to find the correct place to put the active number into!

FIGURE 23-24

We do almost n comparisons at each step

We put all that together and get an average running time of n^2, where the linear time to go through our numbers combined with the linear look left insertion at each point make it a pretty slow algorithm. If we are running insertion sort on an already sorted list, the running time is O(*n*) because our inner loop, which (on average) runs about *n* times, will run exactly once. The first item it compares against will indicate that our active item is in the right location already, so the bulk of the work is in just moving from left to right. This is why insertion sort is not a terrible choice when sorting partially sorted items, nor is it a terrible choice when dealing with small lists of values.

Now, it isn't all bad news for all you insertion sort afficionados, though! It isn't memory intensive at all. Insertion sort takes up a constant amount of memory, so keep insertion sort at the top of your pile if you need to sort numbers (slowly) but are memory constrained.

Conclusion

Insertion sort is not very efficient from a speed point of view. It is, however, very efficient from a memory point of view. To see how insertion sort compares with other sort algorithms, check out Table 23-2.

TABLE 23-2   Insertion Sort versus the Other Sort Algorithms by Speed and Memory Characteristics

Name	Best	Average	Worst	Memory
Quicksort	$n \log n$	$n \log n$	n^2	$\log n$ (average)
Mergesort	$n \log n$	$n \log n$	$n \log n$	n (worst case)
Heapsort	$n \log n$	$n \log n$	$n \log n$	1
Timsort	n	$n \log n$	$n \log n$	n
Bubblesort	n	n^2	n^2	1
Selection sort	n^2	n^2	n^2	1
Insertion sort	n	n^2	n^2	1

Overall, there are better sorting algorithms to use. Unless you are sorting a small quantity of numbers, or you really need to take advantage of its sweet constant memory usage, it's best to stay as far away as possible from insertion sort.

SOME ADDITIONAL RESOURCES

? Ask a question: **https://forum.kirupa.com**

Errors/Known issues: **https://bit.ly/algorithms_errata**

Source repository: **https://bit.ly/algorithms_source**

24

SELECTION SORT

A slow but very easy-to-comprehend sort algorithm is **selection sort**. Its approach is very simple. Let's say we have a list of values that we want sorted (Figure 24-1).

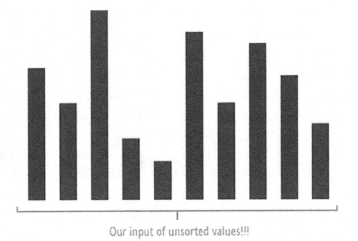

Our input of unsorted values!!!

FIGURE 24-1

Our starting unsorted values

Selection sort works by finding (aka selecting) the smallest item in your entire list. Once it finds that smallest item, it showers it with love and praise and makes it the first sorted item in a region it carves out called the **sorted region**. Our selection sort then goes out and finds the next smallest item in the list. Once it finds that item, it places it directly after our earlier smallest item in the sorted region. This whole process of finding the next smallest item and shoving it in the sorted region repeats itself until there are no more unsorted items left.

All of this probably doesn't make a whole lot of sense. It is also boring, so let's fix that with some pictures and stuff in the next section.

Onward!

Selection Sort Walkthrough

Since I am extremely lazy, let's just continue with the input of bars you saw earlier. Our goal is to use selection sort to sort the bars from shortest to tallest. Along the way, we also learn a thing or two about how selection sort actually works. Hopefully.

First, putting on our selection sort mask, we are going to assume the first item is the smallest item in the list (Figure 24-2).

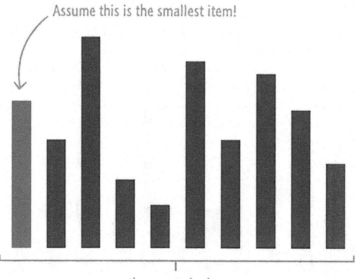

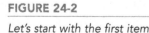

FIGURE 24-2

Let's start with the first item

Before you start jumping up and down about the absurdity of this, hold on a second. The next step is to see if the first item is indeed the smallest item in our list. To answer this, selection sort walks through the entire list and compares the size of each item with our current smallest (and first) item (Figure 24-3).

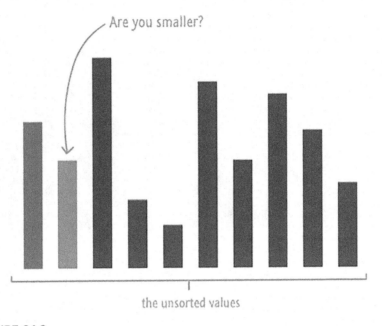

Are you smaller?

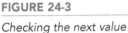

the unsorted values

FIGURE 24-3

Checking the next value

Usually, the first item is rarely the smallest item for long. When selection sort encounters an item that is smaller, **this new item becomes the new smallest item**. As you can see, this happens immediately in our example, for the next item is smaller than the first item (Figure 24-4).

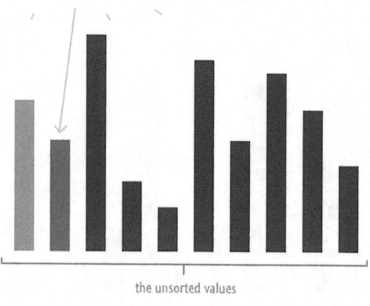

All hail the new smallest item!

the unsorted values

FIGURE 24-4

Currently our smallest item

At this point, we have a new smallest item. Just like before, though, it is premature to call it a day because we have examined only two values so far. Our quest to find the smallest number needs to continue, so we compare our newest smallest value with the remaining items in the list to see if another item will take the smallest item crown.

During this trip, we'll frequently encounter a number that is larger than our current smallest value (Figure 24-5).

When that happens, we simply skip over it and move on to the next item and repeat the comparison (Figure 24-6).

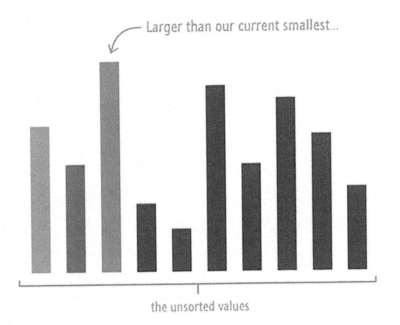

Larger than our current smallest...

the unsorted values

FIGURE 24-5

Continuing to go down the list to find our smallest item

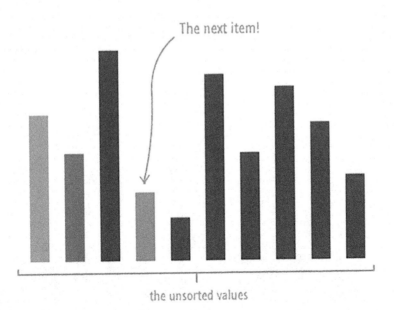

The next item!

the unsorted values

FIGURE 24-6

A new smallest item has emerged

Selection sort goes through the entire list until it has selected the smallest item. For this example, that's the bar shown in Figure 24-7.

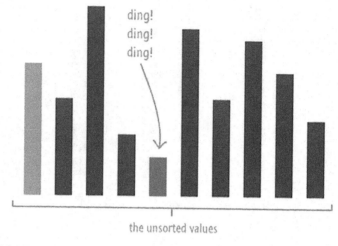

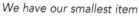

FIGURE 24-7

We have our smallest item

All that is left is to move this number to the mysterious sorted region that I alluded to earlier, and let's assume that we are going to carve our sorted region from the beginning of our list. To do this, our next step is to swap our smallest item with the first item we started with—the first item in our unsorted region (Figure 24-8).

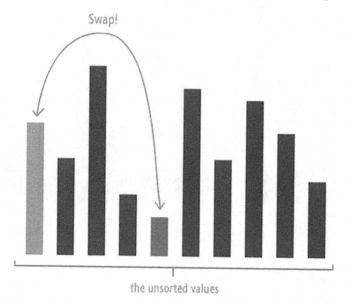

FIGURE 24-8

Swap the smallest item into the first place

Once this happens, **our list is partially sorted with the smallest item leading the way**. The rest of our list is still unsorted, though (Figure 24-9).

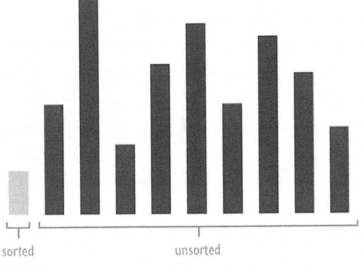

sorted   unsorted

FIGURE 24-9

We have a sorted region and an unsorted region

The sorted region contains one item. The unsorted region contains everything else. Now, here is where things get a little repetitive and painful . . . for your computer. We repeat all of these steps on the new first item in our unsorted part of the list.

Inside the unsorted world, there is now a new smallest number in town (Figure 24-10).

Just like before, the new smallest number is the first item. As selection sort goes through the unsorted items to find the smallest item, that will change. To be more precise and foreshadowy, it will change to the bar shown in Figure 24-11 after all of the unsorted items are examined.

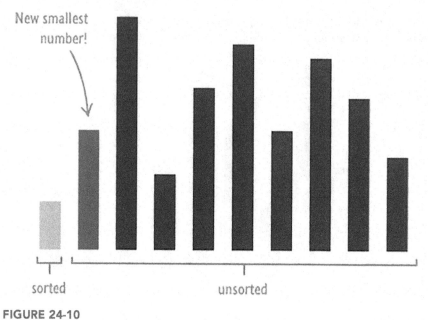

FIGURE 24-10

Checking with the next number

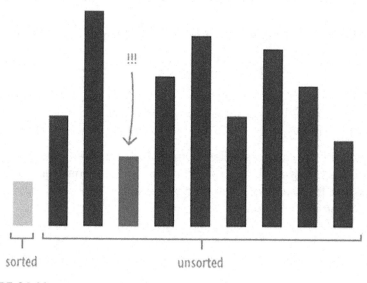

FIGURE 24-11

Finding the next smallest item

The next step is for this item to be swapped with our first unsorted item with the sorted region of our list getting one more entry (Figure 24-12).

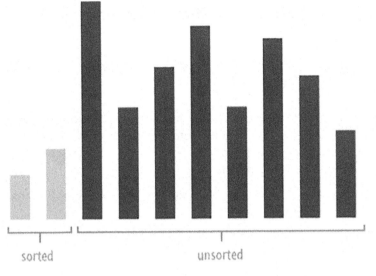

sorted   unsorted

FIGURE 24-12

Swapping to have our second-smallest item in the right spot

This process of finding a new smallest number and swapping it into the sorted region repeats until we have no more unsorted items (Figure 24-13).

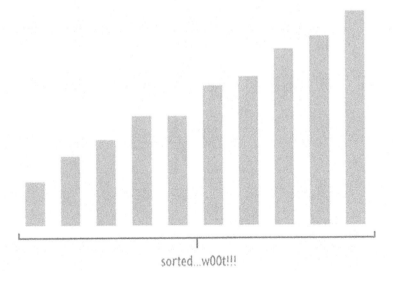

sorted...w00t!!!

FIGURE 24-13

Fully sorted list

Now, next is where I would normally do a detailed walkthrough using real numbers instead of bars of varying heights. Given how straightforward this algorithm is, let's just skip all that and go to the boring stuff.

Algorithm Deep Dive

Selection sort works very predictably. It goes through our list of data to find the smallest number, the next smallest number, and so on. Once it finds the smallest number, it places it in the sorted region. There is a lot of flexibility in how we want to implement this sorted region.

The sorted region could be at the beginning, as it was in the examples we've looked at so far (Figure 24-14).

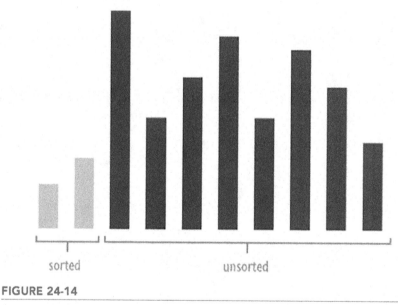

sorted   unsorted

FIGURE 24-14

Two regions

It could also be at the end (Figure 24-15).

If we really want to be different, we can use an entirely new list to store our sorted items (Figure 24-16).

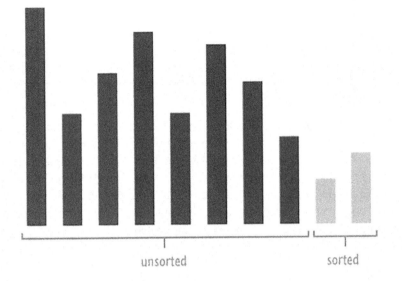

unsorted   sorted

FIGURE 24-15

There is no right or wrong way to organize our list

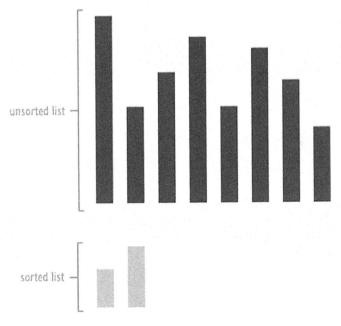

unsorted list —

sorted list —

FIGURE 24-16

It is also common to maintain two lists

For the most part, given how most list-like data types work in many languages, placing the sorted items at the beginning is straightforward to implement. Placing them at the end or creating an entirely new sorted list requires a little extra effort on your part. Pick whatever makes your life easier. The performance and memory characteristics of all three approaches are pretty similar, so you don't have to factor those in as part of your decision.

Speaking of performance and memory, selection sort isn't a fast algorithm for sorting data. Because we pick an unsorted item and compare it against every single other unsorted item, we are doing a whole bunch of comparisons. **Basically, it runs in n^2 time.** From a memory point of view, insertion sort is very good. It doesn't take up much memory beyond any extra objects needed for storing our input. That shouldn't be too surprising because almost all of our sorting-related shenanigans are done in-place on the input itself.

The JavaScript Implementation

We are almost done here. The last thing to do is to look at an example selection sort implementation in JavaScript:

```
function selectionSort(input) {
  for (let i = 0; i < input.length; i++) {

    // assume the item in the first position is the smallest
    let smallestPosition = i;

    // go through the unsorted region
    for (let j = i + 1; j < input.length; j++) {

      if (input[j] < input[smallestPosition]) {
        // a new smallest number is found
        smallestPosition = j
      }
    }

    // swap the min value if it changed
    if (smallestPosition != i) {
      let temp = input[smallestPosition];
```

```
      input[smallestPosition] = input[i];
      input[i] = temp;
   }
  }
}

let myinput = [24, 10, 17, 9, 5, 9, 1, 23, 300];
selectionSort(myinput);

alert(myinput);
```

The JavaScript doesn't veer too far from the English description you saw in the previous two sections. The outer loop represented by the i variable is responsible for going through each item in the list, and its position marks the dividing line between the sorted and unsorted regions of our input (Figure 24-17).

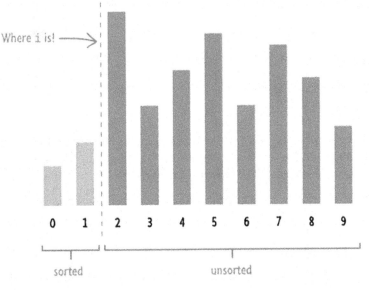

FIGURE 24-17

The i variable divides the sorted and unsorted regions of our input

The inner loop represented by the talented j variable is responsible for comparing the item at the outer loop's position with every remaining item in the list.
Figure 24-18 is the time-consuming and slow part that selection sort is famous for.

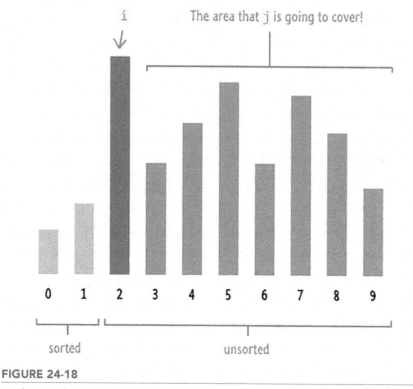

FIGURE 24-18

Looking at the two loops

As for other interesting landmarks in our code, the `smallestPosition` variable stores the position of the smallest item. It starts off as the first item in the unsorted region and then (potentially) changes as the inner loop does the checking against every remaining item in the unsorted part of the list.

Once the smallest item has been found, that item gets swapped with the element at the `i` position. The code for that looks as follows:

```
if (smallestPosition != i) {
  var temp = input[smallestPosition];
  input[smallestPosition] = input[i];
  input[i] = temp;
}
```

Just because I like to optimize some small details for easy wins, I do a check to do the swap only if our smallest item is indeed different than the item we started off with. While that doesn't happen often, it is worth adding the check to avoid some unnecessary operations. You can safely skip that `if` statement if you can sleep well at night without it.

Conclusion

Selection sort makes up the large number of sorts that is easy to understand but not very fast. To see how selection sort compares with other sort algorithms, check out Table 24-1.

TABLE 24-1 Selection Sort versus the Other Types of Sort Algorithms by Speed and Memory Characteristics

Name	Best	Average	Worst	Memory
Quick sort	$n \log n$	$n \log n$	n^2	$\log n$ (average)
Merge sort	$n \log n$	$n \log n$	$n \log n$	n (worst case)
Heap sort	$n \log n$	$n \log n$	$n \log n$	1
Timsort	n	$n \log n$	$n \log n$	n
Bubblesort	n	n^2	n^2	1
Selection sort	n^2	n^2	n^2	1
Insertion sort	n	n^2	n^2	1

If I were you and looking for a slow sort algorithm that is easy to implement, I would probably choose insertion sort over selection sort any day of the week.

SOME ADDITIONAL RESOURCES

? Ask a question: **https://forum.kirupa.com**

Errors/Known issues: **https://bit.ly/algorithms_errata**

Source repository: **https://bit.ly/algorithms_source**

25

MERGESORT

One of the most popular sorting algorithms you'll bump into is **mergesort**.
It was designed in the 1940s when dinosaurs roamed the jungles (Figure 25-1).

Mergesort was developed
around this time!

FIGURE 25-1

*Dinosaurs doing dinosaur things. (Source: Winsor McCay, Gerdie the
Dinosaur, animated short film, 1914. https://en.wikipedia.org/wiki/
Gertie_the_Dinosaur#.)*

Ever since then, mergesort (and variants of it!) can be seen everywhere—ranging from sort implementations in the Perl, Python, and Java languages to sorting data in tape drives. Okay, maybe the tape drives bit isn't relevant today, but mergesort comes up in a lot of places due to its efficiency.

In this chapter, we take a detailed look at how mergesort does its thing and wrap it up with a simple JavaScript implementation that brings it to life.

Onward!

How Mergesort Works

Trying to understand how mergesort works might seem overwhelming at first, but let's take it easy by walking through an example. In our example, we have nine numbers that we'd like to sort (Figure 25-2).

FIGURE 25-2

Another list of unsorted numbers

One quick aside. I should mention that mergesort is a **divide-and-conquer algorithm** . . . and it is quite shameless about that. All that means is that mergesort performs its magic on numbers by dividing them into smaller and smaller sections first. Right now, we have nine numbers that we threw at mergesort. The first thing mergesort does is break that up into two halves (Figure 25-3).

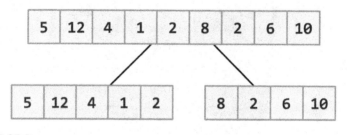

FIGURE 25-3

Break our list into two halves

Our original input is now divided into two sections. Next, we continue dividing by breaking our two sections into four sections (Figure 25-4).

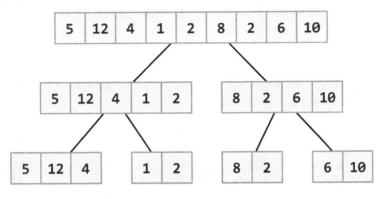

FIGURE 25-4

Continue dividing our input

We keep dividing these sections until we are left with just one number in each
section and can't divide any further (Figure 25-5).

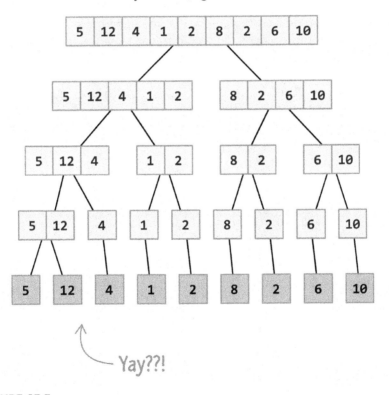

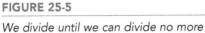

FIGURE 25-5

We divide until we can divide no more

At this point, we have a bunch of individual values that look identical to what we started with. That's not the goal of what we set out to do, but this is an important part of how mergesort functions. At this stage, we have a bunch of arrays of size 1. These arrays are inherently sorted because we can't sort single array elements further. All of this is to say that...we are done dividing! What we are going to see next is a whole lot of merging and sorting—aka the conquering part.

Let's start with the first two sections (Figure 25-6).

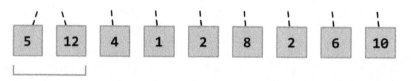

FIGURE 25-6

We are going to start sorting

We are now going to sort and merge these numbers together. As part of the merging, we also do a sort to ensure that the numbers in the combined section are arranged from smallest to largest. Because we are dealing with only two numbers, this is pretty easy for the 5 and 12 (Figure 25-7).

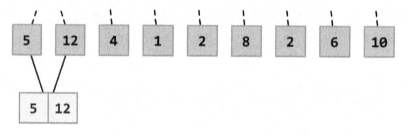

FIGURE 25-7

Each segment is sorted and combined

We now repeat this process for the next two sections made up of the numbers 4 and 1 (Figure 25-8).

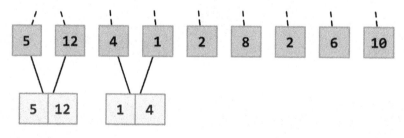

FIGURE 25-8

Repeat this process for each divided section

Just like before, we combine the two sections into one section. The sorting part is clearer this time around because the original arrangement wasn't already sorted. We start with a 4 and 1, and the merged arrangement is 1 and 4. Pretty simple so far, right?

Now, we keep repeating this merge and sort operation on each pair of sections until we run out of sections (Figure 25-9).

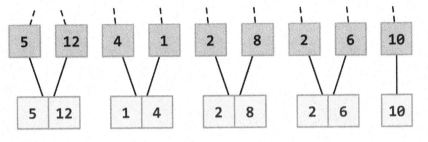

FIGURE 25-9

Our first round of merging and sorting is complete

If we have a number that is the odd one and can't be a part of a merge and sort . . . like our number 10 here, that's okay. Stop making fun of it. We just carry it along for the next round of merging and sorting and hope its luck improves!

Earlier, we were merging pairs of sections that were made up of one number. That was easy. This time around, we are going to continue merging pairs of sections, but each section will contain two numbers. Take a look (Figure 25-10).

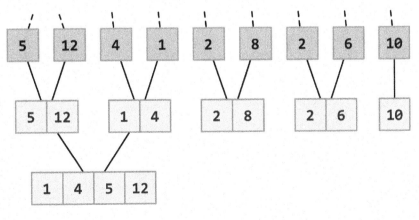

FIGURE 25-10

We keep merging (and sorting) sections

Instead of the merged section containing two numbers, it now contains four numbers, all in perfectly sorted bliss. We repeat this process for the remaining sections as well (Figure 25-11).

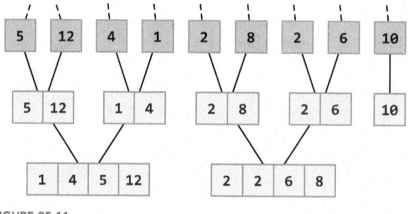

FIGURE 25-11

Our sections keep getting merged

The number 10 continues to be the odd one out and isn't quite in the right position to be sorted and merged, so we drag it along for the next round (Figure 25-12).

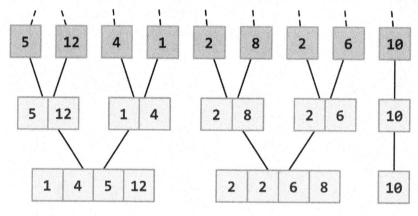

FIGURE 25-12

The 10 value is special

By now, you should start to see a pattern emerge. We are nearing the home stretch here, so let's continue merging and sorting with the next row (Figure 25-13).

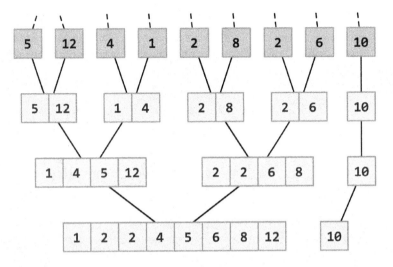

FIGURE 25-13

More merging is happening

This almost looks fully sorted! We have just one more round to go, and to those of you deeply worried about the number 10 . . . it makes the cut this time around (Figure 25-14).

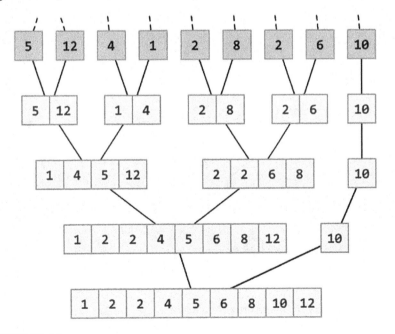

FIGURE 25-14

Our final sorted list

Woohoo! We now have a sorted list of numbers. There are no more sections to merge and sort, so we are done. As a quick recap (and to reminisce about all the good times we had), take a look at the full list of steps we performed to sort our initial collection of numbers (Figure 25-15).

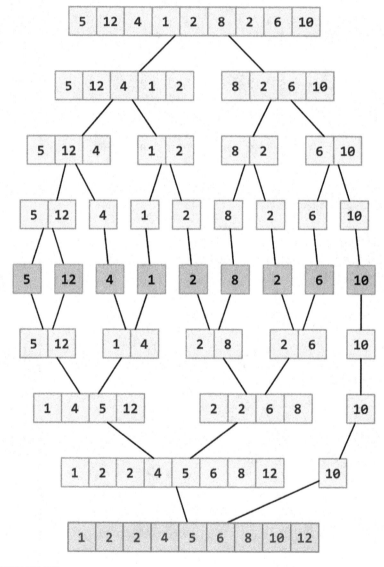

FIGURE 25-15

The path mergesort took to sort our numbers

This giant list of steps is a visual representation of mergesort—with all of its dividing and conquering goodness!

Mergesort: The Algorithm Details

The hard part is getting a good handle on how mergesort actually works. If everything in the previous section made sense to you, you are in great shape for the additional boring (yet important) details that you will need to know. Ignoring all of the diagrams and fancy explanations, mergesort simply does two things:

1. Divides (and divides, and divides, and . . .) its input into subsections until there is only one element left in each section.

2. Merges (and sorts) all of its subsections back into one big section that is now sorted.

It does all of this in $n \log n$ time, and the following tree representation highlights why that is the case (Figure 25-16).

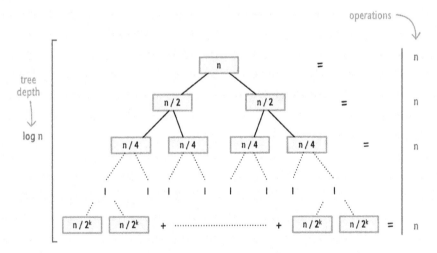

FIGURE 25-16

Operations and tree depth visualized

To put it in plain English, that is pretty fast and efficient for a sorting algorithm. The depth of your typical mergesort implementation is $\log n$, and the number of operations at each level is n.

When it comes to how much space it takes, things get a little less rosy. Common mergesort implementations take up **2n space** in worst-case scenarios—which is not terrible, but it is something to keep in mind if you are dealing with sorting within a fixed region of limited memory.

The last detail is that **mergesort is a stable sort**. This means that the relative order of items is maintained between the original input and the sorted input. That's a good thing if you care about things like this.

Looking at the Code

Now that you've learned how mergesort works and covered some boring details about its complexity, it is time to look at how all of that translates into JavaScript. Following is what my version of the JavaScript implementation looks like:

```javascript
function mergeSort(input) {
  // Just a single lonely item
  if (input.length < 2) {
    return input;
  }
  // Divide
  let mid = Math.ceil(input.length / 2);
  let left = mergeSort(input.slice(0, mid));
  let right = mergeSort(input.slice(mid));
  // recursively sort and merge
  return merge(left, right);
}
function merge(left, right) {
  let result = [];
  // Order the sublist as part of merging
  while (left.length > 0 && right.length > 0) {
    if (left[0] <= right[0]) {
      result.push(left.shift());
    } else {
      result.push(right.shift());
    }
  }
  // Add the remaining items to the result
  while (left.length > 0) {
```

```
    result.push(left.shift());
  }
  while (right.length > 0) {
    result.push(right.shift());
  }
  // The sorted sublist
  return result;
}
```

If you want to see this code in action, just call the mergeSort function with an array of numbers as the argument:

```
let example = [4, 10, 11, 20, 5, 3, 4, 1, -20];
console.log(example);
alert(example);
```

As you follow through the code, notice that there is absolutely nothing interesting going on here. It's just a lot of loop and array manipulations that make up the divide and merge/sort conquer operations.

Conclusion

If you want to sort a large list of values, you can't go wrong by using mergesort. It is fast, uses up a reasonable amount of memory, and (unlike quicksort) is stable. Now, before we call it a night and party it up with mergesort at the local paintball range, Table 25-1 compares mergesort with various other popular sorting algorithms and their performance and memory characteristics:

TABLE 25-1 Mergesort versus the Other Sorting Algorithms by Speed and Memory Characteristics

Name	Best	Average	Worst	Memory
Quicksort	$n \log n$	$n \log n$	n^2	$\log n$ (average)
Mergesort	$n \log n$	$n \log n$	$n \log n$	n (worst case)
Heapsort	$n \log n$	$n \log n$	$n \log n$	1

Name	Best	Average	Worst	Memory
Timsort	n	$n \log n$	$n \log n$	n
Bubblesort	n	n^2	n^2	1
Selection sort	n^2	n^2	n^2	1
Insertion sort	n	n^2	n^2	1

SOME ADDITIONAL RESOURCES

? Ask a question: **https://forum.kirupa.com**

Errors/Known issues: **https://bit.ly/algorithms_errata**

Source repository: **https://bit.ly/algorithms_source**

26

CONCLUSION

If you are reading this, you have nearly reached the end of this book! Congratulations. I hope the preceding chapters gave you a better appreciation for how our computers represent data and think (in their own 101010101 ways) through common computer problems. Let's wrap up all of the preceding content by talking about how this book came about.

How this Book Came About

As was all the rage with the cool kids back in the early 2000s, I majored in Computer Science. I probably shouldn't have, but I liked computers. I liked science. How difficult could this be? Fast forward to a few years in my undergrad program, and my feelings about *Computer* and *Science* was at a low.

My disdain for computer science wasn't because I disliked the material. Far from it! I loved the idea of working with computers and learning all about the hardware, the software, and how complex problems can be broken into chunks a computer can solve. The **problem** was (and still is) that I just happen to learn better if the content is engaging. The material for the many algorithms-related classes I had to take was far from that.

If you show me walls of text, numbers, and equations, my brain is not interested in figuring out what is going on:

Walls and walls of text!

If you show me the same information more visually with a bit of personality and clarity, it's a different ball game. Things make sense:

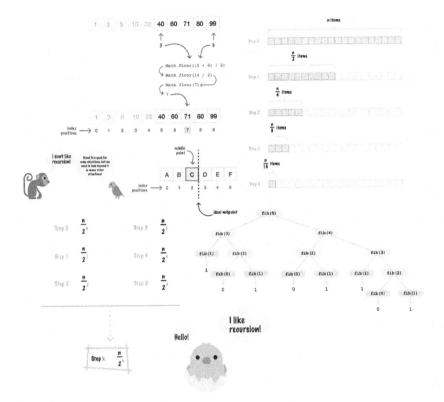

A more visual and engaging way to learn complicated topics

Unfortunately, the former was the entirety of my computer science education. This was all happening at MIT, a place well known for its Computer Science program and quality of teaching. My classmates also did just fine. The teaching material just didn't resonate with me. This was very much a *me* problem.

As many *me* problems go, it was up to me to figure out a graceful workaround. To better help me understand all of the arcane algorithms topics that I kept getting confused by, I started to take all of the material from my lectures and books and reexplain and rewrite them for myself in a more approachable way:

1. If something sounded boring, I made it sound more interesting.

2. If a topic didn't explain the importance of why it needed to be learned, I dug into the motivation and convinced myself of why it matters.

3. If an explanation was really complicated, I expanded it into more simple terms and tied it back to concepts I could relate to.

4. If there was a giant wall of text, I drew diagrams to help me represent the same material more visually

These activities helped me to better appreciate how algorithms truly worked, and they also had the important side-effect of being the source material for this **Algorithms** book you are seeing.

I hope this book hits the mark if you were looking for a reimagined way of explaining very dry and boring algorithms-related topics. In many ways, this is the book I wish I had all those decades ago when I was learning about algorithms and data structures.

One more thing!

I greatly enjoy hearing from readers like yourself about what you liked, didn't like, and more. Please feel free to contact me by posting on https://forum.kirupa.com, and I will reply to you very quickly...in O(1) time!

Cheers,

Kirupa ☺

Index

Register Your Product at informit.com/register

Access additional benefits and save up to 65%* on your next purchase

- Automatically receive a coupon for 35% off books, eBooks, and web editions and 65% off video courses, valid for 30 days. Look for your code in your InformIT cart or the Manage Codes section of your account page.
- Download available product updates.
- Access bonus material if available.**
- Check the box to hear from us and receive exclusive offers on new editions and related products.

InformIT—The Trusted Technology Learning Source

InformIT is the online home of information technology brands at Pearson, the world's leading learning company. At informit.com, you can

- Shop our books, eBooks, and video training. Most eBooks are DRM-Free and include PDF and EPUB files.
- Take advantage of our special offers and promotions (informit.com/promotions).
- Sign up for special offers and content newsletter (informit.com/newsletters).
- Access thousands of free chapters and video lessons.
- Enjoy free ground shipping on U.S. orders.*

* Offers subject to change.
** Registration benefits vary by product. Benefits will be listed on your account page under Registered Products.

Connect with InformIT—Visit informit.com/community

 Pearson

Addison-Wesley • Adobe Press • Cisco Press • Microsoft Press • Oracle Press • Peachpit Press • Pearson IT Certification • Que